The Humanities and the Dream of America

The Humanities and the Dream of America

GEOFFREY GALT HARPHAM

The University of Chicago Press ❋ Chicago and London

GEOFFREY GALT HARPHAM
is president and director of
the National Humanities
Center, Research Triangle
Park, North Carolina.
He is the coauthor of
*A Glossary of Literary
Terms, Ninth Edition*
(2008), and the author
of seven books, most
recently *The Character of
Criticism* (2006).

The University of Chicago Press, Chicago 60637
The University of Chicago Press, Ltd., London
© 2011 by The University of Chicago
All rights reserved. Published 2011
Printed in the United States of America

20 19 18 17 16 15 14 13 12 11   1 2 3 4 5

ISBN-13: 978-0-226-31697-0 (cloth)
ISBN-13: 978-0-226-31699-4 (paper)
ISBN-10: 0-226-31697-1 (cloth)
ISBN-10: 0-226-31699-8 (paper)

Library of Congress Cataloging-in-Publication Data
Harpham, Geoffrey Galt, 1946–
   The humanities and the dream of America / Geoffrey
Galt Harpham.
      p. cm.
   Includes bibliographical references and index.
   ISBN-13: 978-0-226-31697-0 (alk. paper)
   ISBN-13: 978-0-226-31699-4 (pbk. : alk. paper)
   ISBN-10: 0-226-31697-1 (alk. paper)
   ISBN-10: 0-226-31699-8 (pbk. : alk. paper)
   1. Humanities—Study and teaching (Higher)—
   United States. 2. Philology—United States—History.
   3. Endowment of research—United States. I. Title.
   AZ503.H37 2011
   001.3071'173—dc22   2010018450

Chapter 1 originally appeared as "Beyond and Beneath
the 'Crisis in the Humanities,'" in "Essays on the
Humanities," *New Literary History* 36, no. 1 (2005): 21–36;
reprinted by permission of Johns Hopkins University
Press. Chapter 2 is a revised version of "Roots, Races,
and the Return to Philology," *Representations* 106 (Spring
2009): 34–63; reprinted by permission of University
of California Press. An earlier version of chapter 3
appeared as "Between Humanity and the Homeland: The
Evolution of an Institutional Concept," *American Literary
History* 18, no. 2 (2006): 245–61; reprinted by permission
of Oxford University Press. Chapter 7 is a revised version
of "The Depths of the Heights: Reading Conrad with
America's Soldiers," *Profession 2008*, 74–82; reprinted
by permission of the copyright owner, The Modern
Language Association of America.

♾ The paper used in this publication meets the
minimum requirements of the American National
Standard for Information Sciences—Permanence of
Paper for Printed Library Materials, ANSI Z39.48-1992.

For John Birkelund, Francis Oakley, and Carl H. Pforzheimer III,
distinguished supporters of the humanities in America

Contents

Introduction: The Humanities as a Foreign Language

What, exactly, is the protocol when you are addressing a public audience and the air is pierced by a call to prayer? This happened to me in the spring of 2009 in Istanbul, where I was giving a series of lectures at Turkish universities (Ege, Hacettepe, Bilkent, Atatürk, Koç, Bahçeşehir, Haliç, Kadir Has; I regretted being unable to visit Boğaziçi). My subject on most of these occasions was the subject of this book, the humanities. After giving this lecture a couple of times, I had, as it were, thrown my compass overboard, and spoken without a text. This had enabled me to improvise according to the mood of the moment, but, I discovered, it also made it possible for me to be thrown completely off track when the passionate wail of the *azan* came drifting over the city and, through an open window, into the lecture hall.

What to do? Should I wait several minutes until it ended? Or should I treat this intrusion, which is heard five times a day, in the same way one might treat the sound of a thunderstorm or a conversation outside the room, and try to talk over it? How, in general, was this handled in classrooms, business meetings, or daily life? I scanned my audience, over a hundred students and faculty, for clues. An overwhelmingly Muslim country, Turkey had been for eighty years a proudly modern and secular nation. But in 2002, the nation had elected a government that described itself as "Muslim democratic" (and was described by others bluntly as Islamist), creating considerable anxiety among those who valued Turkey's secular traditions, and uncertainty in me about which way the wind was blowing in this particular room. Were my listeners secularists—in which case they might expect and wish me to treat the call to prayer as a mere aural feature of daily life that deserved no particular acknowledgment? Or were they Muslim democrats, in which case they might expect that even a non-Muslim like me would show respect by pausing in my merely academic, not to mention secular and humanist, discourse until the song ceased? Flummoxed, I simply stopped speaking, looked at them looking at me, and then, having lost my train of thought, started speaking again—about what, I cannot recall—with the call to prayer continuing and my audience still apparently attending, to at least one of us. As for me, I was listening to the *azan* even as I spoke. What a sound! Even if you have no idea what the voice is saying, and even if you know that the voice is not speaking to you, it is impossible not to feel somehow called, summoned, drawn out of yourself.

A teachable moment; and as with many such moments, one learns what one already knows. Recollecting my confusion in tranquility later on that evening as I sat on the balcony of my hotel overlooking the Bosphorus, I realized that many of the ideas I had been trying to talk about in my lecture not only were crowded into that moment but had achieved greater clarity and provocative force than I had been able to give them. These included many of the notions customarily associated with the humanities, which, we are told, inculcate, often through attention to works of art, a sense of other minds and cultures; require and reward attention to formal and textural features as well as to literal or manifest meaning; invite individual interpretation and inference; cultivate the faculty of judgment; awaken a sense of values; engage the emotions as well as the intellect; enlarge our imaginative capacities; challenge, deepen, and enrich our understanding of the world; provide fertile ground for the growth of self-knowledge; and, under the right circumstances, open the way to tolerance, restraint, humility, and perhaps even wisdom. It was, I reflected, possible to extract for the purposes of pedagogy each of these points from this incident, in which, arrested by the appearance of an aesthetic form—a voice coming not just from outside the room but from a long cultural and religious tradition that was decisively "outside" my own—I had been shocked into an apprehension of otherness, thrown back on my own uncertain resources, forced to make a judgment involving values, challenged in my self-sufficiency, enriched, and perhaps even, eventually, made more tolerant and wise. It was as if "the humanities" themselves were carried on the breeze that brought the sound of that voice.

It would have been appropriate for the humanities to be in the air in Istanbul, the site of a pivotal moment in the history of the humanities, the founding by the Austrian Jewish émigré philologist Leo Spitzer of the School of Foreign Languages at the University of Istanbul in 1933. Invited by Ataturk, the leader of the new Turkish state, to modernize the Turkish university, Spitzer sought to create a program that would bring to this ancient city the advances in philology and linguistic scholarship that had been won by European scholars; after three years, he was succeeded by another German Jewish émigré, Erich Auerbach. The two took different approaches, with Spitzer learning Turkish (and writing an article called "Learning Turkish") and the more resistant Auerbach retaining a resolutely European cosmopolitan orientation.[1] Together, however, they were largely responsible for preserving the distinguished tradition of European philology during the war years. As the account in chapter 2 of this book shows, the version of philology represented by Spitzer and Auerbach was a kind of redaction, a tradition purified of some of the scholarly and even moral aberrations that had corrupted it during the preceding century and a half—specifically, the deep investment of linguistic scholarship in race theory and in learned forms of anti-Semitism, an investment that had made philology into a half-willing, or in some cases fully conscious, scholarly contribution to the less learned kind of anti-Semitism from which Spitzer and Auerbach had been forced to flee. Emerging from hiding in Istanbul with two luminous and even heroic champions, philology, under the new name of comparative literature, was washed clean of its own history, so that, through a kind of collective recovered memory some forty years later, it could come to seem a model of pure, rigorous, and meaningful humanistic scholarship.[2] But while the work of Spitzer and Auerbach may not have been fully representative of the philological tradition, it gave birth to a new understanding of the possibilities of scholarship. According to Steven Marcus, Auerbach's synthetic masterpiece *Mimesis* "made the modern idea of the humanities possible."[3] That philology had been forced into a kind of exilic chrysalis, only to reappear transfigured as "the humanities" lent, I thought, an impressive depth to my ruminations in this city on the current condition of the humanities.

But as I considered this depth, the real character of the momentary discomfiture I had experienced that afternoon suddenly snapped into focus. For what I really felt, as I anxiously scanned the faces of my audience for some clue as to what was expected of me, was *foreign*—specifically, American. I had not felt this way heretofore. So friendly, responsive, and immediately welcoming were my hosts, my audiences, and those trying to sell me rugs that it was easy to get lost in a fantasy of Turkish-American solidarity bleeding into a universal Family of Man. But over the preceding couple of weeks as I gave this talk—called "The Humanities in America"—to audiences around the country, I had the unsettling intuition that I understood my audiences less and less, and this had led to my becoming less rather than more assured in my presentation. The sense that I was not completely in command of the situation had begun at my very first lecture, when, in an attempt to make a friendly connection with my audience, I had mentioned that I was reading the novel *Snow* by Orhan Pamuk, the Istanbul native and 2006 Nobel laureate in literature. An erect young woman approached me afterward to inform me, in a tone that did not invite dialogue, that Pamuk had betrayed his people by speaking publicly of the Armenian "genocide"; with his Nobel money in hand, she noted acidly, he had not raised the issue again. Nor did I.

The real problem, I began to realize, was that I had presumed that my audiences and I shared a common language, when in fact we only shared common words, or rather common sounds. I had been making arguments about the "state of the humanities" in the belief that we all knew what the humanities are. Reading their reactions as I spoke, I had, over successive lectures, given a progressively more elementary presentation, ultimately zeroing in on the simplest possible subject: what the humanities are, that is, how I understood the concept. I was not trying to dumb it down—my audiences were sharp, attentive, and impressively well informed. I was simply trying to focus attention on the point where I might be instructive rather than mystifying, the point of possible dialogue. The basic proposition, I was starting to feel, was not altogether clear and needed explaining in a way that it would not in the United States. Even though the ostensible subject of the humanities is humanity as such, not all humans had felt a need to organize courses and programs of study based on this subject. Just a few years ago, or a few miles away, the educational system had no category of "the humanities." The University of Damascus, for example, has Faculties of Agriculture, Economics, Dentistry, Pharmacy, and Shari'a, but no "humanities." (There is a Faculty of Literature and Humanitarian Sciences, which does not sound like the same thing.) When I spoke with individuals about the humanities, I sensed that while the word was familiar to them, it was problematic in a way that it was not for me; it was almost a foreign word of some complexity, with uncertain nuances and implications that had not yet been fully mastered.

And so, at this final talk in the series, I was trying to wind back the tape and begin at the very beginning, establishing the most basic definitions. My strategy was to unpack a single sentence: *The scholarly study of documents and artifacts produced by human beings in the past enables us to see the world from different points of view so that we may better understand ourselves.* I was attempting to pull several rabbits out of this hat, including the premises that the humanities have "the text" as their object, humanity as their subject, and self-understanding as their goal. As noncontroversial as these points were to me, I felt a certain risk in making them, conscious that my audience might have been offended at the obviousness of my presentation. But as I spoke, I imagined that they were not offended. In fact, through the myriad ways a silent audience can communicate with a lecturer, my listeners seemed to me to be particularly focused, almost as if they found the argument interesting.

Looking back, I think that what might have interested them—presuming they *were* interested, and interested in what I was saying as opposed to the way I looked and talked; presuming, that is, that we had a shared understanding about the event we were all participating in—was not the very general statements above, but their constituent elements. Within that first premise about the humanities having the text as their object, for example, I had identified several subpremises—first, the mere fact that the text has an objective form suggests that a competent reader can describe and understand its abstract structure of meanings; second, the inability of the text to speak its own meaning requires one to use imagination as well as understanding; and third, the act of reading puts each reader into a virtual community with all other possible readers, a community not limited by nationality, race, religion, gender, age, or any other factor except literacy. In the United States, such statements would elicit indifferent assent. But here, none of these were so self-evident.

Take the first fact, that the text is right there before you, promiscuously available for inspection by you or anyone else. The silent implication—is it not?—is that knowledge can be attained without the guidance of external authority. In the United States and other Western countries, literacy is understood to be an integral part of a modern secular democracy; its value goes without saying. In a Muslim democracy, however, the idea that people can decide important questions for themselves might not be as enthusiastically embraced. The same lack of enthusiasm might greet the prospect of individuals creatively speculating about the meaning of a text, or entering into an imagined global community of readers. In the United States, all these points would be dully incontrovertible. But here, they seemed to be assertions rather than mere premises, and something in the quality of my audience's attention suggested to me that these assertions might be more than interesting, even perhaps politically and culturally controversial. (After all, if my listeners had not been fascinated, would they not have left the room to pray?)

My seemingly tautological second point, about humanity as the subject of the humanities, ran an even greater risk of dullness. But its status, too, is context-sensitive, truer in some places than in others. In order for this point to be as benignly instructive as I intended, my listeners would have to share my understanding of the individual as an autonomous creative agent. If they did not, my argument might seem misguided, ideological, even plain wrong. I wanted, of course, to avoid such a reaction, but how could I presume that *humanity* meant the same thing to my Muslim and perhaps Islamist audiences as it did to me? And, given this train of thought, what was left of my third point, that the goal of the humanities is self-understanding? Did this concept not presume a certain view of the "self" as something puzzling and problematic, something that can be understood only with difficulty, something elusive and withholding—but something worth the effort, something whose secrets are supremely valuable? If a given culture was hostile to the entire project of modernity, regarding it as alien and impious; if that culture regarded "humanism" and "individualism" as forms of idolatry; if they believed that the very idea of progress carried negative rather than positive connotations, then surely the idea of the human in that culture would differ in very significant ways from my own. And if the human was construed differently, then so, too, would the humanities be construed differently—if they were construed at all.

In such a culture—which may or may not have been the culture I was in at that moment; I imagined that many of the people seated before me were themselves undecided or uncertain—the humanities would lack the American tradition of cultural prestige, the association with fundamental questions of human existence that for many years ensured that, even when they were "in crisis," the humanities were still the object of public concern. Here, it seemed, the humanities had a different—a less central, less conflicted, and less controversial—role to play in the educational system and in the culture of the nation. And so, if I began my visit with the casual presumption that the humanities are a global undertaking that had been advanced with particular success in the United States, I ended convinced that the humanities reflect a specifically American or at least Western, modern, and secular version of human being and human flourishing, and that the entire concept might be a mere provincial prejudice.

>>><<<

I have included in this book the culprit ahistorical essay that served as the basis of that talk. I wrote it shortly after I became the director of the National Humanities Center in 2003 as a statement of broad principles that I have seen no reason to disown despite my deepening awareness of the limitations of their appeal or applicability. All the other essays included here were written with the intention of restoring the strangeness to a concept that has become dulled over the years as it has been both battered and banalized. Each essay focuses on a moment, an incident, or an issue where the premises underlying the humanities become visible. My taste and training lead me to focus on literary studies, in which most of the basic premises of the humanities come into focus.[4] This is not a consecutive history or a map of a wide and diverse terrain, but a series of incisions intended to expose some of the sources of both blindness and insight of which the humanities are capable. The entirety is grounded in the recognition that, while the phrase "the humanities" seems to refer to the study of the human as such, the actual practice of the humanities is inflected in various and surprising ways by its complex history and the context in which it arose.

While the term in its contemporary sense is native only to the United States, it has now become sufficiently disseminated that Turks, for example, will gather to hear a talk on the subject. But the meaning of the term is not constant across space any more than it has been across time. Whereas, in the United States, the humanities are associated with such notions as "self-enrichment," "individual interpretation," "distrust of received opinions," "tradition," "culture," or "what it means to be human," in other countries the term has fewer such associations. Indeed, it sometimes seems to signify primarily "America," and often marks an attempt to conform the local system of higher education to that of the United States. Elsewhere, other terms have a prior claim: *sciences humaines* in France and other Romance language cultures ("human sciences," including economics, history, psychology, political science, linguistics; emphasis on empirical method; often in association with *sciences sociales*); *Geisteswissenschaften* in Germany or Germanic cultures such as the Netherlands ("science of spirit": philosophy, theology, jurisprudence, sociology; no arts); arts and letters in Britain. Tellingly, there was until quite recently no entry, not even a cross-reference, for *humanities* in the *Oxford English Dictionary*, which defines *humanist* as "a student of human affairs, or human nature"; nor does the eleventh edition of the *Encyclopaedia Britannica* (1910–11) contain any article on "the humanities." But in all these countries and many more, "the humanities" has recently appeared alongside these more indigenous terms, sometimes complementing them, sometimes competing with them, sometimes signifying cultural maturation, and sometimes being taken as a sign of creeping Americanization. In no other country does the term carry precisely the same conceptual baggage, imply the same goals and aspirations, or respond to the same fears or crises as it does in the United States.

This is not, of course, to say that the humanities sprang suddenly from American soil, without antecedents. The history that culminates in the humanities is long, complex, and generally misunderstood where it is not ignored. I cannot rehearse it all here, but those who are interested can find no better guide than Francis Oakley's brief but commanding book *Community of Learning*,[5] which tracks the tumultuous history of the concept of liberal education, in which the humanities have come to play a central part. Oakley begins his story in classical Greece, not with the conventional starting point of Plato's Academy, but with a debate between the "philosophical" orientation of the Academy and the "rhetorical" system espoused by Isocrates, which proceeded from a quite different understanding of the aims of education. Students at the Academy were formed into a kind of religious order, a philosophical cadre devoted to the dialectical quest for truth. Isocrates' students, by contrast, more closely resembled today's students in that they paid fees and saw themselves engaged in a preparation for life—specifically, in an ethical pedagogy that linked rhetorical expertise with what might today be called leadership studies. The curriculum they followed was literary rather than philosophical, and required the memorization of vast tracts of Homer, in whose work the desired virtues were both exemplified and given the highest expression. For Isocrates, the goal was not the liberation of the mind from ignorance, but the training of the mind for the assumption of civic and political responsibility.

While many of the most impassioned and pious defenses of the humanities today invoke the names of Socrates, Plato, and Aristotle, Isocrates was actually the dominant figure in his time and for many centuries thereafter. With the fall of the Greek city-states, the Platonic model of education went into eclipse: Rome had greater need for men who could administer the empire than for philosophers on an endless quest for wisdom. Cicero's *artes liberales* represents a more normative version of the rhetorical agenda, and it was this program, rechristened under the influence of Petrarch as *studia humanitatis*, that gradually stiffened into the medieval trivium and quadrivium. As Oakley says, the historical norm in the history of higher education between the time of the Roman Empire and the eighteenth century was clearly rhetorical-oratorical rather than philosophical: during that millennium and a half, the dominant form in which the classical tradition was continued was a program based not on science or philosophy but on literary or rhetorical performances (Homer, Euripides, Demosthenes, Menander) presented as a series of monumental achievements to be studied and admired (52). Most interestingly, the classical tradition was preserved not in the Latin West, which was devoting its energies to a highly professionalized scholastic training in philosophy, law, medicine, and particularly theology, but in the East, in Constantinople. Deep beneath the footprints of Auerbach and Spitzer were far older traces, deposited in a different stratum altogether. As I lectured throughout Istanbul, I could imagine that I was standing on ground zero of the humanities, where the *artes liberales* had been faithfully transmitted through long centuries. In other words, as far as the humanities were concerned, I was the latecomer and my audiences were the natives.

Isocrates' rhetorical tradition may have had a long run, but it never succeeded in shaking off its philosophical rival, and traces of both traditions can be detected in modern attitudes toward liberal education. In *Orators and Philosophers*,[6] Bruce Kimball identifies the attitudes associated with each strain. In what Kimball calls the "liberal-free" orientation, Plato's legacy lives on in the form of an emphasis on political and intellectual freedom, an implicit trust in the unfettered intellect, a high value accorded to critical reasoning, an anti-elitist insistence on original equality and individual interpretation, and the conviction that education is an open-ended quest for truth, all of which are gathered into a project whose goal is personal development considered as an end in itself. In the *artes liberales* tradition deriving from Isocrates, the stress falls not on the development of the individual but on the formation of virtuous citizens through the stipulation of moral norms, the identification of a canon, the development of a cultural elite, and a pragmatic accommodation to the realities that responsible authority must confront. The first tradition is critical, corrosive, subversive of habits and identities, searching, unsettled, and centered on the rational individual; the second is consolidating, reverential, aristocratic, and centered—with the gradual decline of religion as the central organizing force of higher education—on the concept of culture. As both Oakley and Kimball note, both traditions live on in colleges and universities today in confused codependency.

These two traditions do not correspond precisely to the more familiar distinction between science and the humanities, but are rather two ways of thinking about the means and ends of education as such. Still, it is clear that the liberal-free tradition is oriented toward what we now call science. Plato began his comeback with the rise of the German research university in the early nineteenth century: in the new academic ethos, *Wissenschaft* (knowledge) was placed on an equal footing with *Bildung* (the formation of character through the pursuit of learning), and the door was opened to a philosophical restoration, which rapidly became associated with science. The emphasis on research placed a premium on the skeptical or questioning attitude, the free application of reason in the service of critique, and originality, all of which contributed to the science-based "knowledge revolution" of the nineteenth century. The famous description of science by Vannevar Bush, science advisor to FDR and Harry Truman, as an "endless frontier"[7] perfectly captures the philosophic-scientific orientation of the liberal-free tradition.

For many decades, resistance to the "endless quest" tradition was centered in England, where Matthew Arnold and John Henry Newman held fast to the rhetorical ideal and the tradition of humane letters. This tradition entailed a very finite quest with a determined goal, which Newman, in his epochal *The Idea of a University* (1852), defined as the production of "gentlemen." In *Culture and Anarchy* (1869), Arnold argued for an educational system based on the inculcation of culture, which he characterized as "the study of perfection," as opposed to the study of science, the "sheer desire to see things as they are."[8] T. H. Huxley responded to Arnold with a vigorous defense of science, to which Arnold replied that science failed to provide any contact between knowledge and "our sense of conduct, our sense of beauty," and left unsatisfied the fundamental desire of human beings for a full life: "Letters," Arnold declared, "will call out their being at more points, will make them live more."[9] To both Newman and Arnold, the idea of research seemed a German fetish. The very first sentence of *The Idea of a University* declared that the university was properly dedicated to "the diffusion and extension of knowledge rather than the advancement"[10]; research, Newman argued, was a valuable but somewhat specialized activity best allotted to learned societies, academies, or curious individuals. This attitude survived in the most distinguished institutions in Britain until quite recently. As late as the 1950s, A. L. Rowse reported, an Oxford don could speak freely and contemptuously about "that state of resentful coma dignified by the name of Rezearch"—a term of opprobrium, worsened by being pronounced with a German accent.[11]

At the beginning of the twentieth century, then, two forces, conceptually and historically distinct but conjoined in practice, were contending for the soul of higher education. The battle was joined primarily in the United States, where the increasingly influential German system—which involved departments of certified professionals engaging in specialized research, major courses of study, electives, honors programs, and a growing emphasis on science and research—met with a powerful countermovement that stressed breadth as well as depth, where the classics were treated as an antidote to the excesses of romanticism and the chaos of modernity, and where the culmination of an undergraduate education was often a class in theology or moral philosophy, often taught by the president of the college. Some institutions specialized. Johns Hopkins was "liberal-free" in its research orientation at its founding in 1876, while its near neighbor St. John's College in Annapolis has offered its students an intensified form of *artes liberales* since 1937. Others, such as Columbia University beginning in 1919 and the University of Chicago in 1930, tried to have it all, committing themselves both to ambitious research programs in the graduate program and, at the undergraduate level, to a morally instructive immersion in the heritage and tradition of the West, a project that was accomplished at both institutions by a program centering on canonical texts, or, as they became known, Great Books.[12]

It was during the tumultuous time between the two world wars that the modern concept of the humanities began to crystallize in the American academy. The first "Program in the Humanities" appeared at Princeton in 1930; at roughly the same time, the University of Chicago replaced the "Faculty of Arts and Letters" with the "Division of the Humanities"; Harvard, Yale, Stanford, and Columbia made comparable changes shortly thereafter—in some cases simply in order to create, as one writer put it in 1940, "a field comparable in breadth to the Social Sciences and the Natural Sciences."[13] By midcentury, the phrase "the humanities," referring to a collection of academic disciplines devoted to the study of philosophy, literature, the arts, and sometimes history, was appearing with some regularity. Defined in opposition to science, ideology, mechanization, behaviorism, mass society, the overvaluation of rationality, and modernity in general, the humanities were identified with notions of empowerment, liberation, cultivation, civic responsibility, and, almost invariably, ethical behavior and the development of character.

A peaceable kingdom, it would seem; but in fact, ever since the rise of the research ethos, humanists had been on the defensive, thinking of themselves, in Steven Marcus's phrase, as "an embattled cultural patriciate ... custodians of a civilization under siege from alien, if not extraterrestrial, forms of life."[14] The most widely known champions of the movement that became known as the New Humanism were Harvard's Irving Babbitt, author of *Literature and the American College* (1908); Princeton's Paul Elmer More, editor of *The Nation*; and later, Columbia's Norman Foerster, editor of the 1930 volume *Humanism and America*,[15] which defined the movement's classicizing, moralizing, and anti-Romantic attitude. The New Humanists always felt outgunned, with the entire institution of higher education moving in what they felt was precisely the wrong direction, toward professional education, pragmatism, eclecticism, and self-indulgence. But in the postwar period, with science assuming an ever-larger role in the nation's priorities, and consuming more and more of the resources available to higher education—and with the humanities themselves becoming more professionalized and committed to research—all humanists had reason to think themselves engaged in some kind of combat. The contest was invigorating: the quarter century following the war, when the phrase "the crisis in the humanities" was first heard, is, as David A. Hollinger has written, now remembered as the golden age of American universities, "a time of robust confidence" within the humanities in particular, with burgeoning numbers of students and faculty.[16]

The often idealizing and universalizing discourse of the humanities obscures the drama of their appearance in the tumultuous interwar period and their consolidation as a discourse of crisis in the immediate aftermath of World War II. But as I argue in chapter 6, the driving force behind the concretization of the humanities after the war was almost nakedly strategic and political—the desire to strengthen the American nation by producing citizens capable of the confident exercise of the freedoms available in, and protected by, a modern democratic culture. The humanities during this time were founded on explicitly American notions of human nature, human culture, and human flourishing, and were promoted by those who saw these notions, and the nation that sponsored them, as being under threat in a dangerous world. Liberal education, in the form of what the influential "Redbook" produced at Harvard in 1945 called "general education," advanced the idea that learning experiences ought to be conducted in a spirit of free inquiry without regard to vocational or professional utility. According to the authors of the Redbook, the humanities were to be the heart and soul of general education, a moral kernel in colleges and universities, whose overall mission was to produce virtuous, cultivated, responsible, and well-rounded citizens.

Three features of this abbreviated account should be emphasized. First, the history leading up to and including the modern humanities is characterized at every point by tensions, divisions, and conflicts both internal and external. It is impossible to discover anywhere in that history a moment that would not deserve the name of crisis. Within the humanities, the descendants of the "orators" and the "philosophers" have never called a cease-fire, and the debate between qualitative and more scientific or evidence-based approaches is a constant feature of professional discourse. Within the university, humanists have felt if not always like a cultural patriciate, at least embattled, and often at a pronounced and growing disadvantage compared to natural science, social science, and especially professional education.[17] And beyond the walls of academe, the humanities have been either promoted as a way of combating some danger to the polis or accused of being that danger. Quite apart from the intentions of most of the quiet individuals responsible for teaching and research in the humanities, the humanities have always been embroiled.

The second point is less obvious: it is that the modern institution of the humanities, like the educational programs that preceded it, has consistently assigned to itself the task of articulating distinctions between optimal or fully realized human being and either subprime human being (slaves, women, noncitizens, barbarians) or, what sometimes comes to the same thing, nonhuman being. At the heart of the Platonic Academy was the Aristotelian conviction that humankind is the creature who desires to know; at the heart of the modern humanities is a less narrowly focused but still definite account of humankind as a creature endowed with several unique capabilities. Each of the modern humanities disciplines takes sectoral responsibility for exploring one of those capabilities: history, the capacity for significant action; philosophy, the capacity for reflection; the study of the arts, the creative capacity. The precise questions to which the humanities furnish imprecise, partial, and indirect answers are, What is humankind? What does it mean to be human? and What makes a significant/ worthy/fulfilled life?

The third point is that these questions, while universal in form, grew from American soil in the sense that they reframe a proposition that has been part of the most heroic formulations of the American character or national mission since the founding of the Republic: the idea that American citizens have as a birthright privileged if not exclusive access to the fullness of the human condition. The "whole man" celebrated in the Red Book is not precisely the culturally enriched gentleman of Newman or Arnold, and not quite the questing youth of the Platonic Academy or the sober citizen of Isocrates; he is, rather, an exemplary American in the postwar era, as determined by a committee at Harvard University.

No advanced training is required to ponder the human condition, but in the United States this pondering has been allocated, as it were, to the educational system and specifically to the humanities. Other disciplines offer knowledge about things; the humanities offer knowledge about human beings, and thus imply a promise of something more than information, an awakened understanding of oneself as a member of the human species, a heightened alertness to the possibilities of being human. The possibility of a genuinely transformative self-understanding is at once the loftiest goal of the humanities and an enduring source of the crisis "in" the humanities. For what knowledge can measure up to this possibility? What must we know in order to feel that we truly know ourselves? And how is the classroom or the campus equipped to provide such knowledge? No lecture, no seminar, no examination, no research assignment, no office hour, no syllabus can produce the life-changing wisdom that the humanities seem to offer, or satisfy the unfocused yearning that they solicit.

Still, education at all levels fails in its mission of preparing people individually and collectively for an uncertain future if it conceives of its task solely in terms of job training, or even as information transmission. With their unresolved mingling of the liberal-free and the *artes liberales* traditions, the humanities remain themselves unresolved, and thereby keep open the promise of a kind of knowledge that cannot be either divorced from or reduced to information. As I try to demonstrate in chapter 5,

Shakespeare's *Henry V* is a different play, even a different kind of document, when used in a course in management or leadership than when studied in a literature class. It is also, of course, a different play when studied in a rural high school, a community college, an elite research university, or a suburban living room. But the most interesting contrast might be between the approach that would be taken in an institution where the category of the humanities is in place and an institution where some other term is used to organize the curriculum. I wonder, in this respect, if the intensely personal, direct, and unpredictable classroom experience I describe in chapter 7 would have been possible if the general context were not humanities, but *Geisteswissenschaften, sciences humaines*, or arts and letters.

That experience was, for me, a compelling instance of the power of the humanities to elicit, facilitate, and validate learning experiences that go beyond the acquisition of information or the application of method, even beyond the refinement of sensibility, and that reach out toward some apprehension of the human condition. Is there something in the history and culture of the United States that provides a welcome context for such experiences, or are versions of such experiences possible anywhere? If they are, are they seen as experiences of the sort that education, especially higher education, ought to be providing? Would they have the same value and meaning? Would they be seen as moments in an itinerary of self-understanding that would serve the long-term interests of society? Or would they be understood as useless distractions from the main point of education, destructive of social order and national identity? Perhaps my audiences in Turkey understood these questions better than I, and were posing them silently as I spoke.

The humanities were born in crisis and do not do well out of it. They seem to be at their best when they are losing ground, or when the ground is moving under their feet. While they make, or seem to make, an appeal to tradition, they have always been responsive to changes in the cultural weather, and their successive revisitings of the textual, artifactual, and material remains of the past enable this change to be marked and measured as the record of the past is scrutinized once again from the perspective of the present. As the world turns, the humanities turn with it: they contribute to the turning and are themselves turned. No discipline is fixed, no sector of knowledge clearly delimited, no distinction is absolute, not even the most fundamental one of all, between science and the humanities. Both of these come out of the "philosophical-scientific" tradition, and both were, for a long gestational period, folded together in the dark chrysalis of philology, which also contained, in larval form, the social sciences. Disciplines are defined by their essential subjects. And if the subject of the modern humanities is human beings considered as such— in human terms, on a human scale, as actors, creators, and thinkers—then any knowledge that illuminates this subject should be considered humanistic, inside rather than outside the circle.

The humanities do not own the project of human self-understanding; by long-standing convention, they merely supervise it. Human self-understanding can pursue many paths. Over the past generation, while the humanities were recovering from an extended infatuation with antihumanist theory, the sciences have been taking over the inquiry into the human. Advances in computer science, genetic engineering, evolutionary biology, and neuroscience have contributed immensely to our understanding of fundamental human capabilities and faculties, and this rumbling avalanche of facts and theories is not just adding to the sum of knowledge but changing the nature of the disciplines, and the relationship of discipline to discipline. A new set of understandings, armed with powerful technologies that expand the scope of our agency, is even changing the human itself: what seemed fundamental or immutable a few years ago no longer seems so today, and limits once thought absolute are being breached every day. Humanists now face the disconcerting but exciting prospect of watching their subject mutate before their eyes. Once again, they are losing ground, and must find a way to adapt themselves to this new crisis. At this time in particular, they must be especially responsive to changes in the weather. If those with the right knowledge base and disposition can find a way to collaborate with the sciences—not as bystanders or commentators, and not as junior partners in a biology-based spirit of consilience, but rather as coinvestigators in a synthetic project of human self-understanding—they might not look like humanists of the past, but they would still be fulfilling the humanities' original and abiding mission.

1

Beneath and Beyond the "Crisis in the Humanities"

I

One of the many curious facts about academic life in America is that very few people who work in the humanities ever think about them. Unlike academic departments, the category of the humanities seems even to humanists themselves a mere administrative convenience, a kind of phantom entity rather than a real principle of identity; and like all things administrative, it is resisted with indifference. The humanities are something like "North America," a level of organization with neither the urgency of the local nor the grand significance of the global.

But to many outside the university, it is the departmental structure that seems arbitrary and even artificial, while the larger classifications—humanities, social sciences, mathematics, and natural sciences—really describe something. From this point of view, the distinctions between the fields of the humanities are less important than the features they hold in common. Scholars working in the humanities would be well advised to sensitize themselves to this point of view; for if, in addition to thinking of themselves as specialists in a given discipline, they could also think of themselves as humanists, they could see how their work contributed to a larger project, how its distinctive emphasis fit together with others both humanistic and nonhumanistic. They would then be in a better position to understand their actual and potential contributions to knowledge as a whole and even to the culture at large. They would, in other words, be better able to address one of the most stubborn dilemmas in higher education, the perennial *crisis in the humanities.*

Virtually every survey of American higher education over the past half century has noted this crisis. Almost since the time of the Hindenburg, it seems, scholars have been crying, "Oh, the humanities!" Sometimes the crisis—whose dimensions can be measured in terms of enrollments, majors, courses offered, and salaries—is described as a separate and largely self-inflicted catastrophe confined to a few disciplines; sometimes it is linked to a general disarray in liberal education, and sometimes to the moral collapse and intellectual impoverishment of the entire culture. But one point emerges with considerable regularity and emphasis: humanistic scholars, conflicted and confused about their mission, suffer from an inability to convey to those on the outside and even to some on the inside the specific value they offer to public culture; they suffer, that is, from what the scholar and critic Louis Menand calls a "crisis of rationale."[1]

Curiously, and disturbingly, Menand, a prominent humanist himself, sees no easy way out of this crisis and makes no attempt to formulate what he describes as the missing rationale for humanistic study. He is especially vexed by the "predictable and aimless eclecticism" fostered by a contemporary mood of "postdisciplinarity," in which tenured scholars feel licensed to abandon their training in order to pursue such topics as (in Menand's hypothetical example) "the history of carrots, written in the first person." If the professors abandon their disciplines, Menand notes, students facing an uncertain economic future might well wonder why they should devote themselves to reading literature, history, or philosophy.

Talk of crisis has been around for so long, however, that it has become simply incorporated into the most accustomed ways in which humanistic scholars understand themselves and their work. Once considered an affliction, crisis has become a way of life. What would the humanities be without their crisis? So inured have scholars in the humanities become to talk of crisis that many have almost been content to have a crisis rather than a rationale; in fact, it sometimes seems that the crisis *is* the rationale in that some scholars seem less interested in exposing students to the wisdom of the ages, the magic of art, and the rigors of history than they are in being observed in a dramatic, and sometimes entertaining, state of self-doubt.

A clearly articulated rationale for humanistic inquiry would, however, help displace the attention from the professor to the profession, and also to focus the profession's attention on the community whose support it seeks and whose long-term interests it aspires to serve. On the other hand, an inability or unwillingness on the part of humanists to give some account of their work that makes apparent its distinctiveness and value to the larger culture actually damages the disciplines themselves and makes it more likely that the humanities, currently hanging on to "North American" status, might actually start to look more like South or Central America.

II

If traditional rationales for humanistic study were to be condensed into a single sentence, that sentence might be the following: *The scholarly study of documents and artifacts produced by human beings in the past enables us to see the world from different points of view so that we may better understand ourselves.* This banal formulation may seem to have limited interest for us, but if we probe it a bit we can discover, preserved in the amber of tradition, elements that retain a certain enduring and even unexplored vitality. Examined closely, the sentence contains three distinct premises, that the humanities have the text as their object, human beings as their subject, and self-understanding as their purpose.

1. *Textuality.* As a valuable 1981 study, *The Humanities in American Life*, authored by the Commission on the Humanities says, "the humanities employ a particular medium . . . the medium is language," specifically textual language. I believe that the word *employ* refers directly to humanistic scholarship, and somewhat less directly to the materials being studied, which can be texts either in the narrow, literal sense or in the more expansive sense that emerged about forty years ago, in which any material artifact—a cityscape, a carved bone, an earthwork, even a spoken word—could be considered a text. The key fact is pastness: as the authors say, the "turn of mind" distinctive of the humanities is "toward history."[2] Once again, this formulation pertains to both the practice and the object of humanistic scholarship: humanists study documents produced in the past, and produce, in turn, other documents destined to become part of the historical record.

This textual-historical orientation sometimes gives to the humanities a backward-looking cast, especially by comparison with an image-and-technology-dominated mass culture. In such a context, the text-dependency of the humanities has sometimes seemed an archaic holdover, like a vestigial tailbone in primates that serves no present purpose. Feeling vulnerable on this point, humanists have responded either with an uncritical embrace of technology or with a stubborn defense of traditional textuality, neither of which has served them especially well.

The concept of the text is not neutral or natural, and is therefore not immune to criticism. As Richard Lanham pointed out in the dawning days of the Web in 1993, the printed text bears within itself a certain ideology, encouraging what he regarded as dangerous illusions about the possibility of objectivity and the separability of mind and voice. By comparison, he argued, technology restores to discourse the enlivening qualities of consciousness, mobility, play, and personality. An accomplished rhetorician,

Lanham was unashamedly excited by the prospect of navigating sprawling networks of information unfurling before him, experiencing the heady sensation that he was becoming more spontaneous, improvisational, and even creative than seems possible while merely staring at a book. The comparison Lanham and others drew could hardly have been more extreme: on the one side, the dead text, wedged in among countless others in the catacombs of the library, requiring a sterile discipline of linear tracking by a solitary reader; and on the other, the live electronic network, with virtual arcades of possibilities created moment by moment by our own choices, our own desires, our own improvisatory expertise—the medium itself seeming to hold out a promise of infinite, immediate, transparent, and universal communication. Comparing the traditional form of the printed text with the vital and adaptive information networks available on the Web, Lanham warned that if humanists could not find a way to accommodate themselves to the new age, they might not survive its advent; or as he put it, "the 'humanist' task may pass to other groups while the humanities dwindle into grumpy antiquarianism."[3]

But the book is not precisely the text. Digital technology erases some features of the book, but textuality as such has survived the technological revolution intact. Indeed, one might even argue that electronic technology does not replace the text but actually extends, supplements, and radicalizes other features of textuality by increasing our power to switch between texts of various kinds, and to take in writing, image, and sound at once. This retention and extension of the text are very good things, because textuality carries with it a number of invaluable entailments unrecognized by Lanham and others who celebrated the technological revolution as a fundamental alteration in the concept of information itself.

First, the material stability of the text, in both traditional and digital environments, implies a reassuring possibility of definite knowledge; and since the text represents intentions and agency, this implication extends to things not directly present to our senses. Reading a text, we are encouraged to seek the truth by observation, inference, and speculation, and are fortified in thinking that our search can produce results. Moreover, the very inertness of the text, its material indifference to our needs, helps produce that peculiar kind of intellectual pleasure distinctive of reading, a kind of weightlessness or freedom from immediate concerns; and we realize this benefit even in an electronic environment where we are not limited to the form of the book. This pleasure is accompanied, especially for the scholar, by a distinct sense of power. Since the truth of the past exists largely in textual traces, it must be assembled in the present, and can always be reassembled from a different point of view, with different emphases, presumptions, and priorities. In return for their focused attention on the object, readers—especially scholarly readers—are granted a license for a highly pleasurable act of synthetic speculative understanding that goes well beyond what is immediately or indisputably given.

Since it is, in theory, equally accessible to all readers, the text is also a public medium, creating around itself an invisible community of those who have or may yet read it. All texts are written from within some cultural tradition, and most groups or individuals look to the archive of the past for keys to their heritage and thus to their identity. But even though the access to a given text is determined by a host of local and contingent factors, the community implied by textuality itself is inclusive rather than exclusive because it is predicated on a particular kind of action rather than on identity. Indeed, one enters this community only after implicitly agreeing to submit to a task of reading that is in some ways depersonalizing, in that it involves a provisional suspension of identity and even, in certain cases, puts that identity at risk by subjecting it to new information, new stimuli, new questions, new stresses. The world pours forth from texts in response to disciplined interest.

And so, although reading may awaken or refine elements of our individual character, and although the information we get from texts may be highly particular, the fact that reading is a labor that all can, in theory, undertake means that the heritage we glean from texts is a human as well as a local possession: textuality as such is organized around the principle of universal communication across time and space, and constitutes a continuous and theoretically unbounded archive. That quintessentially American figure, Thoreau, had absorbed a vast range of knowledge from traditions other than his own, including classical philosophy and history; his "On Civil Disobedience" was read eagerly by that definitively Indian figure Gandhi, who learned from him (and from Emerson, Ruskin, and Tolstoy, as well as from Indian philosophy) the principles of nonviolent protest; this philosophy was then absorbed by a theology student in Chester, Pennsylvania, named Martin Luther King, who gave it memorable expression in the course of that characteristically American protest movement, the civil rights struggles of the 1950s and 1960s, struggles that were directly inspirational to Nelson Mandela and others fighting apartheid in South Africa.

No responsible scholar believes that humanistic study directly fosters private virtue and responsible citizenship. On the other hand, most scholars do believe that by engaging in humanistic study, they are doing something worthwhile in a larger sense; they are simply uncertain about how to connect this larger public good with their private scholarly activity. In a penetrating assessment, "Humanities and the Library in the Digital Age," Carla Hesse makes a fresh attempt, arguing that traditional textuality provides a "space of reflexivity" that takes concrete form in libraries, "our most cherished spaces of contemplation and reflection upon human values."[4] Especially by comparison with the ecstasies that greeted the first days of the Internet, the state of mind associated with reading a book is stubbornly antiutopian, in part because of the measured pace of reading. This pace, which can seem to be out of step with a world devoted to the principle of acceleration, is, Hesse argues, deeply rooted in the history of our democratic ideals. As a "*slow* form of exchange," she says, the book implicitly "conceives of public communication not as action but rather as reflection upon action" (115). A "logic of deferral" structures books, and this deferral opens a space for a "deep investigation, concentration, reflection, and contemplation" (116). Hesse links the capacity for self-reflection with self-representation and self-constitution, and therefore with self-governance. She concludes this majestic argument with the assertion that the humanities, rooted in a principle of reflective delay that is rendered almost visible in the book, reinforce and promote, even if they cannot guarantee or secure, the development of "accountable citizens of a democracy" (117).

That we have access to the past only through texts suggests that the past is not a constant, pressing burden, but a subject that engages our attention on a voluntary basis. We can, if we choose, close the book, or log off. And so, even without claiming that the humanities have a direct positive impact on private character or public citizenship, we may say that the textual emphasis of the humanities implies, as it were, the possibility of truthful knowledge (and the symmetrical, equally bracing, possibility of error), the act of reflection, and the cultivation of democratic citizenship, and fosters as well a sense of freedom and power opening onto an undiscovered future.

2. *Humanity*. According, once again, to *The Humanities in American Life*, "The essence of the humanities is a spirit or an attitude toward humanity. . . . [The humanities] show how the individual is autonomous and at the same time bound, in the ligatures of language and history, to humankind across time and throughout the world" (3). Reading more than a generation after these fine phrases were written, it is easy to detect in them a certain worldview, emphasizing both individual autonomy and universal harmony, that may reflect "American life" at the dawn of the Reagan era more accurately than it does humanity as such. The formulation does, however, contain a germ of constant truth in its insistence that the humanities are inconceivable without some idea of the human.

This idea is, I think, usefully indicated by a statement made by the first director of the National Humanities Center, the philosopher Charles Frankel, who said in 1978 that "the humanities are that form of knowledge in which the knower is revealed.

All knowledge becomes humanistic when we are asked to contemplate not only a proposition but the proposer, when we hear the human voice behind what is being said."[5] These sentences do many things at once, with an appearance of unstressed ease. First, they liberate the humanities from a given set of academic disciplines by stressing a "form of knowledge" that can be found in any discipline.[6] The study of the law, for example, is not part of the humanities, but when legal scholars trace the evolution of the thought of a Holmes, a Marshall, a Frankfurter, they are approaching the law humanistically, as the product of a "human voice." Even mechanisms can be approached in this way. In Michael Ondaatje's great novel *The English Patient*, a British officer during World War II instructs a young man on how to defuse undetonated bombs. "People think a bomb is a mechanical object, a mechanical enemy," he says; but if you want to survive, you must consider the bomb and its detonating device as a tactic, a piece of strategy designed to confuse, and then to kill, the person attempting to defuse it. You must learn to see the bomb humanistically; or, as he puts it, "you have to consider that somebody made it."[7] If bomb detonation can be humanistic, literary study may be mechanistic: bibliography, prosody, or some forms of textual editing, for example, are aspects of a humanistic discipline, but to the extent that they set aside the "human voice," they cannot, on Frankel's account, be considered properly humanistic.

One could quibble about such matters endlessly, but the larger point is that scholarship in the humanities is defined by its concern with the subject of humanity. Humanists operate on a human scale; they treat their subjects not as organisms, cells, or atoms, not as specks of animate matter in the vast universe—nor, for that matter, do they treat them as clients, patients, customers, or cases—but as self-aware individuals conscious of their existence. Humanistic knowledge is centered in texts (in the broadest sense of the term) produced by human beings engaged in the process of reflecting on their lives. At the core of the humanities is the distinctively human capacity to imagine, to interpret, and to represent the human experience.

Beneath the fact-oriented focus on the text (Frankel's "proposition") is a more speculative engagement with the process by which the text was produced, the creative act of "the proposer," with all its contexts. This emphasis on the human act of creation is not noncontroversial; it has, in fact, been one of the most contentious issues in intellectual history over the past century, as one discipline after another has sought to modernize or postmodernize itself by eliminating the human voice from the object of study. Throughout the reign of antihumanistic high theory in the humanities (roughly 1968–90), the most advanced thinkers regarded the very notions of human being, human nature, and human voice—not to mention the individual human subject—as nothing more than ideologically generated mystifications. As an alternative, many tried to produce a pure description of linguistic or discursive facts. Attempts to construct a "history without human nature" (Michel Foucault), to describe an "inhuman" language (Paul de Man), or to trace the movements of an ideological "process without a subject" (Louis Althusser) represented some of the great triumphs of this point of view, triumphs that really did create a crisis in the humanities because they resulted in humanistic disciplines becoming more and more technical, empirical, and analytic—and doing so, strangely enough, while some scientific fields were aggressively taking up issues traditionally allotted to the humanities, such as free will, moral judgment, creativity, and consciousness.

The issue came to a head in a 1970 debate on Dutch television between the scientific linguist Noam Chomsky, speaking in English, and the philosopher and historian Michel Foucault, speaking French. One can only wonder what the original viewers made of this event, but in the years since 1997, when a translation of the transcript was finally made widely available to English readers, the debate has become recognized as a rare occasion when two extraordinary minds engaged each other directly and at length at the level of fundamental principles, with Chomsky arguing for a concrete account of human nature as the indispensable foundation for any kind of political or ethical vision, and Foucault insisting that "human nature" was a sentimental illusion held over from an earlier, less critical, less scientific era.[8] The long discussion at last converged on the question of the ends of social struggle. For Chomsky, justice was the single goal of protest, while for Foucault power was the only plausible motive. In a statement that lingers in the mind, Foucault declared to an appalled Chomsky that "one makes war to win, not because it is just" (136).

I cannot fully represent here the nuances of this debate, but it is clear that Foucault's account is singularly impoverished as an explanation of anything that happens in the human realm and seems more suited to explaining events in the animal or even the vegetable world, in which the reasons for acting are unmediated by any consideration of higher purposes or ultimate ends. With respect to the human world, Foucault explains effects, perhaps, but not causes: his account abruptly short-circuits the inquiry into motivation by eliminating the mass of reasons, rationales, and rationalizations that determine human will or intentionality. Chomsky's insistence not only on "justice" but, in a larger sense, on the place of ideas and ideals points to an indispensable humanistic premise, that human action is not entirely blind but is informed by arguments and undertaken for reasons that, unlike "making war to win," are not immediately apparent or directly manifest in the action itself. This assumption of *depth* in human action and indeed in human being constitutes one of the most crucial premises of humanistic inquiry.

The concept of depth also leads directly to one of the salient features of the human mind, and the key to the "conception of the human" that is reinforced by humanistic study: the fact that the mind operates on many levels or modalities at once, including many of which it is unaware. Human intentionality is irreducibly complex; it can never be grasped by a single principle of explanation. Many would accept this proposition when applied to large-scale collective actions such as the French Revolution, the cold war, or the Great Depression, but it is just as true of actions committed by an individual, of individual expressions, and even of texts written by individuals. As a product of human agency, the text is a record of many intentions and processes, some available to the author in the form of consciousness, and others that are hidden and strictly unconscious. In literary study, as in legal theory, the "original intent" of the author is sometimes advanced as the ultimate explanatory principle, but conscious intentions are remarkably difficult to establish, hard to sort out, and often altogether irrelevant.

For most texts, we can safely presume that the author intended to write these particular words, but not why. The reasons one may have for writing are legion: to pursue fame, wealth, or sexual success; to impress the world as a clever person; to give voice to the wisdom of the nation; to prove that one is not the little fool one's mother had always thought one to be; to redeem one's reputation from the disaster of the last book; to pass the time by writing rather than by undertaking some more arduous pursuit, to fill one more page with writing before knocking off for lunch. Such intentions may be vividly present to the author; they may alternate or mingle with each other and with countless others over the course of composition; they may determine a great deal about the text—and yet they may never crest the surface of the text, may never find direct expression at all. They may in fact be unrecoverable, especially by comparison to unconscious intentions, by which I mean not only the classical Freudian traumas but also a host of other energies of which the author is never fully conscious. The social, historical, economic, and ideological systems in which we all swim without really being aware of them can, to a retrospective examination, actually be more legible in, and therefore more revealing about, a text than the author's conscious intentions when writing. Recognizing that texts are determined, and overdetermined, by forces of which the author is not consciously aware, the humanistic approach begins with the assumption that the text requires multiple explanations, each of which might be an answer to a different question.

Overdetermination, the premise that the real forces determining the text exceed anything the author could consciously know, means that human behavior and expression have a virtually infinite capacity to respond to queries put to them, and exceed any given explanation of them. If this were not true, we would long ago have stopped reading Joyce, Dickens, Shakespeare, Goethe, Austen, the Bible, or Homer, and would have replaced them with their definitive explanations, reaping the rewards of certain knowledge efficiently packaged. We would have contented ourselves with single histories, single biographies, single interpretations. But under the presumption that human behavior and expression are bottomless in their depth, humanistic study produces not certain but *un*certain knowledge, knowledge that solicits its own revision in an endless process of refutation, contestation, and modification—a process of conversation. Humanists aspire to speak the truth, but none would wish to have the very last word, for such a triumphant conclusion would bring an end not just to the conversation, and not just to the discipline, but to the human activities of rereading, reconsidering, rethinking, reflecting.

The underlying aim of humanistic study is always to construct, through the materials provided by the text, an understanding of a human intention, an account of how and why this particular text came to be the way it is, the conditions under which the text emerged. We are not in search of the conscious mind of the historical author, something we can never fully know. We are trying to specify as far as possible the range and sensitivity of that mind, in both its conscious and unconscious dimensions. Milton, for example, thought himself to be a Puritan poet whose task was to justify the ways of God to man; but over a hundred years after he died, William Blake argued that Milton's sympathetic treatment of Satan demonstrated that the poet was "of the devil's party without knowing it"; then, about a century and a half later, the critic William Empson argued that Milton was actually criticizing the moral character of God as the Bible represented it; a half century later, Stanley Fish demonstrated that the effect of reading *Paradise Lost* was to force the reader to venture interpretations that were subsequently discredited by the text—in other words "falling" and experiencing one's own fallibility—so that the theological message of the poem was reinforced by the reader's line-by-line experience. Each of these readings constituted not just an event in the history of Milton criticism but also a moment in cultural self-understanding, as *Paradise Lost* was refashioned as a contemporary document, participating in contemporary debates. On each occasion, the image of the mind of Milton was reconceived as Milton was discovered to have a host of new intentions "without knowing it."

On those fascinating occasions when the meaning of a canonical work is powerfully disputed and a new account advanced, the premises of humanistic scholarship as a whole are laid bare. On such occasions, what had passed for common sense about the past is overturned, and we are forced to confront an unsuspected volatility and depth in the text, in history, and in our view of history. We confront, that is, not just a new interpretation of a text, an event, a person, but the larger possibility that everything we had relegated to that species of inertia we call the past might be altered, even radically so.

This leads to a further point: that humanistic study inculcates a heightened awareness of our power over the past. Under normal circumstances, a desire to change the past is associated either with such counterfeiting romantics as Gatsby, who fabricates a glamorous history for himself, or with totalitarian dictatorships, with their encyclopedias in three-ring binders for easy elimination of patriots-now-adjudged-to-have-been-traitors. The protocols of scholarship—the rigorous observation of fact, the appeal to evidence, the conventions of public debate—can contain or regulate the potential for distortion implied in this power to alter the past, but they cannot eliminate it. Nor should they, for such power is the driving force behind our interest in the past in the first place. As the philosopher Ernst Cassirer noted long ago, "symbolic thought"—the kind of thought in which the humanities specialize—is the best antidote to "the natural inertia of man," and serves as the basis of man's "ability to constantly reshape his human universe."[9] What are we doing when we read, if not changing the past, and doing so for our own present purposes? In humanistic study, we confront not just our ancestors but also our own capacity for determining who our ancestors were, and thus for determining who we are or might become. This capacity should be treated like fire, with great respect for its power to create and to destroy.

3. *Self-understanding.* As Frankel indicates, the humanities are a "form of knowledge in which the knower is revealed." This is the most vital and distinctive aspect of humanistic inquiry, but also the most mysterious and the most easily misunderstood. When people tout the moral value of the humanities—when they claim that the humanities inculcate principles of citizenship, refine one's sensibility, or increase our distinctively human potential—they are claiming, in essence, that humanistic knowledge produces an identifiable positive effect on people. Frankel's formulation is a useful corrective to this claim, for he does not say that humanistic knowledge improves the knower, only that it "reveals" the knower, a very different thing. This curious phrase refers to one of the effects of reading, with its responsibility to get it right, to apprehend the text without distortion or projection. Engaged in this project, we are subjected to a constant discipline in which we are implicitly required to examine and correct ourselves. To be sure, we would labor under the same imperative if the thing under inspection were a fossil, a meter reading, or a pitched baseball. But these tasks do not reveal the knower in the same way as approaching a text from a humanistic point of view. The crucial additional fact about that point of view is indicated by the presumption of "depth," which implies that the text is the record of a human intention to communicate through the use of signs. Signs refer us to a mind, and so bring us into the presence not just of significance—which could be attributed to a cloud, a bullet, a footprint, a snowflake—but of meaning. A deep object is a meaningful object; and it is in the process of examining the object, probing its depth and constructing the mass of intentions behind it, that we discover depth and meaning in ourselves.

To read is to struggle to understand a mind that struggled

to express itself, and this shared struggle is one of the bases for communication between author and reader. To enter into silent dialogue with an author, we must suspend our distinct identities and presume that his or her mind is like ours in this and perhaps other respects. We do not make the same presumption of equivalence about the people described in literary or historical works, and so have a less intimate relationship with them. Reading about people may enrich our imaginative *experience*, but reading words in search of the human presence behind them strengthens our imaginative *capacity*, forcing us to reenact in our own minds the drama of other minds and even to feel their thoughts and sensations as if they were our own. Identification with an author is considered by many scholars to be a primitive and precritical response, but no act of reading, no matter how sophisticated or advanced, can do without it, and the most powerful criticism has it in abundance. The criticism of Stephen Greenblatt on Shakespeare, Leo Steinberg on Michelangelo, Edward Said on Conrad, Eve Kosofsky Sedgwick on Henry James, and Helen Vendler on Keats has this in common, that it not only imparts detailed information about texts and their contexts, but also conveys a deeply personalized sense of intimacy or intellectual sympathy with a mind. When, in a defiant mood, humanists insist that their "soft" disciplines are actually *more* difficult and require *more* intelligence than the "hard" sciences, they are thinking about the discipline imposed by the other mind, which cannot be measured or directly observed, which is not necessarily self-aware or self-consistent, but which must still be somehow apprehended and understood. In the humanistic text, even "the facts" are humanized and must be grasped mind to mind as well as mind to object, and this difficult process exercises both the intellect and the imagination.

True humanistic scholarship insists on this double discipline, which untrained readers find easy to avoid. Consider, for example, the figure of Léon, the callow young clerk who becomes Emma Bovary's lover in Flaubert's great novel. Léon first earns Emma's ardent trust in the course of a rapturous conversation on the power of literature to uplift the soul and touch the heart. "One thinks of nothing," he says, "the hours slip by. Without having to move, we walk through the countries of our imagination, and your thought, blending with the fiction, toys with the details, follows the outline of the adventures. It mingles with the characters, and it seems you are living their lives, that your own heart beats in their breast." "That is true!" Emma exclaims, "that is true!"[10] We fear for Emma at this point, not just because we sense her dangerous attraction to a man who is not her husband, but also because Léon's discourse suggests not a disciplined understanding of the text that also yields an augmented self-knowledge but a kind of free fall; we sense that he can lose himself without losing much, and that if Emma were to lose herself to him, she might lose everything.

One can also go wrong by failing to lose oneself at all, a failure given memorable form in the portrait of Emma's other lover, the callously opportunistic Rodolphe. At one desperate point, Emma tells Rodolphe that she loves him, that she will be his slave— sentiments that seem to him entirely appropriate, as he has heard them from a succession of mistresses. As Flaubert's narrator comments, "He was unable to discern, this man of so much experience, the nuances of feeling that may reside in common words" (138). Hearing a formula for abject devotion, Rodolphe takes it at face value, indifferent to the possibility that the passionate and inexperienced Emma may have deployed conventional phrases to express feelings of great depth and poignancy. In Rodolphe, Flaubert describes a mind unable to surrender its own self-interest, incapable of exposing itself to the "human voice" of others—in short, a mind deficient in true humanistic sensibility. Rodolphe never makes a presumption of equivalence, never places himself on the same footing as others, never apprehends depth, never truly communicates. This may be why he is never shown in the act of reading, except when he peruses his own letter of farewell to Emma, a grossly duplicitous and hypocritical text whose rhetorical finesse he greatly admires. Rodolphe's wide experience has provided him with a certain cunning, but has locked him into himself. It is Flaubert's final, devastating point that the world does not punish such people, but torments their victims without end.

We can contrast both of these antihumanistic types, one deficient in intellect and the other in imagination, with Flaubert himself, who wrote in one of his famous letters to Louise Colet, "I am Madame Bovary." What could he have meant? Perhaps he was saying that he, like Emma, was pouring his heart out to the Léons and Rodolphes, not to mention the Charles Bovarys, of the world. He may have been confessing that his heroine was just a masked version of himself, confirming the recurrent suspicion of readers since Baudelaire that Emma has a "masculine" character. But the most productive explanation concerns the extreme state of empathetic identification he entered into while composing the novel, a state that caused him virtually to live the experiences of his characters, even to the point of having "a distinct taste of arsenic in my mouth" when he wrote of Emma taking poison. Flaubert understood that vomiting one's dinner, as he did when writing of Emma's poisoning, is a form of hallucination dangerously close to insanity, but he understood, too, the difference between hallucination and a genuinely creative state of mind. "I know those two states perfectly," he wrote; "there is a gulf between them. In genuine hallucination there is always terror; you feel that your personality is slipping away from you; you think you're going to die. In poetic vision, on the contrary, there is joy. It is something that permeates you. Nevertheless, here too you lose your bearings."[11]

The mark of "poetic vision" is a sudden sense of creative power as one sheds one's limitations and enters into an expanded field of possibilities. Something of this sense, in diminished forms even farther from terror or hallucination, is available to readers, whose work is still creative, still imaginative, even though it results in no tangible product and merely comprehends the product of another. For the act of reading involves us not only in the experiences of the people described but also, in its word-by-word tracking of the act of creation, in the life and mind of the writer as well. In this respect, too, humanistic understanding is inescapably dual—on the one hand, a liberation from the confines of the mundane self through an immersion in the lives and thoughts of others, a loss of bearings; and, on the other, a vicarious or secondary participation in the author's act of creation that enhances and strengthens our imaginative powers. These effects may seem to be limited to the individual reader, who is given a sense of pleasure and power without cost, and this ethos of self-enrichment was indeed the emphasis and the effect of much traditional humanistic pedagogy. But a new self-understanding can be experienced as an understanding of a new self, and a new relation to others. Such an understanding cannot always be confined to those still, sweet moments spent alone with a book. It is no accident that moments of great vigor in the world of humanistic scholarship are so often concurrent with transformational moments in society at large.

III

With their orientation toward human acts of reflection and representation, their invitation to a loss of self, their investment in unconscious forces, and their confusion of intellect and imagination, the humanities represent by their very nature a crisis in that institution dedicated to research and knowledge, the academy. Each discipline within the humanities is also in a state of crisis, for the larger, discipline-transcending subject of humanity hovers over all of them, providing an ultimate justification for them but also making each seem fragmentary. History cannot tell us the whole truth about the past, nor literary study about literature, nor philosophy about truth. Each of these disciplines picks out a certain aspect of human existence, with the clear if implicit understanding that these aspects represent only segments of the totality. The concepts of the division of labor, collaboration, and codependence inform all the humanistic disciplines, which are in principle porous and exposed to the others.

The humanities must understand this condition as its strength, not its weakness. They must insist on the possibility of trans- or multidisciplinary approaches to fundamental problems. This insistence must extend, too, beyond the humanities. One of the most promising features of the present moment is the new urgency gathering at the interface of the humanities and nonhumanistic disciplines as they confront not only such new subjects as genetic engineering, environmental trauma, and the cognitive capacities of animals or machines but also, and most intriguingly, such traditional subjects as the origin of language, the grounding of ethical imperatives, and the distinctive features of a specifically human being. None of these subjects can be satisfactorily addressed by a single discipline, but all of them concern fundamental issues relating to humanity; and the humanities, whose special province is questions of meaning, history, and value, must now reconceive themselves as the natural sponsor of the debates and controversies that swirl around such issues. The confrontations that result from these debates will, in a sense, threaten the disciplines that engage in them, for the sovereignty or adequacy of each will be called into question by the others. But the promise of genuine advances in knowledge and the rejuvenation of the disciplines that accompany these advances more than compensates for this threat.

Paradoxically, these advances can only be made if the disciplines remain strong. Committed to partial knowledge and limited vision, the disciplines represent indispensable guardrails against runaway amateurism and what Menand called aimless eclecticism. "Postdisciplinarity" is clearly not the most productive response to a crisis in traditional disciplinarity, since what is needed today is more not less discipline, and stronger not weaker disciplines. Scholars in the humanities must not confuse a hospitality to innovation and reconfiguration with an indifference to rigor and accuracy, for it is only with the guidelines and conventions established by disciplines that progress in knowledge can be measured; indeed, the disciplines can only undertake in good faith the kind of internal self-revision that is periodically necessary if they are powerful and confident to begin with. Only strong disciplines can grow and modify themselves in productive ways.

One sign of such power and confidence is a willingness to engage in dialogue with a nonacademic audience, a willingness signaled by an approach to advanced thought that makes scholarship accessible to thoughtful people outside the discipline. Scholars cannot expect the public at large to be fascinated by specialist work, much less by the history of carrots written in the first person; but one test of work in all fields is the degree to which it contributes in some identifiable way to a purpose beyond that of the accumulation of knowledge for its own sake. Humanists ought, I believe, to get in the habit of articulating the possible relations between the work they do and some purpose the nonacademic public can understand. There is, of course, no guarantee that the public will approve of that purpose or the means of achieving it, but if the case is not made, the public can hardly be blamed for its indifference or even its distrust. Scholars might find it useful to think of their scholarly identity as but one of a nested series of identities, with each communicating with the others and accommodated within a single individual. If they performed this thought experiment, they could then ask themselves how their scholarly work contributed to purposes that could be grasped by a citizen, a teacher, a parent, an institutional employee, a taxpaying citizen. And so, if I began by urging humanists to cultivate the view from the humanities rather than from the department or the specialist subfield, I would like to close by urging them to imagine, at least, an even larger perspective that looks still farther, out beyond the academy itself.

The humanities should represent both the conservation and accurate transmission of the past and the imaginative cultivation of the future. At every point in humanistic inquiry, the actual meets the possible in an encounter whose results cannot be predicted in advance. "Crisis" in this sense is not a threat or a disaster but one perhaps overly dramatized way of describing a permanent feature of the humanities, one that humanists would do well not just to accept but to promote with all the resources at their command.

2

Roots, Races, and the Return to Philology

Consequences of philology: arrogant expectations; philistinism; superficiality; overrating of reading and writing; Alienation from the people and the needs of the people. . . . Task of philology: to disappear.
«FRIEDRICH NIETZSCHE, "We Philologists"»

Returning to Philologies

So little did Edward Said and Paul de Man have in common, so different and even opposed were their understandings of the methods and aims of scholarship, that it was easy to overlook points of contact or continuity between them. These came into sharp focus, however, with the posthumous publication of Said's *Humanism and Democratic Criticism*, whose central chapter was titled "The Return to Philology," the very same title that de Man had used more than twenty years earlier for one of his most programmatic and polemical essays. The currents of agreement between these essays ran deep, beginning with their diagnoses of the state of criticism. Literary studies, they said, seem to have lost sight of the object, so that the discourse of criticism was filled with windy pronouncements about what Said called "vast structures of power or . . . vaguely therapeutic structures of salutary redemption," statements referring not to texts but, as de Man put it, to "the general context of human experience or history."[1] They agreed, too, on the reason for this loss of focus: the decline of philology in professional training. Criticism without philology, they said, was nothing more than the professional form of the pleasure principle. Only a penitential return to philology, which Said described as the "detailed, patient scrutiny of and a lifelong attentiveness to" the text, would restore the integrity of scholarship (*HDC* 61).

Although neither gave evidence of actual philological expertise, both de Man and Said suggested that the origins of their own advanced practices were to be found in this most traditional, indeed regressive, of all scholarly practices. As de Man said in a typically ironic and defiant passage, "technically correct rhetorical readings may be boring, monotonous, predictable, and unpleasant, but they are irrefutable" (RP 19). For his part, Said did not aspire to either monotony or irrefutability, but he took as his heroes the great Romanist philologists Erich Auerbach, E. R. Curtius, and Leo Spitzer.[2] In a further coincidence, both Said and de Man wrote their essays a year before their deaths: returning to philology seems to be an urge experienced by those confronting their own mortality.

Within this broad spectrum of agreement, however, there were a series of jarring differences. For Said, the object of philological attention, the text, is best conceived as a window onto a particular historical world. In order to grasp that world, one must "put oneself in the position of the author, for whom writing is a series of decisions and choices expressed in words" (*HDC* 62). These choices constitute the process of aesthetic creation, which, because it constructs a counterworld, represents an "unreconciled opposition to the depredations of daily life" and to the "identities . . . given by the flag or the national war of the moment" (63, 80). For Said, philology leads directly from the text to an empathetic encounter with a masterly author, a deep and direct immersion in the historical world that author inhabited, and privileged access to the author's heroic resistance to the actual, most particularly to the ideology of nationalism. The political indifference of many, if not most, philologists notwithstanding, Said argued that "reading is, fundamentally, an act of perhaps modest human emancipation and enlightenment" (66). De Man, by sharp contrast, regarded language in mechanistic and explicitly nonhuman terms, and scholarship as a technical rather than an interpretive or evaluative exercise. He urged scholars to concentrate on linguistic forms for their own sake, focusing on "the structure of language prior to the meaning it produces" (RP 25).

It seems strange that the leaders of two such divergent critical movements should have ended their careers and indeed their lives with the same diagnosis of criticism's current state, and the same cure; and stranger still that both should have claimed to be the true heir of the philological tradition. Strangest of all, however, is the fact that Said and de Man used the same word to denote such utterly different things: intimacy, resistance, emancipation, and historical knowledge for Said, and, for de Man, a harsh and explicit corrective to precisely such humanistic fantasies, as he regarded them. It is as if each had appropriated the term *philology* for his own purposes, without regard to its meaning.

These curiosities invite us to probe more deeply into philology itself; more important, they awaken us to the complex of desires, needs, and longings that have troubled and animated literary study and humanistic scholarship in general.

It is tempting, reading Said and de Man, to think that one of them must simply have gotten it wrong, but philology actually answers to both of their accounts. De Man thought of philology as a positive science, a technical and systematic investigation of texts, beginning with the establishment of the correct text, by restoration if necessary, and emphasizing accurate description and linguistic analysis. While "philologists" in the Renaissance devoted themselves to preserving and printing authoritative editions of ancient manuscripts, de Man seems to be referring more specifically to the "new" or "modern" philology invented at the end of the eighteenth century by F. A. Wolf, who applied to the texts of Homer the methods of meticulous textual scholarship recently developed for the study of the Bible.[3] In his major work, *Prolegomena ad Homerum* (1795), Wolf argued, on the basis of an erudite study of the language of the texts, that the Homeric epics were composed and transmitted orally, and existed as a loosely connected sequence of songs for about five hundred years before they were written down. Wolf treated the surviving texts not as transcribed Homeric utterances but as transcriptions of transcriptions, each one potentially harboring an authentic but encrypted Homeric voice that had to be liberated by painstaking scholarly labor from the impurities that had over time corrupted it. Wolf's professional distrust of the text as given may have compromised the authority of Homer as the historical author of the text, but it marked a significant advance in critical sophistication. Subsequent philologists embraced the presumption that the text was a tissue of appearances whose most elementary features had to be determined by scholarly methods. Scholarship in the wake of Wolf became skeptical and aggressive, even as it confined itself to preliminary matters.

Wolf defined philology as the application of a defined methodology to a limited field of evidence, an empirical practice that prepared the way for the consideration of questions of meaning and value, which would be achieved by other means. After Wolf, philologists devoted themselves to marking the first occurrences of words or usages, determining the geographical range of certain linguistic forms, noting spelling variations, identifying the sound-structure of words and phrases, and tracking shifts in meaning over time. They counted, measured, and compared; they recorded anomalous instances of verb forms, case terminations, inflections, and moods. They developed methods of comparing grammars and classifying languages into families. The work was arduous, a series of microdescriptions with little opportunity for synthesis, judgment, or reflection.[4] Devoting themselves to the study of texts written in ancient languages—Old Norse, Zend,

Old Slavic, Sanskrit, and especially ancient Greek—scholars scarcely lived in the world, their asceticism becoming legendary. As the linguist Roy Harris comments dryly, "We are told that such-and-such a scholar paid no attention to the fall of Napoleon, or the Russian revolution, so engrossed was he at the time in the libraries of Paris or St. Petersburg."[5] Those engaged in such work may have denied themselves many worldly felicities, but they were consoled by the thought that their labors yielded certain knowledge free from abstraction and uncontaminated by interests, desires, or extraneous ends. Moreover, they could, in moments of pride, reflect that their project was reserved for the tiny number of focused intellects capable of years of tedium in pursuit of irreducible fact. They could tell themselves that everything depended on their selfless devotion. As the Byzantinist Ihor Ševcenko puts it, philology even today consists primarily of "constituting and interpreting the texts that have come down to us. It is a narrow thing, but without it nothing else is possible."[6] Associated with a deep erudition accumulated over the course of a disciplined life, philology shaped, as Gerald Graff notes, the pedagogical practices, based on rote learning, recitation, and the examination of linguistic details, of the most prestigious American universities well into the twentieth century.[7] By affiliating deconstruction with this narrow but indispensable thing, de Man was clearly attempting to cast his own practice not only as a traditional pedagogy but as a kind of first knowledge that subtended and enabled all other kinds of understanding.

Philology was, however, also understood in very different terms, not as an empirical study of a limited field but as a speculative undertaking oriented toward deep time and distant things. In "We Philologists," written in 1874, Nietzsche registered his contempt for most philologists, whose work impressed him as an absurd combination of inconsequentiality and hubris. But writing just a few years later in *Daybreak* (1881) as the philosopher of "untimeliness," he summoned up the vision of a rare but authentic philological practice:

Philology is that venerable art which demands of its votaries one thing above all: to go aside, to take time, to become still, to become slow—it is a goldsmith's art and connoisseurship of the *word* which has nothing but delicate, cautious work to do and achieves nothing if it does not achieve it *lento*. But for precisely this reason it is more necessary than ever today, by precisely this means does it entice and enchant us the most, in the midst of an age of "work," that is to say, of hurry, of indecent and perspiring haste, which wants to "get everything done" at once, including every old or new book:—this art does not so easily get anything done, it teaches to read *well*, that is to say, to read slowly, deeply, looking cautiously before and aft, with reservations, with doors left open, with delicate eyes and fingers.[8]

As a careful reader of Nietzsche, de Man was undoubtedly thinking of this memorable passage when he promoted deconstruction as a way of suspending the rush to interpretive closure by attending to the structure of language prior to the meanings it produces. But de Man most certainly did not intend to affiliate deconstruction, as a practice of "technically correct rhetorical readings," with the kind of unfocused rumination Nietzsche describes here. It appears, in other words, that de Man's call for a return to philology registered only one of its aspects—its modest but honorable narrowness—but that there is more.

This "more" was present from the beginning, but not in the form of a simple addition or complement. Wolf's work, to take the example nearest to hand, emerged from and supported a larger movement of "philhellenism," an enthusiasm for the culture of ancient Greece. This enthusiasm was associated with his famous predecessor, Johann Joachim Winckelmann, the most influential advocate for a view of classical Greek culture as a singularly rich embodiment of certain values, including an organic unity of man and nature, a vibrant civic culture, a free and harmonious development of human capacities, and a passionate cultivation of beauty. Wolf joined other "neohumanists," including Winckelmann, Herder, Lessing, Schiller, Hölderlin, the Humboldts, Goethe, and Hegel, in regarding Greece and Rome not merely as admirable in themselves but as inspiring models for contemporary culture and institutions. In the neohumanist ethos, the Greeks were thought to offer Germans a happy example of the youthful freshness of life, exemplifying above all the unity of soul shared by an entire people that would inspire Germans in the wake of the devastations of Napoleonic rule.[9] The singularly creative essence of Greek culture was, they thought, encoded in the language, whose very grammar represented a kind of elementary philosophy. Wolf's work was important in this context because an accurate text would, it was thought, permit the genius of the Greeks to shine through all the more clearly. The Prussian state supported Wolf and his students, because it recognized in philology a tool for promoting a movement of cultural solidarity and renovation that would not be restricted to philosophers, and would not be based on reason alone. As Lionel Gossman says, the philhellenistic movement that gave philology its original point and purpose was "one of the more ingenious and deceptive disguises adopted by the Romantic revolt against the Enlightenment."[10] While Wolf and his successors may have seen themselves as disengaged from contemporary political and ideological struggles, they made no effort to distance themselves from the cultural-political project of rendering the vivifying spirit of ancient civilizations in a form that could inspire imitation.

It is ironic, to say the least, that philology, which Said credited with constituting a resistance to the "identities given by the flag or the national war of the moment," emerged in its modern form in the context of a state-sponsored attempt to foster cultural solidarity. Said may have failed to note the irony because, like de Man, he wished to extract and preserve just a portion of philology, which was crystallized in Wolf's statement of his task: to retrieve, from the corrupted extant texts, the "pure, genuine form which first poured from [Homer's] divine lips."[11] Such a project required not just vast knowledge and a long attention span but—most important to Said—the kind of responsiveness and imagination that would enable the scholar to draw inferences about other minds and cultures from a close study of textual evidence. Imagination was required for such work, and indeed for everything a philologist did. Only inspired guesswork amounting to divination could identify vanishing traces of one word in another, or derive words in different languages from a common source in a prior language. One of the most striking features of the new philology, and the one that Said wished to retrieve and reactivate, was a speculative boldness that many today would consider unprofessional.

Required of even the most basic philological procedures, this boldness was deployed on an ever-larger scale as the discipline matured. At the very beginning, Wolf declared that his ultimate goal was to articulate *"the philosophy of the history of human nature in Greece."*[12] A big job; but over the course of the nineteenth century, philology developed even greater aspirations. Wolf's most accomplished student, Philip August Böckh, saw philology as a master-discipline encompassing a total knowledge of antiquity, including history, geography, mythology, law, religion, art, epigraphy, and what might be called social history—in a phrase that became famous (to philologists): the "knowledge of the known." The scope of philology came to include not just Greece but also the civilizations that lay behind Greece, cultures long since vanished, whose migratory movements and even ways of thinking might be reconstructed on the basis of linguistic study. In *On Language* (1836), Wilhelm von Humboldt argued that philology could disclose the origins of myths, religions, and even national characteristics—the elements of a *Volk*. Each language, he said, represented a unique expression of a nation's "mental power," a distinctive way of solving the universally imposed "task of language formation."[13] After studying a number of languages, the philologist might be able to construct a general typology of languages, which could then inform a historical understanding of the principles of cultural development and a philosophical understanding of the phenomenon of human culture as such. At the end of his labors, the philologist might even be privileged with a glimpse of the ur-language, or *Ursprache*, from which all others had evolved, and thus of the thought-forms prevailing at the origin of human civilization itself. A prodigious vista opened up before the scholar, such that a dry stick like Mr. Casaubon in George Eliot's *Middlemarch* could imagine that as a consequence of decades of dreary toil, the key to all mythologies was within his grasp.

Philology became new or modern when it found a way to conjoin a limited empiricism to a speculative practice with no limits at all, when it discovered a route that led from the close study of the text to the language of the text, and from there to the author, the culture the author inhabited, other cultures, the origins of cultures, and finally to human origins and the mysteries surrounding those origins. In the new philology, the "art of the goldsmith" extended from textual microdetails to questions of profound historical, philosophical, and moral significance, for there was no weak link in this golden chain, no knowledge that could be considered irrelevant.

Given the magnitude of the questions it addressed and the commitment it demanded of the scholar, philology came to be respected, at least in Germany and France, as the highest form of modern scholarship, the vanguard discipline of modernity itself. Writing as an eager young man of twenty-five, in the wake of the events of 1848, Ernest Renan predicted the dawn of a new day of progress and science, with philology in the lead. The "modern spirit," he wrote, "that is, rationalism, criticism, liberalism, was founded on the same day as philology. *The founders of the modern spirit are the philologists.*" He defined the discipline that eventually came to be known for its antiquarian narrowness as nothing less than "the *exact science of the productions of the human intellect*," a master discourse that epitomized the scientific spirit as such; all advances made by humanity since the fifteenth century, he contended, were attributable to the philological spirit.[14] To its partisans, philology embraced everything, and almost every person, of consequence. Nietzsche, for whom a genealogy of morals lay well within the compass of philology, counted Goethe, Wagner, Schopenhauer, and Leopardi as philologists of the highest rank. Heidegger was placing himself in the great tradition when he attempted to recover the primordiality of Being through a study of

words. No task was too great for the philologue. As Said noted, in
the nineteenth century the term itself seemed to include "both a
gift for exceptional spiritual insight into language and the ability
to produce work whose articulation is of aesthetic and historical
power"; "there is," he concluded with a guarded admiration, "an
unmistakable aura of power about the philologist."[15]

In short, the fear voiced by Said and de Man—that critics un-
moored from philology might indulge in statements about vast
structures of power or the general context of human history—
was for nearly a century and a half proudly announced as the
defining characteristic and entire point of philology itself.

Neither Said nor de Man emphasized the way that the ascetic
rigor of philological discipline—the commitment to empiricism, erudition, narrowness, and method—translated into critical power in the form of speculative freedom and the authority
to pronounce on issues of immense moment. They merely sought
to roll back the tape of the history of scholarship and begin again,
with criticism established on the foundation of a safe, limited,
honorable practice. It is, however, difficult to imagine that two
such charismatic scholars did not also respond to the aura of
power that gathered about the philologist, and that, in seeking
to return to philology, they were not also looking to recapture
that aura. They undoubtedly recognized that the otherworldly
authority of philology derived from the fact that it was strictly a
preliminary procedure, unimplicated in cultural, political, or ideological agendas. Accordingly, both offered carefully delimited
and partial versions of philological practice that stressed such un-
exceptionable virtues as attention, care, and rigor. De Man simply ignored the historical and speculative dimensions, and while
Said criticized scholars such as Renan who could be accused of
Orientalism, he saw their work as a perversion of true philology. The question raised by their work is, then, not just whether
scholarship would be well served by a return to philology, but
whether an essential or authentic philology of unimpeachable
intellectual credentials could be identified and rescued from its
actual historical practice.

Language, Origins, and Race

In fact, philologists in the nineteenth century were already raising this question, and were answering it by insisting that their
discipline should be considered a true science, a refined and sophisticated practice that could bear comparison to biology, phys-
ics, chemistry, anatomy, electricity, botany, anthropology, and
above all geology. "There is no science," Max Müller wrote, "from
which we, the students of language, may learn more from than
Geology."[16] From the philological perspective, ancient languages
were like fossils or petrifactions, and gave access to past human
experience in the same way that rocks displayed in a museum
revealed the geological record. "In language, as in pure amber,"
one scholar wrote in 1858, "the ideas, hopes, mistakes, experiences,
follies, joys and sorrows of preceding generations are preserved,
in clear, transparent beauty, for our constant appreciation and
enlightenment."[17] Indeed, words were superior to rocks in that
while the latter could only be observed, analyzed, and described,
words could speak their own truth. "And how," this writer continued, "is the silent past of language made, under the reviving
touch of philology, all vocal of itself again." But as this comment
suggests, philology, the discipline of the reviving touch, was also
felt to command powers that were not strictly scientific, even
approaching the occult. It represented, in fact, a sublime non-
conflict of the faculties: as this long essay concludes, "the study
of language rises, under the light of true philology, like all high
philosophy, into the very charms of poetry" (ibid., 507).

Staking claims to the status of poetry, philosophy, and science—and to a transcendence of disciplinarity as such—philology represented itself as an "untimely" form of knowledge that
was completely independent of political or ideological ends. And
yet, the defining feature of philology in the nineteenth century
was that, persuaded of the scientific solidity of its means and
the sublimity of its ends, it was repeatedly appropriated by, and
even affiliated itself with, projects that were neither scientific nor
sublime. The most telling instance was the deep investment of

linguistic scholarship in the concept of race. The ambitious and high-minded attempt to disclose a history as well as a characterological analysis of peoples and nations through a genealogical study of language had, as a corollary, an inquiry into the origins and characteristics of races. The appeal of race, for those interested in language, was that it provided a strong way of conceiving of linguistic groups as kinds of people whose ways of life could be observed; the appeal of philology, for those interested in race, was that it provided an equally strong—that is, empirical and objective—way of describing the capacities and dispositions of those groups.

The point of origin for this particular strand of the history of philology was the 1786 address by Sir William Jones to the Asiatick Society in Calcutta, in which Jones argued that the resemblances between Greek, Latin, and Sanskrit suggested a long-extinct common source for all three.[18] This hint provided linguists with a new task that took them far beyond Homer and ancient Greece. The reconstruction of the history of humankind through comparative linguistic study led directly to spectacular and altogether unexpected discoveries about linguistic genealogies, and forced a rethinking of the origins of European culture. The "discovery of a fissure in the European past," as Tomoko Masuzawa has called it, created a stunning new historical and secular genealogy that located the origins of European culture in a part of the world that had hitherto seemed exceedingly remote to most Europeans, and yet devoid of exoticism or even interest—and, incidentally, radicalized the difference represented by the Jews.[19] As this project advanced, philological distinctions hardened into ethnological or biological distinctions: the terms *Indo-European* and *Indo-Germanic*, which the German scholar Franz Bopp, building on Jones's insights, had proposed in *Comparative Grammar* in 1833, were understood by many to be "racial" as well as linguistic categories.[20] Linguists found it increasingly difficult to sustain a methodological distinction between language and its speakers, and many failed to see the point of the effort, since the idea of race was so helpful in concretizing the conclusions of linguistic scholarship.

A generation before Bopp, a philhellenic philology was already racialist in that it was explicitly "anti-Judaic." Its enthusiasm for ancient Greece was all the more intense for being pitted against Jewish religion and culture, which were thought to exemplify such qualities as mechanism, abstraction, dualism, and lifelessness.[21] In his later teaching, Wolf himself specifically excluded the Hebrews (along with Egyptians, Persians, and other Oriental nations) from the tiny group of ancient peoples distinguished by a "higher" spiritual culture. The philological inquiry into the historicity of languages, which, after Wolf, rapidly replaced the great curiosity about the origin of language as such—the subject of Herder's 1772 Berlin prize essay—produced the discovery that Sanskrit was an older language than Hebrew, which therefore could not be an "original," much less a "sacred" language. And when scholars compared the expressive capacities of different languages, they almost invariably concluded that those from which most modern European languages had derived were superior to Semitic ones.

Friedrich Schlegel, for example, praised the "inflectional" capabilities of Sanskrit and its descendants by comparing it explicitly with the limited resources of the "agglutinative" Semitic languages. He cautioned against the temptation to rank cultures on this basis, and noted in particular "the lofty power and energy of the Arabic and Hebraic languages," but this point was largely lost even on his most sophisticated readers.[22] Referring to Schlegel's comparative study of grammars, von Humboldt argued that the "Sanscritic family" demonstrated a uniquely generative power, possessing virtually as an organic fact a "stronger and more variously creative *life-principle* than the rest" (ibid., 183; emphasis in the original). The people who invented these languages were, he held, naturally more robust and creative than other peoples. After von Humboldt, scholars were increasingly committed, not just to articulating cultural differences on the basis of linguistic differences, but also to affirming the supremacy of the groups that had settled Christian Europe.

The decisive, if in crucial ways ambivalent intertwining of linguistics and race theory took place in the course of an extended, mutually provocative and productive dialogue between the human and the biological sciences. In order to grasp the full dimensions and implications of this intertwining, we must take a short detour into the fascinating dialogue between philologists and Charles Darwin, in the course of which linguistics and biology came to identify themselves as joint partners in a shared enterprise. At the beginning of this exchange, philology was by far the more advanced and prestigious science; long before he committed himself to any definitive formulations about the origin of species, Darwin was impressed and intrigued by the implications of linguistic scholarship. In notes made during the 1831–36 *Beagle* voyage, he reflected that

> at least it appears all speculations of the origin of language.—must presume it originates slowly—if their speculations are utterly valueless—then argument fails—if they have, then language was progressive.—
>
> We cannot doubt that language is an altering element, we see words invented—we see their origin in names of People.—sound of words—argument of original formation—declension etc often show traces of origin—[23]

At the time he wrote these words, Darwin little understood the significance that philology would hold for his own work; indeed the jottings quoted here are contained in a notebook he later titled "Old and Useless Notes." But he was beginning to assemble the elements of his theories of descent with modification and natural selection, and was keenly interested in solid information about origins of any kind.

Darwin undoubtedly thought that "we cannot doubt" the "altering" and "progressive" character of linguistic development because it had been so persuasively demonstrated by philological science, which showed how linguistic forms derived from, and often retained traces of, earlier forms. Genealogy, Darwin was beginning to believe, provided the foundation for a natural or true system of classification. By the time he was finally ready to publish *On the Origin of Species* in 1859, Darwin was confident that his convictions were supported, not only by his own researches and those of other naturalists, but by the accumulating force of analogies that linked his speculations to the hard facts of philology.[24] At key moments in *Origin*, he drew on these analogies, noting, for example, that "a breed, like a dialect of a language, can hardly be said to have had a definite origin"; or by beginning his exposition of the idea that a natural system is "genealogical in its arrangement, like a pedigree," by commenting that "it may be worth while to illustrate this view of classification, by taking the case of languages."[25]

These almost incidental comments still do not indicate the real importance for Darwin of the analogies between language and species. *Origin* was concerned only with plants and animals, with but a single passage at the end indicating the real target, which would be revealed only twelve years later with the publication of *The Descent of Man*: "In the future, I see open fields for far more important researches. . . . Much light will be thrown on the origin of man and his history" (*Origin*, 527). One reason that the extravagantly cautious Darwin was able to contemplate a shift in terrain from plants and animals to the far riskier subject of human beings was that the defining human trait, language, had already been proved by philology to behave in "Darwinian" ways. In *Descent*, Darwin even conceded his debt to Müller, with whom he had by then been corresponding for many years, saying that "the survival or preservation of certain favored words in the struggle for existence is natural selection."[26]

Philology thus provided invaluable support to the theory of evolution. But the lines of influence extended in both directions, with the passages in the *Origin* having an impact on philologists that can hardly be overstated. That Darwin had enfolded language into an overarching and compelling theory of nature represented an invaluable vote of confidence for a linguistic science that was still, for all its achievements, striving to establish its scientific credentials. Philologists were also quick to recognize that the theory of natural selection provided something philology badly needed and did not have: an explanation of why certain variations were preferred over others. Grateful for this, they embraced Darwin even more warmly than he had embraced them.

Perhaps the most compelling feature of Darwin's presentation, from the philological perspective, was the single illustration in *Origin*, which represented in the form of a branching "tree" the genealogical descent of the various species of a genus (*Origin*, 129). This illustration, combined with Darwin's use of the evocative phrase the "great Tree of Life," encouraged those philologists who had been experimenting with such representations as ways of illustrating the history of languages (ibid., 156). August Schleicher, the first philologist to use tree diagrams in this way, was particularly excited by Darwin's figure. Although Schleicher's own thinking was soaked in German Romanticism, he immediately became Darwin's most prominent German apologist, writing a small tract called *Die Darwinische Theorie und die Sprachwissenschaft* (Darwinian Theory and the Science of Language [1863]),[27] in which he contended that philology provided direct empirical evidence for Darwin's ingenious suggestions and hypothetical scenarios, making speculations into facts.

Tree diagrams were one of the great achievements of nineteenth-century philology. They provided a compelling and easily grasped form for understanding the large movements of linguistic change, the stages in which the bewildering variety of modern languages emerged from a single fountainhead. But just as important, tree diagrams greatly facilitated the easy flow of analogies between the human and the biological sciences. Premised on the new-philological belief that languages were natural objects, tree diagrams also supported by sheer force of form the more specific argument developed by Darwin, that all natural objects including languages were governed by the principles of descent with modification and derivation from a common source. Although both the metaphor of the linguistic family and the tree diagrams that charted their genealogy are now regarded as incomplete and misleading, they seemed to many in the mid-nineteenth century to be authoritative because they made lucid sense of the immense tangle of empirical data and speculative inference concerning linguistic development. Their explanatory power was only increased by the fact that they seemed to compensate for the loss of the biblical narrative of human history by suggesting on scientific grounds that the stories of Eden and Babel were true in essence if not in particulars, and that there was once a single language, the language of humanity, spoken by all people. A truly brilliant invention.

One of the most enthusiastic and polemically effective of Darwin's philological admirers was Max Müller, a German-born comparative philologist and Orientalist who settled in England in the late 1840s to study Sanskrit in the collection of the East India Company. Müller was not primarily interested in race or even in language, which engaged his attention primarily as sources of information about the origins and growth of religions. But he, like Schleicher, insisted that biology and linguistics provided mutual confirmation through their joint embrace of genealogy. In the first series of his wildly popular *Lectures on the Science of Language* (1861–63), he described the scene of language in explicitly Darwinian terms as a process of "natural elimination," a *"struggle for life* ... which led to the destruction of the less strong, the less happy, the less fertile words, and ended in the triumph of *one,* as the recognised and proper name for every object in every language."[28] While such cross-disciplinary influence is still possible today, the greater crystallization and professionalization of the disciplines in our time has made this kind of cross-pollination less likely to occur than in the mid-nineteenth century, when, in the words of Stephen G. Alter, "the metaphoric mind of nineteenth-century science" produced a number of "striking conceptual transfers" between disciplines, of which the flow of analogy between biology and language was the most consequential.[29]

Analogies flowed particularly freely in the work of the German naturalist and philosopher Ernst Haeckel, one of those distinctively nineteenth-century titans who, like Müller, published in a range of fields, the breadth of which is indicated by the fact that he coined the terms *phylum* and *ecology*, as well as the phrases "ontogeny recapitulates phylogeny" and "the first world war." Three years before the appearance of *The Descent of Man*, Haeckel proposed, in a book modestly titled *The History of Creation*, a theory of human evolution from primates.[30] Many of the particulars of his account were controversial from the outset because they lacked adequate scholarly support, but Haeckel was able to buttress his claims about evolution by pointing out that they were entirely consistent with the findings of philology. Using fancifully drawn tree diagrams illustrating the evolution of species, Haeckel argued that the crucial evolutionary leap took place when "Man-like Apes" acquired "articulate human language," thereby becoming transformed into "Ape-like Man," the next-highest branch on the tree of life. Language was not only an acquisition but a transformative agent. According to Haeckel, "the highest authorities in comparative philology" had demonstrated that language had an "ennobling and transforming influence upon the mental life of Man," effecting a "real and principal act of humanification."[31] In *The Evolution of Man*, written six years later, Haeckel again called attention to the "remarkable parallelism" between the evolution of languages and that of organic species: "Indeed it is hardly possible to find an analogy better adapted to throw a clear light on many obscure and difficult facts in the evolution of species, which is governed and directed by the same natural laws which guide the course of the evolution of language."[32]

The rapid advance of philology and evolutionary science in the mid-nineteenth century was partly attributable, then, to the fact that each discourse supported the other by addressing key points that neither could solve on its own. The effect of this collaboration was to create the appearance of a powerful scientific consensus around the proposition that the deepest mysteries of language and species were capable of being solved through the application of genealogy. This consensus lent scientific authority to the racial theorizing to which, as we have seen, philology had already begun to commit itself. And this authority was brought to bear on the question of questions: what was the fabulously fertile first language, and who spoke it—and, just as important, what contemporary group could lay claim to representing a continuation of the pure strain, the original human condition? The question may have been antiquarian and Romantic (especially German-Romantic) in character, but it was addressed by philology as a problem of science.

One problem, from our perspective, is disturbingly evident in Haeckel's confident statement that "the Caucasian, or Mediterranean man has from time immemorial been placed at the head of all races of men, as the most highly developed and perfect."[33] But this manifest problem had roots in an earlier decision by Max Müller and others to call aboriginal language, the common ancestor of Greek, Latin, and Sanskrit, "Indo-European," and in his further decision, which seemed innocent enough at the time, to refer to the speakers of Indo-European as "Aryans." In so doing, Müller was appropriating the name of a tribal group that had been the object of intense and often wild speculation and mythologizing in German thinking since the late eighteenth century. His authority in this respect was Schlegel, who had proposed in 1808 a connection based on linguistic evidence between Indians and Nordic peoples. In 1819 Schlegel gave to the ancestors of both peoples the name Aryan, a word he connected to *Ehre*, or honor.

Müller included among the descendants of the Aryans not just Germanic peoples but all Europeans and many others as well. He suggested that the Aryan homeland, the *Urheimat*, was either in the Caucasus Mountains between the Caspian and Black seas or, more likely, in the Pamir Mountains in Central Asia (now Tajikistan); others put it in Persia, Anatolia, Lithuania, the Ukraine, the Himalayas, southern Germany, the Euphrates Valley, southern Sweden, the Boreal Pole, and even North Africa. Like most who speculated about the Aryans, he posited a restless and mysteriously driven group that eventually inhabited large parts of India and Russia, as well as Persia, Greece, and most of Europe.[34] Müller's growing stature as a philologist and Orientalist supported his identification of the Aryan homeland, his suggestion that they were the common ancestors of all Indo-Europeans, and his advocacy of the thesis, first advanced by Hegel, that the best proof of their existence and their migrations lay in linguistics.

Within eighty years of Jones's suggestion of a common origin of ancient languages, scholars in Europe had shifted their attention from Hebrew and Greek to Sanskrit, and then from these known "daughter" languages to an unknown language, an Indo-European "protolanguage" that had to be reconstructed from the traces it had left in the languages that had succeeded it. Scholars had also attempted to identify on strictly linguistic grounds a number of ancient groups that had left few traces of their existence. And they had identified the original human horde, its cultural characteristics, its wanderings, and its homeland. Given the paucity of material evidence for lost languages and cultures, philology was challenged to maintain the premise that it was an empirical discipline. As Bruce Lincoln writes, the reconstruction of an ur-language "is an exercise that invites one to imagine speakers of that protolanguage, a community of such people, then a place for that community, a time in history, distinguishing characteristics, and a set of contrastive relations with other protocommunities where other protolanguages were spoken. For all this," Lincoln adds, "need it be said, there is no sound evidentiary warrant."[35] But throughout the nineteenth century, a voracious curiosity possessed of considerable cultural prestige and a methodology that gave its speculations the character of scientific discoveries flourished in the absence of such a warrant. With support from Müller and others, language became widely accepted as a rich and reliable source of evidence, and philology a kind of master-discipline, for theorizing about human origins in general and human races in particular.

This represents one of history's bitter ironies, for Müller came to despise those who, like Comte de Gobineau in the *Essay on the Inequality of Races* (1853–55), used linguistic evidence to argue for racial differences.[36] Gobineau adopted von Humboldt's claim that language was an index of the "mental power" of a people, substituted "race" for "people," and added the assertion that race was the most powerful explanation for human difference in general, particularly the difference between healthy and degenerate civilizations. He voiced another commonly held view when he wrote that Aryans were not simply an ancient race but the most masterly and "creative" of races. And he spoke to a smaller but still sizable and committed group when he argued that the corruption or contamination of Aryan stock by Semitic or other blood, wherever it occurred, constituted a species disaster. For those who, like Gobineau, were committed to the principle of human difference rather than human unity, one of the key facts about Aryan migrations was that Aryans had conquered and intermarried with local populations everywhere they went, but had never intermarried with Jews.

Müller rejected all such arguments and the motives that drove them. He believed as a matter of faith in the unity of the human race—indeed, he believed in an "original pair," which seemed to him common sense and sound science—and held that philology was premised on that unity. He argued, in fact, that the Aryan (Indo-European), Semitic, and "Turanian" linguistic families all derived from some even earlier source, a Central Asian tongue spoken at the dawn of human existence.[37] And, in his later statements at least, he insisted on the wickedness of racial theory and its utter irrelevance to linguistic scholarship. On historical and moral grounds, he repudiated the notion of Aryan racial superiority, and deplored the fact that linguistic evidence was conscripted in support of such arguments. He singled out for special opprobrium the United States, where "comparative philologists have been encouraged to prove the impossibility of a common origin of languages and races, in order to justify, by scientific arguments, the unhallowed theory of slavery. Never," he asserted, "do I remember to have seen science more degraded than on the title-page of an American publication in which, among the profiles of the different races of man, the profile of the ape was made to look more human than that of the negro."[38] But he was not always careful to make his ideas clear, and some of his ideas, particularly on the genesis of metaphor and myth as "diseases" of language, were themselves unclear—or, worse, clear but wrong, even obtuse.[39] He insisted that philology was a science, but sought to use this science to disprove the notion that humans had evolved from primates, to demonstrate the presence of the divine scattered throughout nature, and, ultimately, to reveal Christianity as the unconscious goal of all human history.[40]

Müller's commitment to the symphonic unity of humankind was unwavering, but his understanding of race was uncertain and inconstant. Race occupied a region in his discourse somewhere between the literal and the metaphorical, the biological and the linguistic. "Not a single drop of foreign blood has entered into the organic system of the English language," he wrote in his *Lectures*; "the grammar, the blood and soul of the language, is as pure and unmixed in English as spoken in the British Isles as it was when spoken on the shores of the German ocean" (*Lectures*, 1:70). The ambiguity was aggravated when he spoke, in terms almost worthy of Gobineau, of the "Aryan race," of which, he asserted, English language speakers were privileged descendants. He translated Kant's *Critique of Pure Reason* into English in the conviction that it represented "the perfect manhood of the Aryan mind," and offered it to "the English-speaking race, the race of the future . . . [as] another Aryan heirloom."[41]

The reception of Müller provides sobering evidence of the fate of scholarly ambivalence and nuance when it enters the public sphere. On the basis of the uncertain evidence provided by language, Müller attempted to draw inferences about what he called, with some reluctance, race. Others more interested in race than in language simply ignored Müller's scruples even as they cited him as an authority, and proceeded directly to the comparison and ranking of races, cultures, and even religions, claiming scholarly support for their theses.

Under the reviving touch of the right kind of scholar, language yielded up fascinating new insights, particularly into the Jews. Scholarly arguments about the Jewish character resonated well beyond the walls of universities and learned societies. The work of Müller's friend Ernest Renan was particularly influential. Renan's multivolume history of Semitic languages, like his multivolume history of the people of Israel, was undertaken in the rooted conviction of the profound limitations of the Semitic mind. A professor of Hebrew, Renan devoted much of his life to the study of Semitic languages and history, and he was one of the most liberal and learned minds of his age. Yet his detailed historical and linguistic arguments, stripped of complexity and context as in their public reception they were bound to be, did not contradict a common anti-Semitism that included both Jews and Muslims: Renan is, in fact, the occasion for some of the most powerful condemnatory passages in Said's *Orientalism*.

In contrast to Müller, Renan saw, at the origin of human existence, two groups, Semites and Aryans. Each had contributed to human progress, but, according to Renan, the contribution of Semitic peoples was largely negative. The deficiencies of the ancient Semites were striking: they were incapable of science, philosophy, civilization, personal courage, and tolerance; they were selfish, rigid, and righteous; their culture displayed a "want of fertility both of imagination and language," a "startling simplicity of ideas."[42] All this could be seen in their cultural practices and religious beliefs; but the real mechanism, the determining force behind what appear to be racial characteristics, was neither cultural nor religious; it was linguistic.

Renan held an exceptionally hardwired version of the Humboldtian argument, believing that language, once established, became "a mould, a corset so to speak, more binding than even religion, legislation, manners, and customs."[43] A proper scholarly understanding of Semitic culture could therefore, he thought, best be obtained by a philological study of the Bible and other texts. This study would focus not on words but on a linguistic subunit developed by philology, the "root," the irreducible lexical kernel that, he believed, provided the best evidence of the deep character of the people. In the Aryan languages, nearly all roots, according to Renan, "contained an embryo divinity," while the roots of Semitic languages were "dry, inorganic, and quite incapable of giving birth to a mythology."[44] Bound by the ligatures of their language, the ancient Semites were simply incapable of thinking abstractly, much less metaphorically; and their conjugation of verbs displayed a dismaying primitivism.

There is no question of Renan's admiration for the nomadic peoples of the ancient Middle East, who, he said, "were superior to all the peoples of their day," and "occupy the foremost place in the history of humanity." Jerusalem was for Renan "the religious capital of humanity."[45] But he was convinced that he had discovered in the Semitic languages evidence of a principle of incompleteness so definitive and deep-seated that he could only account for the most monumental Semitic contribution to human civilization, the invention of monotheism, by describing it as a "secret tendency," an unconscious and in a sense unwilled expression of racial predispositions.[46] To be sure, he noted, the world owes the Jews in particular an immense debt. The sublime madness of the prophetic voice, decrying injustice in the name of a higher power, is their invention entirely; the multifarious Aryans, dazzled by the world's variety and distracted by divinities everywhere, would never have discovered that voice on their own. But while the kingdom of Israel was "to the highest degree creative," it "did not know how to crown its edifice"; it was incomplete, a "withered trunk" with but one "fertile branch," Christianity, which appropriated the Semitic religion without assuming the mental and linguistic limitations that had framed it.[47] In a sense, Jews owe Christians as much as Christians owe Jews, because the full glorious potential of monotheism was not realized until Aryans converted to it. Having conquered the world by proxy through Christianity, Judaism, Renan declared, was now effectively dead as a world-historical force.

Comparative philology, the science of modernity itself, provided Renan with scientific grounding for arguments about Semitic inferiority that otherwise would have appeared to be mere conventional prejudice. But so inconsistent was Renan in his use of the term *race* that at times his arguments were indistinguishable from their vulgar counterparts, as tendentious as the popular views they sought to correct.[48] While he argued on occasion that the very concept of race was useful only as a way of thinking about the distant past, and was becoming less and less significant in the liberal and rational ethos of modern times, he also held that there was "nothing shocking about the conquest of a nation of inferior race by a superior race," and even that Christian Europeans constituted "a race of masters and soldiers."[49] Müller and Renan both equivocated on the question of race, but Renan's pendulum swung even farther than Müller's in the direction of Gobineau, with whom Renan corresponded and whom he cited several times as a fellow philologist in his treatise on Semitic languages. Indeed, his commitment to science (as epitomized by philology) caused his pendulum occasionally to swing even farther than Gobineau's. In *Dialogues philosophiques* (1876), Renan entertained the thought of a "factory" for the production of Scandinavian heroes located in Central Asia and organized by the Germans, a nation even then celebrated for its efficiency.[50]

The discourse on Aryans proved to be immensely suggestive across a wide range of political sympathies, influencing not only Gobineau and his sympathizers but also many others who relied on scientific studies of linguistic development to support liberal or moderate arguments about culture. Matthew Arnold, for example, had absorbed, without fully endorsing, the racialized discourse on language, which he deployed in "Hebraism and Hellenism," the famous opposition in the fourth chapter of *Culture and Anarchy* (1882).[51] Unlike some of his neohumanist predecessors, Arnold was neither anti-Judaic nor anti-Semitic; for him, Hebraism and Hellenism represented qualities ("strictness of conscience" and "spontaneity of consciousness") that existed in dialectical mixture in any healthy society. Given Arnold's deferential respect for French and German philology, in fact, it is possible that he based his understanding of these terms not on observations of human beings but on linguistic scholarship. Aspects of his account of "Hebraism" seem to have been drawn from Renan's account of Semitic languages as inflexible and limited; while his Hellenism recalls some of the more buoyant formulations of the philhellenistic cultural project, with its emphasis on an enlightened culture that gave form to the sweetness and light inherent in the Greek language. But it is difficult to maintain that actual Jews are altogether outside the referential field when Arnold describes Hebraism in terms of "stiffness, hardness, narrowness, prejudice, want of insight, want of amiability," or when he draws a sharp contrast between Jewish culture and the "higher" spirituality and deeper humanity of the Greeks, Christians, and Aryans.[52]

These differences played a direct role in his 1891 text *On the Study of Celtic Literature*, where he posited, with linguistic evidence, a distant and long-forgotten commonality between Aryan (more recently, Teutonic and Celtic) and Semitic peoples.[53] The argument borrowed from Müller, who traced the word *Arya* from India to Ireland (*Eire*, rather than Schlegel's *Ehre*), and more directly from the warm-blooded account of Celtic "nobility" in Renan's "The Poetry of the Celtic Races," which began by praising the Celts for their racial purity.[54] "Never," said Renan (who had been born and raised in Celtic Brittany), "has a human family lived more apart from the world, and been purer from all alien admixture."[55] Like Renan, Arnold believed that Celtic racial superiority was a scientifically determined fact, and in claiming a Celtic admixture in the English racial strain, was attempting to provide a biological account for the extraordinary poetic and literary nature of the English. The horrifying tale of the theory of Aryan supremacy had yet to unfold, of course, and the tolerant and reconciling Arnold would have been appalled at the course the story took after it left the hands of scholars. And yet, the key premises of the Aryan myth—that long ago, an aboriginal group of people emigrated to the West, becoming Christianized without having passed through Palestine, thus avoiding any contact with Jews; that pockets of post-Aryan purity still existed; that the culture of these pockets was superior in many respects to that of other places, and definitely opposed point by point to that of Jews—were all in place in Arnold's time, firmly *in* the hands of scholars, who regarded them as hard-won scientific knowledge about language.

By the turn of the century, when Richard Wagner's son-in-law Houston Stewart Chamberlain was composing *Foundations of the Nineteenth Century*, a richly confused tradition of scholarship on language, stretching back to Herder, Schlegel, and von Humboldt and including recent eminences such as Müller and Renan, supported in one way or another the concept of race, including notions of racial distinctness, racial comparisons, and racial rankings.[56] Müller had spoken of a "great Aryan brotherhood" based on sameness of blood and encompassing both Europeans and Indians—a concept that, he said, implied a long and peaceable future for the Raj—and Chamberlain agreed, with one exception. Noting that in Sanskrit, *Arya* means "noble, free, or skillful person," Chamberlain simply dropped the then-colonized Indians from the brotherhood. The natural leaders of the human race, he said, were the Aryans, and the natural leaders of the Aryan race were the "Nordic" or "Teutonic" peoples, whose refined features and Indo-European language indicated an ancient and noble lineage, a race whose distinctive talent was to rule. Setting aside Chamberlain's inconvenient identification of the insular English as the best contemporary representatives of ancient Aryan stock, a later generation of German intellectuals drew from him, Gobineau, and Nietzsche ideological and quasi-scientific support for the new strain of racist nationalism. After the Great War, the entire discipline of philology in Germany was dominated by monarchist nostalgia and reaction. Indeed, distinguished linguists were among the most committed academic supporters of the anti-Semitism and xenophobia of the Third Reich, contributing to the effort what Christopher M. Hutton has called "mother-tongue fascism," which must be considered the ultimate inversion and profanation of what was, in Müller's work, a mere suggestion about the speakers of Indo-

European made in the context of an argument about the unity of the human race.[57]

The history of philology in the nineteenth century was dominated not by people like Gobineau and Chamberlain, whose subject was always race, but by people like Wolf, von Humboldt, Müller, Böckh, Renan, and Arnold, learned and large-souled men who thought they were using scientific methods to extend the range of human connectedness, to provide a secular and rational account of human origins, to articulate ways of understanding and valuing cultural differences, and to hold up for inspection those fascinating instances in which an original purity had somehow been preserved. They looked for the clean and simple forms prevailing at the infancy of the language, the race, the species. But the historical reach of philology, the period of time that it could illuminate through empirical evidence, was actually quite shallow in comparison to the vast stretches of time opened up by the theory of evolution; its reach always exceeded its grasp. Moreover, the history of philology is not the whole of history, and the work of these admirable sages lent itself in ways both obvious and subtle to the purposes of others less scrupulous and learned than they, and it was these others who influenced more directly the course of events.

By 1940, philology—that narrow, dull, but indispensable preliminary task, that safely nonideological practice of erudite observation and analysis—had been associated with many of the major movements of the past century and a half, including Romanticism, nationalism, liberalism, Darwinism, and psychoanalysis.[58] Along with several other sciences, including anthropology, archeology, and geology, it had played a key role in breaking the hold on the human imagination of the biblical account of human origins, and had made the human past available for systematic inquiry as never before. These were immense accomplishments, and it was not without cause that philology was commonly held up as the highest form of learning. And yet, it had also been responsible for turning scholarship into a practice of pedantry, and, far more important, had given warrant to generalizations and profundities that lay well beyond the boundaries of any scholarly discipline. Philologists adduced linguistic evidence in support of racialist theorizing, promulgated learned forms of anti-Semitism, represented as a fact of nature the domination of the weak by the strong, and claimed to deduce from the study of language the superiority of western European culture and its dominant religion, Christianity. Many of the intellectual and subintellectual currents of the time circulated through it, and others had brushed up against it, confirming or being confirmed by it.[59] A tree diagram of the intellectual and ideological movements of the nineteenth and twentieth centuries would show many of them branching forth from philology. And so, when some recent American critics wished to recall the glories of philology, they had a wide—a chaotically wide—range to choose from.

Task of Philology: To Reappear

These glories had to be recalled, because philology had been unable to establish itself as an academic discipline in the American research universities taking shape at the end of the nineteenth century. And we can see why: its speculative dimension ruled it out of the sciences, and its empirical and technical character disqualified it from the humanities, as loosely defined as that category was at the time. It did, however, serve as a kind of chrysalis for two discourses that did establish themselves as professionalized disciplines, linguistics and literary studies, both of which defined themselves in contrast to philology, only to return to it in the course of time.

At one time, linguistics based its claim to be a science on the achievements of philology. Müller had in fact predicted that the new discipline of linguistics, then dominated by comparative philology, would eventually have the highest place among the "physical" sciences. His successors tried to make good on this prediction, but did so in a manner that would have astonished him, by rejecting philology. Ferdinand de Saussure, who had made an early reputation as a historical philologist, argued that philology had strayed from its scientific purpose when it turned from the text itself to "literary history, customs, institutions, etc."[60] Linguistics could only become a science, he contended in an argument that founded modern linguistics, by focusing not on the written language but on the system of signs, the code that made communication possible—not a language but language itself, language alone. Philology, which directed its attention to "the picturesque side of a language, that which makes it differ from all others as belonging to a certain people having certain origins," remained stubbornly unscientific.[61] For Saussure, philology was to scientific linguistics as Semites were to Aryans for Renan—historically necessary, but preliminary and incomplete. Saussure began the *Course in General Linguistics* by relegating philology to the domain of "criticism," whose primary historical function was to prepare the way for a truly scientific linguistics, that is, semiology. Each of Saussure's innovations—the shifts from languages to language as such, from words to signs, from history to system, and from the description of particulars to theory—was intended to strengthen the scientific credentials of linguistics by distancing it from philology.

Saussure and his successors created this distance by describing philology as a practice whose deficiencies called forth their own corrections in the form of a superior version of linguistics, which they provided. Benjamin Lee Whorf argued, as Saussure had, that a scientific linguistics was superior to philology because the latter failed to focus on the linguistic object, but indulged itself by "reading off a sweeping survey of . . . history and culture." But Whorf defined the true object of linguistics in terms very different from Saussure—not the system of signs but "the text as text, the exact words and grammar, conceiving this as their paramount duty."[62] And while Saussure thought that philology was logically prior to linguistics, Whorf thought the reverse, that philology should be kept at bay until linguistics had secured the text with an adequate factual description. Linguists after Whorf, including Edward Sapir, Roman Jakobson, Leonard Bloomfield, and Zellig Harris, devoted themselves to forgetting philology altogether. Noam Chomsky delivered the final blow, defining linguistics, with an authority that could not be questioned, as a subdiscipline within cognitive psychology, a purely scientific discipline with no historical dimension whatsoever. From Müller to Chomsky, the field of linguistics turned itself inside out, or rather outside in, moving from history to the brain. Chomsky realized Müller's dream of making linguistics into a "physical science," but did so by purging philology from linguistics altogether.

And yet. While linguistics was discovering more and more ways to purify itself of any philological residue, it was also tracing a circuitous route back to the origin. Chomsky's linguistics rejected everything about philology except for one thing: its original goal, which F. A. Wolf had defined as that of articulating a philosophy of human nature on the basis of a study of language. In retrospect, it is clear that linguistics since Saussure did not reject philology at all, but simply groped toward ways consistent with evolving understandings of science and scientific methods of fulfilling philology's initial ambitions.

The return by linguistics to its humanistic origins was circuitous and delayed; the return by literary studies to its origins in science has been much more direct and insistent, despite an initial rejection every bit as emphatic as that of linguistics. Indeed, the desire to return to philology has been one of the defining features of literary study from the beginning. In Gerald Graff's invaluable account in *Professing Literature*, the university-based discipline of literary study was born of the struggle conducted a century ago between science-oriented philological "scholars" and generalists, or "critics," who thought literature should be studied from an interpretive, humanistic, and even moralistic perspective.[63] At the end of the nineteenth century, the philological project was still so prestigious that at Johns Hopkins, the model of a research university, English was part of the German Department. Elsewhere, however, the appropriateness of a scientific model, with the "degrading vassalage to philology" implied by that model, was being resisted.[64] This resistance gathered strength, and eventually, the generalist-critics won their independence from the scholars. By 1948, René Wellek and Austin Warren were arguing that the word *philology*, lingering on in ghostly form in the titles of journals, no longer described anything concrete in literary studies and should be dropped, a recommendation that was rapidly adopted.[65]

Thus liberated, literary scholars and critics were free to engage in literary history, comparative literature, and the history of ideas. But from the beginning, some critics were haunted by their deed; and, feeling increasingly exposed in the professional ethos of the university, they began to cast longing glances at the discipline they had flung aside, and at the receding prospects of a science of language and literature. Attempts at reconciliation or reclamation were made. Virtually all the surging movements that swept over criticism in the twentieth century were grounded in the fear that a practice of literary scholarship that defined itself too aggressively in contrast to close textual study was in danger of losing its footing and collapsing into unwarranted judgments, impressions, evaluations, projections, generalizations, heresies, and fallacies. Iconoclasts in many ways, Said and de Man were in this respect traditionalists, for the history of literary studies has been marked by a series of returns to philology.

While linguistics, in the course of becoming scientific, found it useful to construct a philology to be rejected, literary scholars have more often found it useful to construct a philology to be admired. In recent years, the humanistic disciplines most drawn to philology have been those that stress the formal or technical study of texts, beginning with medieval studies. In 1990, Stephen G. Nichols edited a special issue of the journal *Speculum* devoted to a "New Philology" that would, he predicted, rejuvenate medieval studies by returning philology to the manuscript culture of the medieval world, a world of variance unconstrained by the regularities and exactitudes of print culture.[66] As part of this movement, Lee Patterson published, in 1994, an essay called "The Return to Philology," in which he argued that medievalists should embrace this new practice "not despite but because of its intractable penchant for pedantry"—a specialty of medieval studies of which critics in less demanding and rigorous fields could use a strong dose for their own good.[67] Calls for a "feminist philology" have been heard since 1987.[68] And a "radical philology" has emerged from within classics, declaring its intention to tackle questions of textual genetics in a spirit of theoretical audacity.[69] Younger scholars in Mesoamerican ethnohistory are attempting to rejuvenate their field by insisting on a "New Philology" that would recognize the importance of native language sources treated with a linguistic and historical approach.[70] Even biblical scholarship has attempted to renovate itself by returning to philology: a collection of essays titled *On the Way to the Postmodern* includes an essay titled "Philology and Power."[71] Jan Ziolkowski's edited volume *On Philology* includes papers given at an unexpectedly exciting 1988 Harvard conference attended by deconstructionists and other theorists, as well as by traditional philologists. And there's more. Sunny Stanford has in recent years become the scene of a Great Philological Awakening, marked by Hans Ulrich Gumbrecht's 2003 book *The Powers of Philology*, which bluntly calls for a return to philology as an antidote to the illicit freedoms of cultural studies, as well as by Seth Lerer's edited volume *Literary History and the Challenge of Philology* (1996), and Lerer's own *Error and the Academic Self* (2002).[72] In 2007 philology acquired a powerful advocate when Michael Holquist, author of "Why We Should Remember Philology," ascended to the presidency of the Modern Language Association.[73]

What most such movements prize above all in philology is its supposed assurance. Whatever its flaws or limitations, many feel, philology knows itself: it is what it is. But a look at recent issues of the scholarly journals whose names retain the term *philology* suggests that the discipline is now characterized by the same loose eclecticism that characterizes literary studies in general. The *Journal of English and Germanic Philology* has published articles such as "The Werewolf in Medieval Icelandic Literature," and "Revisiting *Gisla Saga*: Sexual Themes and the Heroic Past"; *Modern Philology* has devoted its pages to discourses that include "inventing the nation," "William Faulkner's Southern Knights," and "Charismatic Authority in Early Modern English Tragedy"; and *Classical Philology* has provided a venue for essays such as "Horsepower and Donkeywork: Equids and the Ancient Greek Imagination" and "Writing (On) Bodies: Lyric Discourse and the Production of Gender in Horace *Odes* 1.13." The absence in these journals of a hard core of philology as distinct from criticism and literary history suggests that the term now signifies not so much a discipline—in fact, there are no traditional departments of philology in any major university in the United States[74]—as a kind of dream or myth of origins.

It is tempting to see recent expressions of a renewed interest in philology as symptomatic of a discipline that, momentarily uncertain of its object, methods, and goals, tries to anchor itself in its origins, in a time when things were assured, stable, and honorable, when it addressed serious issues in a serious way, when it commanded respect. But a more comprehensive account would begin with the recognition that while interest in philology may have spiked in recent years, it cannot be considered a temporary fascination or even a recurrent mood, but must instead be seen as a permanent and characteristic feature of humanistic scholarship, a deep chord vibrating beneath literary studies in particular. Philology is to modern scholarship what the voice of Homer was to Wolf and the Aryan *Ursprache* was to Müller and Renan, an endlessly tantalizing mirage, the phantasmatic solution to all problems.

The continuing influence of philology on modern scholarship can be detected in three areas. The first is in the concept of the origin. Philology has bequeathed to modern scholarship the conviction that things are explained when their origins have been identified. This assumption commits scholarship to an endless quest, for origins may be construed in any of a number of ways, and every origin has origins of its own. Wolf considered the origin of the Homeric text to be the voice, and therefore the mind, of Homer; but Homer himself sprang from Greek culture, which itself had origins extending all the way back to the origin of humanity. Returning to philology does not solve the problem of origin, for this problem is part of our inheritance from philology itself.

Second, philology has handed down to contemporary scholarship its characteristic duality, a double commitment to an empirical attention to linguistic fact and a more subjective approach to questions of context, meaning, and value. This duality has led to constant uncertainties about the methodology and mission of scholarship, uncertainties for which philology seems to many to be the cure. But once again, we do not solve our problems by returning to philology, for it was in philology that these problems first appeared in the form of a deep equivocation between broad humanistic generalities and narrow empirical science. The difficulties that are, in the view of some, reason to return are in fact the clearest evidence that we have never truly escaped.

Third, modern humanistic scholarship continues to be informed by a key assumption that also guided philology: that a scholarly inquiry into the historical or formal dimensions of the language of the text can illuminate issues of personal, cultural, or national identity. Recent claims that the current interest, especially among literary scholars, in culture simply recodes an older interest in race should be seen in this context, as a confirmation that contemporary scholarship has found yet another way to return to philology.[75]

It is difficult to know how to think about philology, because it is difficult to know exactly what philology is. Its proponents, many of whom stake their advocacy on a clear sense of the distinctive difference between philology and other kinds of scholarship, almost invariably also distinguish between worthy and unworthy aspects of philology, identifying good practices as "radical," "modern," "feminist," or, most often, "new." Nietzsche condemned almost all living philologists even as he extolled the virtues of a rare but authentic philology. Said noted the smothering sense of sterility and pedantry that afflicted most philology, but urged respect for his particular heroes. De Man wanted to return only to rhetorical description, not to the speculative or interpretive side of philology. Advocates of the New Philology in medieval studies reject an older philology because of its association with "political nationalism and scientific positivism."[76] Praised for its single-mindedness, philology is irreducibly complex, and repels as strongly as it attracts.

If it is difficult to know exactly what philology is, we can, however, still discriminate between the right and wrong kinds of return. The right kind of return, I submit, would begin with an act of disciplinary soul-searching that holds up the history of philology as a cautionary reminder that the focused professional attention we apply to the object can make us susceptible to ambush by received ideas passing as common sense, or even as empirical observations. Said and de Man, to take just two examples, might have considered this possibility before promoting a practice that had been intimately entangled with racist and anti-Semitic theories and practices.[77] They were, however, promoting the wrong kind of return, one that sought to use philology as a means of restoring a lost sense of groundedness, assurance, and professional self-esteem. To treat philology in this way, as an innocent form of conscientiousness and scrupulosity, or as what Said called "an act of perhaps modest human emancipation and enlightenment," is to invite it to disappear once again, ushering it out with polite applause. Perhaps disciplines, like nations in Renan's famous formulation, have much to remember and much to forget, and a selective recall is somehow psychically and professionally necessary. But philology cannot be purged of its history any more than contemporary humanistic scholarship can get quit of philology. It is our history, a continuous story leading up to the present, and we must own up to it.

The question is what to make of this genealogical connection. One inference might be that scholars should become more careful, cautious, and respectful of limits lest they fall into the same errors as their predecessors. This is undoubtedly good advice, but philology also has more spacious lessons to teach. If we are truly to assume the full burden of the history of philology, we must also allow ourselves to be instructed, inspired, and challenged by the genuine achievements of the greatest scholars of the philological tradition, who were intellectually curious and ambitious to a degree we can scarcely imagine. Their ambition was the germ of much of what today seems their errancy, but we cannot become virtuous simply by becoming small; nor does our abandonment of any pretense to methodology or any attempt to acquire comprehensive knowledge necessarily count in our favor. A revealing mirror, the history of philology combines in a single image scholarship's highest aspirations and darkest fears. The ongoing challenge is not which to choose but how to tell them apart.

3

Between Humanity and the Homeland: The Evolution of an Institutional Concept

Speaking in Jackson, Mississippi, at the gubernatorial inauguration of Republican Haley Barbour in January 2004, Bruce Cole, chairman of the National Endowment for the Humanities, recalled another inauguration. "In his Inaugural Address," Cole said, "President Bush called on all Americans to be citizens, not spectators . . . to serve our nation . . . to embody the ideas that gave our nation birth. That call," he said, "took on new meaning after the attacks of September 11."[1] On that day, Cole noted, citizens countered evil with "acts of courage and compassion"; and within a matter of months, a righteous nation "defeated a murderous regime, liberated an oppressed people, and literally unearthed a tyrant." All these things were well known to his audience; what might have been less obvious was the critical role played by the humanities.

If any were uncertain what a scholar was doing at this occasion, Cole was not. For, as he understood the matter, the humanities were at ground zero of American civic life. To begin with, he argued, the essence of the citizenship displayed on 9/11 by firefighters, police, and ordinary people was revealed by the humanities, to which we look for the key to "what makes us human: the legacy of our past, the ideas and principles that motivate us, and the eternal questions that we still ponder." Before the first responders responded, they had already responded to the humanities, which help us cultivate the sense of beauty, reveal to us our traditions, and give meaning to abstract concepts such as justice and goodness. The NEH, he pointed out, had been "founded in the belief that cultivating the best of the humanities had real, tangible benefits for civic life," including a deepened understanding of our conflicts in Iraq and Afghanistan. In America, where "wisdom and knowledge" are "essential to our national identity," the humanities are particularly important. Indeed, from one point of view, the humanities were the true object of the 9/11 attacks. As Cole put it,

> the values implicit in the study of the humanities are part of why we were attacked on September 11. The free and fearless exchange of ideas, respect for individual conscience, belief in the power of education . . . all these things are anathema to our country's enemies. Understanding and affirming these principles is part of the battle.
>
> Today, it is especially urgent that we study American institutions, culture and history. Defending our democracy demands more than successful military campaigns.
>
> It also requires an understanding of the ideals, ideas and institutions that have shaped our country. . . .
>
> James Madison famously said, "the diffusion of knowledge is the only true guardian of liberty." Such knowledge tells us who we are as a people and why our country is worth fighting for.
>
> Such knowledge is part of our homeland defense.

If any humanists were in the crowd, they might have been made a bit uneasy by the facility with which Cole described their work in terms of eternal truths, beauty, justice, and the mystery of what makes us human; they might also have been uncomfortable with the smooth transition from timeless values to American national identity and from there to the political and military projects of the current administration. They would almost certainly have been alarmed to hear that they had been the objects of the 9/11 attacks.[2] And they would, one can safely say, have been astonished to hear that the knowledge they professed was a vital part of homeland defense.

From another point of view, however, the really remarkable fact about this speech was that the NEH was being so stoutly defended in the state of Mississippi, at the gubernatorial inauguration of a former chairman of the Republican Party. As recently as 1997, the very survival of the NEH, and that of the even more controversial National Endowment for the Arts, had been in doubt. Enemies of these agencies included Newt Gingrich (who targeted them explicitly in the Contract with America), the Christian Right, the Heritage Foundation, the libertarian Cato Institute, the National Association of Scholars, and even former NEH chairs Lynne Cheney and William Bennett, who charged that the NEH was wasteful, anti-American, anti-family, and elitist.[3] The problem lay not in the subject matter of the humanities but in the ideologues who taught and wrote about them, and in their enablers at the NEH who funneled tax dollars to them. In the end, the NEH survived, if only just barely; and when the world turned in 2001, the agency passed, with the approval of Cheney and Bennett, into more responsible or responsive hands. And the problems disappeared: the nation might be in crisis, according to Chairman Cole, but there is no *crisis in the humanities*, for they, in solidarity with a nation at war, have regained their traditional capacity to ground, vivify, and enlighten. Academics in the audience might have been shocked, once again, to hear this news, because for many, that crisis was so long-standing that it was a threat not to their identity but to the identity itself. Without our crisis, they might have said to themselves, what are we? It was to this question that Cole was providing an answer.

My argument is that the notion of crisis is indeed a constitutive part of the humanities as they have evolved, but that a fuller understanding of that evolution should suffice to protect us against many of the surprises, alarms, and shocks I have been describing. I will be arguing, in true humanistic fashion, that tradition is our best guide to the bewildering present and to the unknown future.

One reason the phrase "crisis in the humanities" arrests the attention is that the humanities seem to be so pacific, benign, meditative, enlightening, enriching; such a pure good. The very notion of a crisis seems like a tragic interference in the noble mission of the humanities, whose interests are essentially identical to those of humankind. But the history of the humanities is a history of struggle, characteristically involving some ambivalence or uncertainty about the consequences of modernity. Evidence of the struggle often has to be reclaimed from the emollient rhetoric that characterizes the discourse of the humanities, but it is never far from the surface, even in what many regard as the founding moment of that discourse.

Renaissance humanism, from Petrarch to Pico della Mirandola, is often depicted as a modernizing movement dedicated to the promotion of individual autonomy, self-realization, and interpretation against traditional sources of authority. With the rise of humanism, it is said, we emerge from the shadows of traditional clerical authority into the sunlight of the modern world as humankind claims its destiny. But the argument informing the humanistic movement was much more specific: it was that the influence of Aristotle and Averroes on Christian theology should be replaced by a different set of influences, including Ciceronian eloquence, Christian piety, and, most crucially, Platonic wisdom. The *studia humanitatis* of the fifteenth century sought to recall humankind to its divine origins through a rereading of the classical and early Christian texts as an extended meditation on ethics whose ultimate goal of personal salvation was manifestly Christian. The immediate target was the kind of professional philosophizing that ruled the universities, a style of thinking that rejected the notions of personal virtues and a personal interpretation of the world in favor of rationalism, the study of logic, and natural philosophy.[4] Renaissance humanism was, as one writer has put it, "an interruption in the development of science."[5] The argument that humankind could, by its own efforts, achieve a glorious destiny actually provoked as a response the theology of the early Reformation, which stressed humankind's total depravity. This theology represented the revenge of modernity in that it emphasized system over individual instance, and observation (of actual depravity) over hopeful illusion. The Renaissance insistence on the autonomy of the individual had, in short, the character of a reaction, and in the "Apology for Raymond Sebonde," Montaigne ridiculed it on those grounds.

Contemporary advocates for the humanities sometimes refer to the Renaissance in their attempts to reclaim an authenticity that we have lost in our corrupt modern times, but the Renaissance humanists saw themselves as living in corrupt times as well. And when we approach the origin of the humanities as an academic project in something like a modern university, we see the same attempt to recover an older tradition from the degenerative effects of modernity. The humanities begin to come into focus, from our point of view, with the critic Matthew Arnold's opposition of culture—the antecedent, anchor, and direct reference point of what we now call the humanities—and anarchy. According to Arnold's *Culture and Anarchy* (1882), modern society was in jeopardy because of the loss of "Christian knowledge" and the tradition of classical *humanitas* that had complemented that knowledge. The sustaining function of that knowledge could, he thought, be assumed in modern times by culture, which summoned people to "total perfection by means of getting to know, on all the matters which most concern us, the best which has been thought and said in the world; and through this knowledge, turning a stream of fresh and free thought upon our stock notions and habits, which we now follow staunchly but mechanically."[6] Like the Renaissance humanists, Arnold favored a Christianized Plato over the mechanic and naturalistic Aristotle, and individual self-realization at the expense of system, science, and method. Although culture was a collective creation accessible in principle to all, the emphasis Arnold placed on individual illumination meant that culture was in fact available only to those who had access to the right kind of learning and the leisure for the right kind of experiences, those in a position to savor both classical "sweetness" and Hebraic "light." An educational reformer, Arnold felt that the schools were the best means of acquiring and disseminating culture. With Arnold, we see *humanism* beginning to morph into the academic form of *the humanities*, passing through the intermediate form of *culture*.

Arnold was strongly influenced by the philologist and educational reformer Wilhelm von Humboldt, whom he described in *Culture and Anarchy* as "one of the most beautiful souls that have ever existed" (chap. 3, no. 35). Arnold praised in particular Humboldt's classically humanist and Enlightenment understanding of the educational value of language and linguistic history. He agreed completely with Humboldt's assessment that philology, which provided objective knowledge of the history of a people, was a more fundamental discipline than the apolitical pursuit of scientific knowledge and the cosmopolitan study of philosophy, desiccated fields lacking true interest or urgency. An education that emphasized philology would have a moral as well as a utilitarian value: pursued in the right spirit, it would produce a deep knowledge of culture, and would lead naturally to *Bildung*, the ennoblement of character.

Arnold's deepest accord with Humboldt concerned the question of the relationship between education and the state. For both men, state control was a means of ensuring uniform quality, avoiding needless specialization, and overriding local limitations or prejudice. More important, however, was the premise that only the state could provide the proper moral context for true education. And on this question, Arnold took an even firmer line than Humboldt, for whereas Humboldt envisioned the distant day when the individual might stand "perfect on his own foundations and . . . do without the State,"[7] Arnold believed that the guiding hand of the state would always be required. His argument took him from sweetness and light and the timeless monuments of culture to this startling conclusion:

> And this opinion of the intolerableness of anarchy we can never forsake, however our Liberal friends may think a little rioting, and what they call popular demonstrations, useful sometimes to their own interests. . . . And even when they artfully show us operations which are undoubtedly precious, such as the abolition of the slave-trade, and ask us if, for their sake, foolish and obstinate governments may not wholesomely be frightened by a little disturbance . . . still we say no, and that monster-processions in the streets and forcible irruptions into the parks, even in professed support of this good design, ought to be unflinchingly forbidden and repressed. . . . Because a State in which law is authoritative and sovereign . . . is requisite if man is to bring to maturity anything precious and lasting now, or to found anything precious and lasting for the future . . . the very framework and exterior order of the State, whoever may administer the State, is sacred; and culture is the most resolute enemy of anarchy. ("Conclusion," nos. 3–4)

As the late Bill Readings wrote, "the University becomes modern when it takes on the responsibility for working out the relation between the subject and the state."[8] In passages such as this, Arnold clearly anticipates a "modern" university in which departments of the national literature assume the role of the "spiritual" center not just of the humanities but of the university as a whole. Declaring culture, in the form of enriched personal experience, to be the noblest and most essential human attainment, and the state as the precondition of culture, he also anticipates the founding, a century later, of the National Endowment for the Humanities, a federal agency that funds teachers of poems, plays, and novels. And he has done so, we must remind ourselves, by way of a vitalistic critique of modern rationality as manifest in science, a repudiation of reformist politics, a veneration for tradition and aesthetic sensitivity, and an implicit endorsement of elite education and the ethos of privilege.

It is deeply ironic that the concept of culture, which emerged once again into prominence in the 1950s in the British academy as a neo-Marxist movement explicitly identified with working-class experience and set against both social-democratic and communist regimes, should have begun life, as it were, as a dependent clause within statism.[9] Those who founded the highly successful movement known as British Cultural Studies cited F. R. Leavis more respectfully than Arnold, much less J. H. Newman; but Leavis notwithstanding, the new concept of culture they espoused was explicitly allied with the discipline of sociology rather than with literary studies or even the humanities. The institutional success of the concept of culture, in this context, came at the cost of its identification with literature and any notion of providing direct service to the state. As Stuart Hall has written, "the truth is that most of us had to leave the humanities in order to do serious work in it."[10]

In the United States, by contrast, an explicitly Arnoldian concept of culture has informed the discourse of the humanities for the past hundred years; even today, Arnold is routinely invoked by educational conservatives (who do not always share his indifference to the question of "whoever may administer the State").[11] Since the beginning of the twentieth century, when administrators at Columbia, Chicago, Yale, and Harvard began to speak fervently about the moral and spiritual benefits of a university education, "the humanities" has served as the name and the form of the link Arnold envisioned between culture, education, and the state.[12] Particularly after World War II, the humanities began to be opposed not just to its traditional foil, science, but also to social science, whose emergence as a powerful force in the American academy was marked by the founding of the Center for Advanced Study in the Behavioral Sciences at Stanford in 1951. To some, the new prominence of social science as a more or less integrated set of mutually sustaining disciplines signaled the capitulation of the academy to the forces of mass society, technology, and bureaucracy. As one writer put it, the social sciences presumed "the meaninglessness of the single event and the single human being in themselves" and the priority of "broad process or general 'laws'"; accordingly, they represented a very intimate threat, "the intrusion of the mode of the natural sciences into the world of human affairs and into man himself."[13] The vocabulary and context are different, but the intellectual issues are the same ones that animated the Renaissance humanists, Humboldt, and Arnold: Plato versus Aristotle, individuality versus system, interpretation versus objectivity, direct experience versus method, unity versus fragmentation, authenticity versus inauthenticity.

These struggles began to be framed as a general crisis in the humanities in the mid-1960s, when a book with the title *Crisis in the Humanities* appeared. The editor, J. H. Plumb, declared his intention to describe and combat "the whole sickening deadening process of increasing specialization" that segmented knowledge into sectors of expertise and blocked a holistic understanding.[14] The essay in this book that remains most resonant today is Ernest Gellner's detailed and anguished description of the consequences of the very recent rise of "knowledge" disciplines, whose new authority had deprived the humanist intellectual of his aura of dignity, "his full cognitive status."[15] Anybody can know scientific facts, Gellner said, and this knowledge does not confer dignity or wisdom on the knower; but a holistic humanistic knowledge had always been "closer to what we *are*, to the life we live, than is the language of science"—so close, in fact, that it might not even be appropriate to call it knowledge (79). To Gellner's dismay and even disgust, the vulgar pursuit of mere accumulative knowledge was dominating the university, shouldering aside the "sensitive, locally rooted, but static and fairly low-productive ways of the artisans. The humanists," Gellner concluded with a melancholy pride, "are the artisanate of cognition" (75).

The same year, 1964, also saw the *Report of the Commission on the Humanities* (a document I will treat in greater detail in chapter 6), sponsored primarily by the American Council of Learned Societies, in a somewhat different context. This report drew the attention of Lyndon Johnson, who used it in pushing for the creation of the NEH the following year. It made clear that this new government-sponsored phase in the history of the humanities was firmly based on Arnoldian tradition, for it described the humanities as "the study of that which is most human," and all but explicitly identified that study with Arnold's concept of culture. "Throughout man's consciousness," the report said, the humanities "have played an essential role in forming, preserving and transforming the social, moral and aesthetic values of every man in every age.... Their subject is every man."[16] To some, such overblown rhetoric constituted its own kind of crisis in the humanities, but to those who supported the creation of the NEH, the humanities were the solution, not the problem, especially when the humanities were identified with the interests of the state. The argument that carried the day then, as now, was that while the humanities addressed and concerned everyone, they spoke with particular force to citizens in a free society in which individual autonomy and personal experience were prized. It was often said during this time—the time of the civil rights struggle, the space race, the Bay of Pigs, the U.S.-Soviet missile gap, the Kennedy assassination, and the cold war—that the humanities could "unify society," often with the strong implication that they were especially good at unifying American society. As one writer put it, the humanities could "play the role of liberator to the American spirit" and fill "the desperate need of the American people to find some constructive use for their increasing hours of leisure."[17] If such claims had been made about the role of the humanities in liberating the German, French, Somali, Italian, British, Bolivian, Navajo, Egyptian, Laotian, or Hungarian souls, they would be considered frightening, ridiculous, deluded, arrogant, or pathetic. But in a public culture in which the free individual was so aggressively and insistently identified with the national identity and the national identity with universal values—a culture in which the capacity to realize a full human essence was considered a national characteristic, even the nation's gift to the species—such claims were none of the above; they were effective.

They were effective most of all in clinching an argument that was essential to sustaining a taxpayer-funded endowment—that the humanities, which are often described even by their advocates as useless on principle, or useless in the best sense, were a matter of national importance. Public Law 89–209, the bill that created the NEH, defined the humanities as a set of disciplines—philosophy, literature, history, and so on, but ended the list with something that is not a discipline at all: "and the study and application of the humanities to the current conditions of national life."[18] Over the years, these conditions have warranted a vast array of grants made to "improve" the quality of life in the United States; at the same time, however, the elitist tendency of the humanities has been underscored through grants to scholars doing specialist work that spoke only to the needs or interests of the scholarly community, if to those. The NEH is dedicated, in a thoroughly Arnoldian spirit, to education, and is informed by the belief that the full experience of the human condition is enriched and even enabled by learning. This belief is not confined to starry-eyed scholars dazzled by the prospect of riches. One can find it even in weightier discourses such as Hannah Arendt's *The Human Condition*, where she wrote that "we humanize what is going on in the world and in ourselves only by speaking of it, and in the course of speaking of it we learn to be human."[19] Learning to be human is still learning, and so, it is argued, advanced scholarship, often at elite private universities, is required. In the United States, the challenge for those who would argue for government support for humanistic research is to find ways of making such research seem useful to a nation that prides itself on its privileged access to the human condition.

I will leave it to others to judge how well Chairman Cole met that challenge on that day in Jackson, Mississippi, in January 2004. I can only say that he performed it in a way consistent with the history of the humanities, a history to which both conservative and progressive forces have contributed. He articulated the importance of cultural tradition as a way of realizing our full humanity, he tied that tradition and therefore that humanity to a certain kind of learning, and he defined the place of that learning in the current national priorities in a way designed to ensure continued funding—which in fact was secured: even as many services have been cut or eliminated, the NEH budget has remained steady, and has even grown slightly since 2004.[20]

Now some humanist scholars might argue that Cole's approach has compromised the independence of the humanities by turning them into instruments of policy on the one hand and an inert ("timeless") tradition on the other. Some scholars, their lives consumed by classes, department meetings, university politics, letter writing, grade sheets, and committees, might find Cole's emphasis on "eternal questions" and the things that "make us human" misguided and even embarrassing; they might feel that government officials invoking universals in a time of war are likely to be engaged in ideological rather than intellectual discourse. And, as a sidebar, some might question the all but explicitly anti-Marxist emphasis of the NEH during the Bush years in its "Heroes of History" lecture series, a celebration of those who have generated more than their share of the best that has been thought and said. But no one can say that Cole's comments represent a radical departure from, much less a betrayal of, the tradition of the humanities as they have been conceptualized and represented. All he has done is to lay bare the mechanism of that tradition—and, indeed, this fact alone might explain the discomfort his rhetoric creates in some quarters of the humanistic community.

Lest we think that the crisis in the humanities is restricted to the problematic way we Americans talk about them, I would like to report a recent experience in which I was asked to review a proposal for a grant from a research council in one of the western European countries. As it happens, the project was on the concept of the state in the educational writings of Matthew Arnold. It was an exhaustive proposal, 7,000 words in length, including a bibliography of over 100 items. It provided a general background and an assessment of the current state of knowledge, a statement of purpose, a list of research questions, and a 1,000-word section on "design and approach." This last section described the process by which a comprehensive database of all Arnold's references to collectivity and community would be compiled, and outlined the methods by which a rhetorical analysis of these references would be conducted. The goal of the analysis would, the proposal says, be to elucidate the way Arnold represents, through a pattern of rhetorical distortions, "the undecidabilities of aesthetic ideology as a discourse of sentimental education which simultaneously aspires to concrete realization in the form of the State and resists the disinterested impersonalisation involved in this realization in the name of self-interested sentiment." This sounds to me more like a result than a plan, but it is a highly useful indicator of the paradigm for humanities research in this environment.

That paradigm is social-scientific, with specific results following from determined methodology. The entirety is unapologetically predetermined, and while the students in Matthew Arnold's ideal schools may have been invited to exercise their imaginations in the contemplation of the treasures of the past, no such invitation would be extended to the as-yet unknown graduate student who would, if the project were funded, simply sign on to it as to a contract, adopting it as the subject of his or her Ph.D. dissertation. This rigorous and highly detailed program suggests virtually no scope for individuality, no space for uncertainty, no need for discovery, no value attached to interpretation, no possibility of instructive interpretive error, no sense that scholarship represents a kind of free self-fashioning, no opportunity (or time) for deliberative reflection—no room, Americans might feel, for the humanities. A subject will have been responsibly covered, and the result will be a new certitude about the undecidabilities of aesthetic education as a discourse of sentimental education, but what of the student—if, indeed, *student* is the right word and not *employee* or *team member*. I hope that the project is funded, but I cannot altogether suppress an "American" feeling that the entire thing is shallow and, in its confidence about the value of its predetermined results, optimistic in a way that humanists in this country find off-putting. Indeed, reading the proposal, I realized that one of the cultural roles played by the humanities in this country has been to counter the epistemic optimism of the sciences, their Enlightenment confidence that the application of rationality and the scientific method will solve the problems not just of science but of the world.

I cannot say how widespread in Europe and elsewhere is the assimilation of the humanities to the model of the social sciences. But to American ears, Cole's invocation of courage, compassion, liberation, and the human legacy sounds—notwithstanding misgivings about intellectual vulgarity, and about the ideological and political motivation of his statement—both reassuring and deeply refreshing. Like American humanists generally, Cole's understanding of the connection between learning and personal and cultural enrichment derives directly from Arnold, while the European model seems, from our perspective, not properly humanistic at all but rather something that belongs to the "human sciences" or, more exactly, to the assemblage of disciplines Wilhelm Dilthey called *Geisteswissenschaften*, including religion, psychology, law, politics, and economics.

For another contrast with American presuppositions, we might look at the mission statement for the Arts and Humanities Research Council, established in 2005 in the United Kingdom. The AHRC lists as its "strategic aims" the following:

- to promote and support the production of world-class research in the arts and humanities
- to promote and support world-class postgraduate training designed to equip graduates for research or other professional careers
- to strengthen the impact of arts and humanities research by encouraging researchers to disseminate and transfer knowledge to other contexts where it makes a difference
- to raise the profile of arts and humanities research and to be an effective advocate for its social, cultural and economic significance[21]

Once a part of the Arts and Humanities Research Board, the AHRC was redefined in 2005 as a subunit in the Office of Science and Technology, which itself was part of the Department of Trade and Industry, along with seven other research councils. By 2009, the AHRC had been reassigned to the Department of

Business Administration and Skills, tightening up its mission as it went. In 2005, when the more humanistic Department of Trade and Industry was running the show, the AHRC included among its goals "to promote awareness of the importance of arts and humanities research and its role in understanding ourselves, our society, our past and our future, and the world in which we live." Four years on, the talk is of "impact" and profile raising.

To American eyes, all this is strikingly deficient with respect to uplifting rhetoric. No fine discourse about values, sensibility, the imagination, humanity, much less about the need to counter tyranny and terror—nothing, just a list of the disciplines supported by this office. Breathes there the man with soul so dead! The contrasting messages of these entities are in fact fully communicated by their places in the larger bureaucratic structure. The AHRC is a microunit in larger entities whose only goals are economic, but the NEH is independent, and while its budget is dwarfed by the National Science Foundation and the National Institutes of Health, it is structurally comparable to them. And in terms of uplift, the self-description on the NEH Web site does not disappoint: "Because democracy demands wisdom, the National Endowment for the Humanities serves and strengthens our Republic by promoting excellence in the humanities and conveying the lessons of history to all Americans."[22] While the NEH has not been altogether apolitical throughout its history, most humanists in the United States who were thinking of applying for support for an original, exploratory, innovative, controversial, or ground-breaking research project would undoubtedly prefer to have their applications judged by an NEH peer review panel than by the AHRC.

Still, some might prefer a drier, less crisis-driven, and less explicitly patriotic approach to the humanities. They might look for ways to make Cole's points in acceptably sophisticated ways that conform to values that a scholar can hold without also holding his nose. They would find it surprisingly easy to do so. They could, for example, defend Cole's idea that the humanities are about "what makes us human" by talking about the importance of the principle of universal values, noting that any challenge to local customs that support the victimization of women, minorities, and outcast groups of all kinds must be based on ethical principles that transcend local customs. They might say that when the rule of law has broken down or become corrupted by power in a rogue or failed state, the international community can only intervene legitimately if it can make the case that human rights are at stake. They could then say that the tradition of the humanities has readier access to a universal understanding of humanity, and thus to a richer and more spacious understanding of human potentiality, than could ever be attained by local law, customary practices, or popular culture. They could note that, even if the interest in universals, human rights, personal fulfillment, and individual interpretation was itself an American parochialism in a fact-based, increasingly factionalized and tribalized world, a legitimate pride could be taken in the fact that these deeply humane interests were shared by the government of the United States, which actually supports their work. *Voila!*

My subject is not truly the NEH or the current administration but rather the contemporary condition and self-understanding of the humanities. Humanists today must, I submit, come to grips with their own tradition. Specifically, they must bring themselves to recognize the problematic fact that when their discipline has asserted itself, that assertion has characteristically been framed in conservative, melancholic, or merely oppositional terms, with humanists positioning themselves on the losing side of a struggle with the mighty forces of capitalism, science, or modernity. In recent years, humanists have been remarkably ingenious and persistent in accessing the sense of exile, marginality, and anachronism that the great humanists possessed and that has defined the humanist malaise since Petrarch.[23] This has traditionally been a very powerful tactic, but it has its downsides, and its usefulness may have been exhausted. If humanists today would reorient their discipline and pull the sword from the stone of reaction, they must rethink a self-description that has in recent years been dominated by terms such as *subversive, oppositional, critical,* and *resistant.* They must ask themselves, in an activist spirit, what great questions, what pressing issues they might have something to contribute to by virtue of their training and expertise; they must ask what responses those questions and issues elicit from the discipline they have spent so many years acquiring.

Not everyone can or should engage great questions directly, but all work in the humanities takes place in a context of concern for issues that are not directly or immediately reflected in the materials under consideration, and if some scholarly work seems more important than others, one reason is that some scholarship—the important kind—establishes a connection between itself and the deeper currents of the culture. In scholarship that is felt to be important by an audience beyond the small group of specialists to which it speaks directly, that connection is somehow available or perceptible; in the work of those critics who seem to mean the most, the connection is rich and inescapable even if still, and necessarily, indirect or mediated. Many of the most interesting questions today seem to "belong" to other disciplines—economics, biology, neuroscience, religion, politics, law, international relations. But humanists are not debarred from any of these questions: all of them have a philosophical or reflective dimension, and many can be represented in narrative form. And one can, of course, always historicize.

In his great and prescient book *The University in Ruins,* Readings wrote that whereas the university was once dedicated to the transmission of a national culture, it is now adrift in a transnational global economy in which the concept of culture has lost its purchase. In such an economy, he noted, the university no longer needs to make transcendental claims for its function.[24] The options left include (a) simply reaffirming a national cultural identity; (b) reinventing cultural identity to include those elements traditionally marginalized or excluded; or (c) abandoning the notion that the mission of the university is linked to the project of realizing a national cultural identity at all. With considerable reluctance, he recommended the third option, despite the fact that this would mean surrendering the claim of service to the state, and even the claim to have a *mission* at all (Readings, 90). Scholars should, I think, set aside this reluctance and assert that the glass is half-full. One of the troubling aspects of the history of the humanities has been precisely this concept of service to the state, which has involved scholars in a project not of their making and for which they have had at best intermittent enthusiasm (largely depending on whoever is administering the state). This project, as we have seen, arose within the emphasis on culture, the erosion of which releases scholars and enables them to discover or forge new attachments, new affiliations, new configurations, new ends. As Readings argued, the postcultural era still has a place and indeed a need for the university, which can ensure its survival by becoming more flexible and adaptable, more ingeniously responsive to market pressures, more supportive of multidisciplinary conversations and temporary aggregations of scholars engaged with particular questions.

Two such questions seem to me immediately pertinent for the most jeopardized portion of the university, scholars in the humanities. Currently, the ancient question of the human is taking radical new forms, but those who are advancing the question most aggressively are, for the most part, unequipped by professional training to address considerations of meaning or value—unable to, as Arnold said, put their work into relation with a cultural tradition. They are largely indifferent to background or context, and to the task of assessing long-range consequences. There is work here for the scholar who could overcome the long-standing humanist antipathy toward the sciences and begin to imagine a disciplinary reconfiguration that would include, within the larger field of the humanities, those areas of science and technology that address the question of the human. This would depend on some cooperation with scientists in various fields, but happily, many of these have recently shown a willingness to speak in the vernacular so they can communicate with a larger audience—the very audience that humanists, speaking in professional tongues, have largely lost. Humanists are natural sponsors of the inquiry into the human, and should make the most of this opportunity.

Religion represents another opportunity for humanistic reconsideration. As even this briefest of surveys suggests, the history of humanism runs parallel to the history of religious thought. Humanistic study has never left religion untouched, which is to say it has never left it alone.[25] If scholars in the humanities today believe that they are professing a mode of understanding with no substantive relation to religion whatsoever, they risk seeming ignorant of their own history and therefore of their own discipline, and thus playing themselves off the field of contemporary concern. For even in recent years, when humanistic scholars have established an agenda that often excludes or opposes religious thought, the two modes have never been altogether distinct. The interests of the humanities and religion converge on a number of issues, perhaps the most significant of which is the role of values and attitudes in shaping knowledge. And on this point, scholars might look to religion as a model of how to promote the idea that knowledge is bound up with values that are not determined by the interests of the state.

The history of the humanities teaches us that tradition is, among other things, an excellent springboard for innovation and progress. The primary fact about tradition, from a humanistic point of view, is not, after all, its inertial insistence on the past but its malleability and responsiveness. Humanists must always respect tradition, but they do not always have to be on the wrong side of modernity or progress; nor are they constrained to understand themselves as mere obedient particles of the state or of global capital. If humanistic scholars could grasp, without reluctance, the full dimensions and implications of the history of the humanities, they could still hope to refashion that tradition in light of current postcultural conditions; for, like a seed in springtime, it is waiting and willing to flower, but only on the condition that it is left buried in the soil.

The Next Big Thing in Literary Study: Pleasure

It may go without saying that literary study today suffers from some kind of evil malady, but that does mean that people have foregone the pleasure of saying it. Indeed, analyses of the decline and fall of English have proliferated to the point where there is a livelier community of discourse surrounding this subject than there is about almost any subject in literary study: the autopsies outnumber the instances. Some of the causes of this decline can be, and have been, laid at the door of the professoriate itself, who are accused of being overly professionalized (although they are in desperate straits, professionally), hyperpoliticized (by those with a political agenda), and elitist (by those who would prefer they turn away from mass culture and stick to the Greats). Other causes, however, are simply attributes of the larger culture: the shortening of the collective attention span through a surfeit of information; the tinnitus effect of a noisy, vulgar, and invasive popular culture; a general tendency to vocationalism and professionalism in higher education; the ceaseless invitation to distraction issued by our increasingly compelling electronic gadgets; the grinding effects of the economics of education; and the atmosphere of nonstop hysteria generated by the media. All these factors work against a discipline that is predicated on discipline, on the ability of people to absent themselves from the world and enter into extended periods of solitude, concentration, and meditation in which they ponder artifacts just for the sake of pondering. But you can only control what lies within your reach, so I would like to talk about what literary scholars themselves have done and what they might do to get out of this situation.

What have they done? The very short answer is that they have by their own actions repeatedly exacerbated an already problematic structural division within literary studies between the undergraduate and graduate programs, and have, as an unintended consequence, weakened the discipline as a whole.

To see how this has happened, we must recall that as recently as the 1940s, the undergraduate programs dominated at all but a few institutions. But after World War II, the federal government began to provide massive funding to universities for scientific research, shifting the center of gravity to graduate programs, especially in science, and producing ripple effects that touched all disciplines including the humanities. Research rather than teaching became the measure by which individuals, departments, and universities were evaluated. And with huge numbers of students entering higher education, graduate programs had to grow in order to keep up with the demand for more professors. For many disciplines, the rapid growth of the graduate program presented tremendous opportunities, but in literary study, these opportunities were accompanied by vigorous reaction.

English departments could not easily convert themselves into engines of research because the study of literature, while elitist in some respects, was founded on the egalitarian presumption that the value of literature was available in principle to all competent readers without recourse to specialist training. As a consequence, the relationship between the undergraduate and graduate programs in English was different from other fields. In mathematics, history, biology, or engineering, undergraduates learn simplified and elementary forms of the kinds of knowledge that are discovered or created by professors, while the graduates learn how to discover or create that knowledge themselves. The standard "Intro" class in a given discipline will have undergraduates reading basic or classic texts in the field, learning how and why the subject is important, and acquiring some sense of methodology. The course, as well as the structure of the major, will attempt to communicate the impression that there is a certain order and sequence to the way one acquires an understanding of the field. Literary study is different. There is no smooth natural progression from an undergraduate encounter with literature up to the professorial level. Indeed, there is an unspoken presumption that most undergraduates take courses in literature not to learn about it but to enjoy it. Learning, in the sense of acquiring a body of information or mastering a methodology, is not the point at all; the point, rather, is to open oneself to the experience of literature. A secondary point, ancillary to this experience, concerns skill. Students are encouraged to develop the ability to say things about literary texts that are meaningful to them in a way that others might find persuasive, in the conviction that argumentation as such is a valuable skill. Say anything you want to about the text, professors tell their students, as long as you back it up with evidence. In a great many colleges and universities, there is no "Intro to English" class at all, because there is no agreement among the faculty on what constitutes a proper introduction to a field in which the goals, methods, basic concepts, and even objects are so loosely defined, and in which individual subjective experience plays such a large part. This lack of consensus has sometimes been lamented, but has never been considered a serious problem.

At midcentury, humanist hostility to science was centered in English departments. This was, after all, the era of C. P. Snow's famous 1959 Rede Lecture, *The Two Cultures*, and F. R. Leavis's blistering response; and many professors of English were not only resentful of the massive amounts of support and cultural prestige that were flowing to science but regarded research even in their own field as an activity best conducted elsewhere, by others, for purposes other than the ones they valued. They believed that while scholarship might be required for the production of literary history, bibliography, and other fact-based approaches, the tone was set and the mission defined by the professors, amateurs in spirit and pedagogues by vocation, who sought to awaken students to the glories of great literature, thereby giving them a gift that would, it was hoped, last a lifetime. As late as 1969, one-third of American professors did not have a Ph.D., and that figure was surely higher in the English department than in the sciences.[1]

At first, even literary criticism had to struggle to be accepted as a legitimate activity for professors of English. As Louis Menand points out in *The Marketplace of Ideas* (2010),[2] it was a hard slog persuading people inside and outside the academy first that literature could actually be studied like other subjects, and second that criticism represented a contribution to knowledge that could bear comparison with those made in other fields. Both arguments eventually prevailed, but did so over the objections of those who thought the modern university an unpromising site for literary commentary. This objection might seem wholly fanciful to many people today, with literary study securely embedded in, and even largely confined to, the university. But Menand's explanation makes clear that for many people, a skepticism about the "contribution to knowledge" made by criticism followed naturally from a certain understanding of the nature of criticism, an understanding that many professionals today still find compelling:

> To the extent that literary criticism is thought of as the possibly idiosyncratic interpretation and appreciation of works of literature and the drawing of moral and other non-aesthetic conclusions from those activities, the university literature department is not especially well suited to the business of producing either interesting literary criticism or interesting literary critics. But to the degree that literary criticism is thought of as a discovery about the nature of literature or of literary language by the application of philosophically grounded methods of inquiry, then the modern academy becomes a relatively congenial place in which to practice criticism (110).

In any event, with all the rewards flowing to those who discovered things about the nature of literature and away from those in the idiosyncrasy and morality business, English was virtually forced to adopt as its primary rationale an agenda that came into direct conflict with what many of its professors were trying to do in the undergraduate classroom. Professors who had considered themselves primarily teachers found their activity devalued in favor of an activity that they felt should not be conducted in the university at all. And this is a relatively recent development: the Modern Language Association's constitution did not add the word *criticism* to its list of the objectives of professional literature and language studies until 1951.[3]

At first, professors could practice criticism with a relatively clean conscience, because the criticism they produced was tightly linked with teaching. The New Criticism was a way of studying poetry that set aside questions of biography, authorial intention, and context in order to focus on the formal linguistic structures of works of art, primarily short poems. Some New Critics did not consider themselves scholars in any sense, but those who did often taught in small colleges, such as Amherst or Kenyon, or in universities with a strong liberal arts orientation, such as Vanderbilt (John Crowe Ransom), Harvard (Ruben Brower), or Yale (Cleanth Brooks). Guided by some of the early essays of T. S. Eliot, New Criticism was all but explicitly postreligious, generating "heresies" and "blasphemies" with inquisitorial enthusiasm even as it insisted that literature was no substitute for religion. And it was a practice born in and made for the undergraduate classroom in that it required close attention to what was in front of the eyes, with no history, context, or general questions permitted to confuse the issue.

But New Criticism was an unreliable ally in the battle against science and research, for other aspects of its practice were easily adaptable to the new spirit. New Criticism reinforced the sense that the study of literature was a discipline like others, and since it sought to be rigorous, precise, and empirical in its methods, it had the effect of accommodating literary criticism to the ethos of science (see Menand, 107–17). Indeed, it was ultimately through the successes of the New Criticism that literary study was able to earn a place in the research university during what Menand describes as the Golden Age of higher education, the years between World War II and 1975 when research funding was plentiful, student enrollments even in the humanities were rising, and the faculty were increasing in numbers and power year by year (64). Indeed, the New-Critical insistence that poetic language objectively displayed qualities of tension, irony, and ambiguity was not only quasi-scientific in itself but opened the door for subsequent approaches that, if they had arrived without New-Critical forewarning, might well have appeared so out of touch with the humanistic spirit of literature that they would have been rejected outright rather than dominating literary study for a quarter of a century. As it was, however, irony and ambiguity slid insensibly into the even more technical terms *undecidability* and *différence*; the premise of the inaccessibility and irrelevance of the author's intentions became the more radical argument that intentions themselves were mere linguistic illusions. And so New Critical humanism prepared the way for a wave of European antihumanism in the forms of structuralism, poststructuralism, and deconstruction.

What made all these theory-based schools of thought into a mighty force that swept over literary studies was the fact that whatever their differences, many of the major figures shared the conviction that our basic ideas about human subjectivity and experience were based on a misunderstanding. The very concept of the subject—the self-determining core of individual identity—was, they said, vastly overrated by a culture that wanted to believe in autonomy; in fact, they believed, individuals and all their acts (including their "cultural" acts) were epiphenomena, determined in their essence by large forces that were of a different kind and operated at a different scale from individuals and groups composed of individuals. Under the influence of theory, literary scholars in great numbers abandoned the human orientation and scale that had always characterized their work and began to talk about things that were much smaller than human beings, such as graphemes, signifiers, or tropes, or much larger, such as "Western metaphysics," "epistemes," or economistic or ideological processes—and to talk about them as if they were independent, even "constitutive," of human agency or human communicative processes. Drawn by the cosmopolitanism, novelty, and intellectual authority represented by theory, literary scholars worked to refashion their discipline, leaving the self-aware and self-determining human being out of it—"effaced," "bracketed," or "under erasure." By comparison with the masterly new force of advanced theory, the humanistic disciplines of literary criticism and literary history seemed woefully undisciplined, and seemed to shrink under its stern gaze. Perspectives usurped the privileged place formerly occupied by works of art: as one critic wrote in 1998, "English has become an intellectual locus where people can study the text of *Sir Gawain and the Green Knight* from a Christian perspective, the text of the O. J. trial from a Foucauldian perspective, and the text of the Treaty of Versailles from a Marxist perspective."[4] Where scholars once discussed Dickens's depiction of women, they now talked about the representation of gender with Dickens as an example, before finally tucking in to a discourse on gender theory minus the distracting examples. With the advent of theory, the graduate program secured its ascendancy over the undergraduate program.

The critical paradigms that succeeded the era of poststructuralist theory moderated but did not reverse the theory-based attention to things other than artifacts created by people. The New Historicism and especially Cultural Studies were informed primarily by nonliterary models of thought, particularly political economy, sociology, anthropology, and Marxist critical theory. While the concepts of agency and especially "resistance" were often touted in these approaches, the real agency was held to lie with segments of society, or patterns of energy circulating through society, rather than individuals; even works of art were treated as the expression or instrument of forces circulating throughout the culture. The center of gravity, in other words, remained outside the humanities, and definitely outside the domain of the literary, for these other, more scientific fields presented greater opportunities for empirical research and abstract theoretical formulations of the kind that could support a research program. The bedrock concepts of traditional literary studies were thought by many to block a truly critical understanding of the ways that culture actually functioned. The humanities were held to be so antithetical to cultural studies in Britain that the leading theorist of cultural studies in Britain, Stuart Hall, wrote that "the truth is that most of us had to leave the humanities in order to do serious work in it."[5]

Professors who theorized rather than illuminated, who published rather than taught, who gravitated toward social science and away from the humanities, generally had a strong professional and disciplinary self-conception. Since the late nineteenth century, professors in virtually all disciplines had—like chemists, psychoanalysts, physicians, lawyers, and other professionals— their own professional organizations, journals, prizes, conventions, and other trappings of an autonomous, self-legitimating professional activity. Professionalism in academic life had always been an unstressed element, especially in literary study, where most scholars scarcely regarded themselves as employees, much less as members of a guild. But spurred by an influential series of articles by Stanley Fish, scholars began in the 1980s to take their professional status more seriously.[6] That meant taking status itself more seriously. Authority and hierarchy became not just brute facts but issues to be debated and goals to be openly pursued. Inflamed by a job crisis that has since become permanent, the annual meetings of the Modern Language Association became not ceremonies of decorous conviviality but scenes of turbulence and upheaval, animated by political insurgencies, theory wars, cross-generational resentments, and a sharpened awareness of the economics of the market. In this highly stressed and volatile context, it was both exciting and reassuring for professors to think that an academic life might be, not just a practice of routine and unmarked constancy undertaken over a succession of quiet decades, but a real career, with the kinds of structure and self-affirmation enjoyed by professionals in other fields, if not their income levels. Under the influence of this new conception of the scholar's working life, the profession, as it called itself with increasing conviction, of literary study discovered a new sense of its own prospects.

These prospects were centered, once again, in research and publication. But the professional ethos not only lent even more urgency to these activities. It underwrote a new conception of literature itself, a "conventionalist" account, in Fish's term, in which institutional practices and vocabularies constitute not just the rules of the critical game but the literary object itself by prescribing the ways in which facts about the object are to be determined.[7] Fish was attacked from left and right, with both sides accusing him of violating the spirit of literary study by promoting ideas that would be more at home in the School of Management than in a department of English.[8] Edward Said, to take a "left" example, held out for "amateurism, the desire to be moved not by profit or reward but by love for and unquenchable interest in the larger picture, in making connections across lines and barriers, in refusing to be tied down to a specialty, in caring for ideas and values despite the restrictions of a profession."[9] To Said and others, the professionalism Fish seemed to celebrate was a self-enclosed and self-protective state of mind devoted to conformism and structure rather than to the openness, freshness, responsiveness, iconoclasm, and free historical imagination that they saw in literary study at its best. However valuable professionalism may be in fostering group self-approbation and support structures, they argued, it was fatally predisposed to agreeability, groupthink, and worldly success. Teachers are in business to help students, they felt, but professionals are in business to help themselves.[10]

But behind this new complaint about professionalism was another version of the tension I have been discussing. Professionalism, many felt, fails to solicit, and even actively suppresses, the undergraduate enthusiasm that is the focus of the undergraduate English program and the basis for the argument that English is an important discipline. In a professionalized departmental environment, the interests and attitudes of research dominated over those of teaching. And dominate they did, taking over the graduate program[11] and even the undergraduate program, which became preprofessional in the sense that the teaching of literature in the lower division was heavily influenced by what was going on upstairs. Many undergraduate courses included a host of secondary works swarming busily around the primary text like drones around a supine queen. These were often theoretical in character; class discussions and writing assignments often focused on theoretical points, and it became fashionable for faculty to promote the idea of undergraduate "research," often into theoretical points, as a valuable activity. Moreover, in their desire to assert a professional identity that could bear comparison with that of scientists, many tenure-track scholars convinced themselves that the best teaching jobs were those that involved the least, or least strenuous, teaching.

In some senses, the battle is over, research has won, and English is a full participant in the mission of higher education to create and discover new knowledge. But in actuality the situation is more complex. While the orientation of the graduate program determines the self-understanding and pedagogical style of a great many professors, the undergraduate approach to literature, as the occasion for a certain kind of experience rather than as a passive body of fact to be learned or a methodology to be mastered, retains much of its former appeal, even for faculty. The result is an exquisite, almost perfect, incoherence: embracing theory and research, as it was virtually forced to do, English has undercut its own intellectual and even moral foundation and alienated its most reliable customers, undergraduates; but by retaining, as it must, the high value placed on literary experiences of the kind that once excited them and continue to excite their students, English has made itself an outlier in the research environment of the modern university.

What to do? One suggestion was proffered by William M. Chace, a former English professor and past president of Wesleyan and Emory, in a 2009 article called "The Decline of the English Department."[12] Chace cites recurrent—indeed, by now traditional—doubts about the viability of English as a scholarly pursuit, and lends these doubts his full support, based on his long experience as a scholar and administrator. His adjectives alone tell the story: incoherent, chaotic, self-centered, comatose, empty (modifying *tank*), bankrupt, déclassé. If nothing is done to stop the slide, he says, English departments will descend to the "moderate dignity" of classics. To avoid such a dismal fate, he offers a two-step program: first, a return to "the aesthetic wellsprings of literature, the rock-solid fact . . . that it can indeed amuse, delight, and educate"; and second, a recalibration of the standards for tenure, beginning with an emphasis on classroom performance, where the focus "should be on the books, not on the theories they can be made to support." As a final insult to the research agenda of most tenure-track professors, Chace adds that English departments should prioritize courses in composition and rhetoric, the "sturdy lifeline" to resources—and the meal ticket for otherwise unemployed graduate students. He says nothing about research or scholarship. There could hardly be a clearer statement of the view that English is essentially an undergraduate enterprise, a field in which little fresh research can be done, where the main project is the awakening of the young to great works of art.[13]

Such a program would represent a crushing reversal for the graduate program, and a blow to the viability of English as a discipline among others in a modern research university. English would be reduced to issuing earnest invitations to students to experience amusement, delight, and edification; to affirming the greatness of great works; to correcting punctuation errors. Facts would be abandoned in favor of values, and what passes for common sense would prevail over creativity and innovation. Chace's proposals would require that English, and English alone among the disciplines, roll back the clock to some point, perhaps mythical, when professors could speak confidently for the cultural inheritance, when beauty was truth and truth beauty.

A better solution would be one that did not humble one side

of the department at the expense of the other, one that unified the undergraduate and graduate programs in a way that made sense of the entire discipline from the lowliest freshman to the most exalted professor. What would such a program look like? On what principle would it be based? How would it define its object and its purpose?

One way to begin thinking about these questions is to ask what draws people to literature in the first place. At the undergraduate level, the answer, I believe, is that literature satisfies the particular intellectual cravings that young people, or at least some young people, have. With its direct but noncoercive address to readers, its invitation to engage with it on one's own terms, literature attracts the serious interest of college-age students, eliciting live or stray psychic energy of the sort that they possess in great abundance, and providing ways of thinking about their lives that their lives themselves do not always afford. For them, the English department is the place in the university where the desire for knowledge braids most intimately with the hunger for experience, the longing for self-understanding, and the wish to connect oneself with something larger or other than oneself. With all these urgencies piling in, the literary experience can be felt as a moment of extraordinary focus and intensity. As Andrew Delbanco has written, "Students who turn with real engagement to English do so almost always because they have had the mysterious and irreducibly private experience—or at least some intimation of it—of receiving from a work of literature 'an untranslatable order of impressions' that has led to 'consummate moments' in which thought and feeling are fused and lifted to a new intensity."[14]

Consummate moments have not been widely celebrated in the professional discourse of recent years. They are too laced with affect to be reduced to knowledge, too disorderly to be accommodated to the rigors of theory, and too individualist to be interesting from a cultural perspective. But they have never entirely disappeared from the scene, because they represent the common experience of the undergraduates who populate classrooms.

Technologically advanced, many of these undergraduates still experience reading literature as, in Robert Louis Stevenson's terms, "absorbing and voluptuous; we should gloat over a book," Stevenson said, "be rapt clean out of ourselves, and rise from the perusal, our mind filled with the busiest, kaleidoscopic dance of images, incapable of sleep or of continuous thought."[15] This deep-purple passage is quoted in a remarkable 1991 essay by Barry Weller that sought to provide a corrective to the then-prevailing accounts of reading, which described the reader as a "locus of will and desire, even when any notion of self—a unified self, at least— has disappeared."[16] On all sides of the critical spectrum, Weller notes, the reader was being described as "strong," "resistant," or otherwise engaged in a scene of power in which the reader either recognized him- or herself in the text and was gratified and empowered, or failed to see him- or herself registered in the text and was bored, discouraged, or enraged. The "curricular accommodations and pluralist rhetoric of the academy," Weller says, "appear to assume that readers cannot achieve pleasure and knowledge without immediate self-recognition or a shared ground of experience" (8). The assumption appears to be that the pleasure of literature is based on self-communion and self-confirmation. If, for example, one is Asian, female, gay, African-American—if one is anything—then one can only be pleased by texts written from that perspective; all other texts become "a ground of intellectual and emotional warfare, where the designs of alien subjects on the subjectivity of the reader must be disputed" (9). Against this model, Weller proposes another that is, he suggests, more in tune with Stevenson and with the common experience of readers.

That experience, Weller argues, is essentially passive: the pleasure it affords is different in kind from the pleasure we take in, for example, seizing our destinies or commanding our fates, or indeed in agency of any kind. While it is pleasurable for professors to be "smart about the formal structure, the semiotic density, the cultural symptoms, or the historical determinations of a poem or story," or to produce a triumphant analysis or a new interpretive discovery, these kinds of pleasure are not as fundamental to literature as the kind of engagement he describes provocatively as "something swoonier, more embarrassing, some possible apprehension of sublimity or self-erasure in the presence of what is not ourselves" (10). Reading of this "almost preconscious" kind does not confirm us in what we already know or mirror us as we already take ourselves to be, but takes us out of ourselves, relieves us of the burdens of selfhood, and sets us free in an alternate universe of possibility.

Reading passively, we learn a fundamental lesson about the human species: that, by virtue of our intellects and imaginations, our destinies are not fixed by our starting positions or immediate circumstances. Weller cites an experience recorded by the scholar Nina Auerbach, who, early in her career, taught Charles Dickens's *Great Expectations* at California State College at Long Beach, a "sprawling, car-choked school between two freeways on the fringe of the barrio."[17] Her students were "blue-collar workers, blacks, Chicanos, foreigners, and housewives," for many of whom college was a strange and estranging experience. In this context, Dickens came unexpectedly alive. "The bullied poor boy, hungry for glorification, whom my present middle-class students [at the University of Pennsylvania] condemn with sanctimonious ease, was heard by his own." You do not have to resemble Pip in order to read your own fate as coded somehow in his, she concludes; "all you have to be is despised." Glossing Auerbach's astonishment that her disenfranchised urban students could respond so powerfully to a fictional British boy, Weller speculates that "suspension of . . . the urgencies of immediate experience . . . was the condition for their passionate embrace of, their triumphant engagement with, *Great Expectations*; they had, in other words, taken the novel in only after they had evacuated themselves so that they were free to inhabit a mobile web of identifications, responding to whatever they chose" (11).

One of the deep pleasures of undergraduate teaching is that it gives the professor the opportunity to facilitate experiences in which self-discovery merges with the discovery of a freedom that the very possession of a self sometimes seems to foreclose. More so than other disciplines, literary pedagogy has the potential to reach deep into a student's growing self-understanding and understanding of the world, and to help him or her imagine other ways of looking at life, and an expanded range of possible futures. One of the most complex but essential things teachers must learn to elicit and to talk about, then, is the particular kind of pleasure that people experience when they read literature.

Literary pleasure is a subject worthy of inquiry. It may be a gift to be simple, but literary or aesthetic pleasure is not simple at all. If it were, we could not take pleasure in representations of human misery, pain, and suffering. The spectacle of Hamlet descending into madness, of the gnawing self-consumption of Dostoevsky's underground man, of the wittily articulated hopelessness endured by Kafka's heroes, even of Anne Frank's unbearably poignant self-discovery, all give us an intense but inexplicable and even disturbing pleasure. Our own reactions seem to implicate us somehow in the suffering we are reading about, and lead us deep into the chasm that separates, but also connects, the aesthetic representation from the thing represented, and thus to the mysterious specificity of art. Other forms of separation are less mysterious. Reading of some pathetic scene of human suffering, we sometimes find ourselves drifting into indifference, distracted, coldly appreciative of a turn of phrase, envious of the author's abilities, irritated by the length of the book. Literature takes us out of ourselves, but by allowing us to take pleasure in representations of pain, or by bringing before us our own capacity for detachment, it can also trouble the image we may have of ourselves as morally sensitive people. Even when we are reading about pleasurable experiences, our own pleasure in reading is of a different kind, and the discrepancy between the events represented and our interest in those events suggests a capacity to take things in a different sense than they seem to demand, an ability to understand something against the grain, construe it according to our own interests, or simply to ignore it. We learn from literature what we want to, when we want to. The sense of freedom we have while reading is truly fundamental: it does not have a defined or assured moral status, and implies that we do not either.

Eliciting literary pleasure would be good work for any teacher, and explaining it would be a useful occupation for graduate students and professors. They would not have to invent the subject. A 1983 book called *Formations of Pleasure*[18] included essays by prominent Marxist critics, with a lead essay from Fredric Jameson that described pleasure as "the consent of life in the body," and concluded with the pronouncement that "the proper political use of pleasure" was "allegorical."[19] More recently, Slavoj Žižek has promoted "enjoyment" as the cornerstone of a Lacanian political theory.[20] But literary pleasure has not had a true theorist (other than Weller) since 1975, when Roland Barthes published his subversive little book, *The Pleasure of the Text*. A proper literary theory of pleasure would not only explain what it is that nonprofessional and undergraduate readers are doing, thus helping to unify the undergraduate and graduate programs. Such a theory could also serve as a bridge to other disciplines, even to scientific disciplines. In fact, literary study now seems to be groping uncertainly toward precisely this form of interdisciplinary collaboration in two areas, cognitive neuroscience and evolutionary theory. I can only sketch out here some paths of exploration that might be pursued.

Many humanists object to the reductive implications of the assumption that brain functions can be localized, a prospect that implies, they feel, a banalized and even a vulgarized understanding of consciousness that ignores the four-dimensional complexity and dynamism of the brain. But in a recent article, the British scholar Philip Davis claims to have discovered a way of bringing together a humanistic understanding of literary language and the information provided by imaging technology to explore "the possibility that the shapes of mentality formed by literary language, in particular syntax, lock into, shift and modify established pathways of the brain."[21] Pleasure is the key. With the help of EEG and fMRI, Davis and two scientific colleagues tested the hypothesis that literary language has an identifiable impact on the brain. They wired subjects up and had them read passages from Shakespeare in which language is used in creative ways, as when the Duke of Albany asks his wife, Lear's cruel daughter Goneril, "*What* have you done? Tigers not daughters, *what* have you performed? . . . A father, and a gracious aged man, him have you *madded*" (quoted on p. 267). Using a language that was still in "rich molten transition," Shakespeare, Davis notes, often effects "functional shifts" of this kind, in which words change their parts of speech. When the subjects encountered such shifts, Davis discovered, a "powerful P600 surge (a parietal modulation peaking approximately 600 milliseconds after the onset of the word that upsets syntactic integrity) is registered on the EEG graph"—and, crucially, with no N400 effect, the "negative wave modulation that occurs 400 milliseconds after the onset of the critical word." Davis infers from this that "functional shift can be seen to have the function of stretching the human mind towards new connections, making the language itself more alive to us, at a level of neural excitement never fully exorcised by subsequent conceptualization" (269).

In Davis's account, functional shifts alert and energize the brain, producing a distinct kind of pleasure in which the brain takes delight in exploring its own capacities. If nouns and verbs are processed in different sectors of the brain, as some neuroscientists believe, then Davis's experiment would encourage the inference that the brain, on confronting Shakespeare's "madded," is forced out of its customary routines and compelled to relocate the word in a different sector of itself, creating new pathways as it does so. That P600 surge might, in short, represent the brain's exultant experience of its own structure and its own power to rearrange that structure—a kind of brain self-awareness. As Davis puts it, "consciousness is called into being when simple automaticity is baulked" (269). Since literary language is virtually defined by its balking of automaticity, literature could be said to represent the state of the brain before the need for efficient communication has dug the channels of convention. And this possibility gives the humanist-experimenter his own variety of pleasure, enabling

Davis to claim that literature is not just a highly sophisticated form of language but the original form of cognition itself. Literary language, he declares triumphantly, is "the best model brain science has to work from, if it is to capture the spontaneous living complexity of the human brain, and not merely limit itself to subjects spotting the color red" (272).

Of course, we did not need fMRI images to know that Shakespeare messes with our minds. Just as interesting as Davis's conclusion, from my perspective, is the fact that in this experiment, the problem was posed and the results interpreted in ordinary language, with technology placed in the service of the humanities. It is a considerable service, because the imaging technology gives the humanist new kinds of evidence, and new ways to talk about, for example, the "embodiment" of thought or the way that literature provokes "self-awareness" in the reader, concepts that have become smooth with use. But the role of technology is not merely secondary: by subjecting literary hypotheses to experimental verification, neuroscience gives the humanist the exhilarating prospect of achieving an empirical foundation for his speculations.

In order to stand on this footing, however, the humanist is forced to leave his zone and venture into a domain where he has no training, interpreting not texts but meter readings or false-color representations of brain activity. Dazzled by the prospects opening up before them, some humanists might lose their wits and abandon all sense of what makes experimental results worth attending to in the first place. Surely, for example, it makes all the difference in the world which brain is being monitored—it would certainly make a difference if the issue were the understanding of the entirety of *King Lear* rather than a single brief passage— but for the purposes of Davis's experiment, a brain is a brain. In a larger sense, one might question the basic pertinence to literature of electroencephalography. The "onset" of a word might be identifiable if the brain in the head had never encountered the word before. But what if it had? And what if other words in the play had prepared the reader for the use of an adjective as a verb? Would these factors not affect the surge? How can we separate the brain's response to syntax from its response to semantics—that is, what if the surge were attributable not to the functional shift Davis describes but to the recognition that Lear has been driven mad by his own daughters? And what about experiences involving greater complexity than the decoding of a single word, such as Cordelia's death scene, which gives many people an almost unspeakably exquisite sense of tragic pleasure? Or the temporal extension of reading, which is constantly recalling, experiencing, and anticipating all at once? What does "the brain" do with uncertainty, confusion, or ambiguity? If we cannot generalize about the brain's response to anything more complex than Davis's example—and if even that example is compromised by methodological problems—then what's the point?

These worries notwithstanding, I would encourage further work in this field, because the failure of some inquiries might stimulate others, and because literary study should be open to neuroscience as it has been open to other forms of science in the past. Way leads on to way, and the real benefit of approaching literature from the perspective of the brain might not be realized in fMRI studies at all, no matter how advanced the technology or refined the experiments. For beyond the technics of neuroscience are other promising projects involving literature and cognitive science that seek to explain how "cognitive cravings" are satisfied and even created by fiction.[22] And behind these is an even more ambitious project seeking to place literary study on an empirical footing.

The Darwinian approach to literature is already far advanced. Having moved beyond the phase of interpreting the novels of Jane Austen or Charles Dickens as dramas of adaptability, fitness tests, and mate selection, Darwinian literary study is now taking on a much more comprehensive project based on the premise that the desire to produce and consume art is itself an adaptation and can be studied as a branch of evolutionary psychology. Like Marxists, Freudians, and Saussureans before them, Darwinians see their task as the complete redescription of the character and ends of literature and literary study in such a way as to make it the queen of the sciences. As the most prominent advocate for Darwinian literary studies, Joseph Carroll, puts it in a breathtaking formulation, "literary Darwinists ... aim at fundamentally altering the paradigm within which literary study is now conducted. They want to establish a new alignment among the disciplines and ultimately to subsume all other possible approaches to literary study."[23]

If they succeed, it will be over the objections of one of the leading Darwinian theorists. In *How the Mind Works*, Steven Pinker argues that the arts are not themselves adaptations, but the byproducts of adaptations that served other purposes altogether. He does not have to illustrate his point in the following way, but he does:

> We enjoy strawberry cheesecake, but not because we evolved a taste for it. We evolved circuits that gave us trickles of enjoyment from the sweet taste of ripe fruit, the creamy mouth feel of fats and oils from nuts and meat, and the coolness of fresh water. Cheesecake packs a sensual wallop unlike anything in the natural world because it is a brew of megadoses of agreeable stimuli which we concocted for the express purpose of pressing our pleasure buttons. Pornography is another pleasure technology.... I will suggest that the arts are a third.[24]

Expressed with maximally provocative élan, this argument enraged Carroll, who replied with a review of Pinker's book (called "Steven Pinker's Cheesecake for the Mind") that begins by describing Pinker with comparable élan as "a popularizer of an unusually high order."[25]

In one sense, the disagreement was sharp and deep. The most fundamental premise of Darwinian literary study is that the capacities to produce and appreciate art are produced and understood according to inborn rules of mental development that are not just contingent byproducts of evolution, as Pinker would have it, but adaptations that have conferred specific advantages. Given our high intelligence and singular ability to generate counterfactuals and hypotheticals, we might well be perpetually lost in a swarming mass of alternatives, paralyzed by possibility while the lesser creatures of the world simply eat and reproduce, eat and reproduce. We might well suffer all the disadvantages of what E. O. Wilson calls our "psychological exile,"[26] with none of the advantages. Literature to the rescue: by producing a representation of consecutive action in the world—events with causes and consequences—literature disciplines and informs the imagination, keeping us on track. And by giving us a sharpened, refined, and evolutionarily useful sense of the subtleties of other minds, literature delivers pleasure mixed with survival skills. As Carroll concludes, "The arts are thus an adaptive response to the adaptive problem produced by the adaptive capacities of high intelligence."[27]

But in another, perhaps deeper sense, there is no disagreement at all, for both literary Darwinians and Pinker concur that the truly fundamental premise is that human nature has been fixed by evolution, which is driven by choices made on the basis of pleasure. Indeed, Denis Dutton's 2009 contribution to evolutionary literary theory, *The Art Instinct*, bears the subtitle *Beauty, Pleasure, and Human Evolution*.[28] As an introduction to his attempt to explain exactly why people experience pleasure in the creation and consumption of art, Dutton explores the virtually universal appeal of realistic depictions of landscapes, with trees, gentle hills, water, seen from a certain height—a "longing" for a soothing landscape that reflects not a lack of artistic sophistication but an ancient interest in an environment rich with nutritional possibilities. Pinker uses a very similar example, describing a 1993 stunt performed by two artists who used marketing research polls to assess the artistic preferences of Americans. The polls confirmed a strong preference for realistic compositions in green and blue, with children, women, animals, and heroic figures—a result that was then replicated in Ukraine, Turkey, China, and Kenya (Pinker, 408). Some of Dutton's examples come from the world of elite art, which is generally "difficult" (that is, Glenn Gould), but Pinker focuses on the kind of art enjoyed by the vast majority of humans, which provides, he says, a better indicator of the place of art in evolved human cognition. Indeed, Pinker argues that when modernist artists began, a century ago, to produce art that omitted all these pleasing features, followed by modernist art critics praising their efforts as extraordinary achievements, they were colluding in a perverse severance of art from human nature, a project that produced status for the practitioners (a consequence of rarity) but disappointment, mystification, and indifference for the audience. In the big picture, we humans prefer calendar art to Kandinsky, and do so, Pinker says, for good evolutionary reasons.

One test of evolutionary criticism will be how it handles the question of literary value, which is to say, the question of complex rather than simple pleasure. This question is insistently engaged by a writer whom every critic, it seems—including Dutton, Pinker, Carroll, and Weller—feels the need to discuss, Charles Dickens. Sophisticated readers concur that Dickens is a great writer who sometimes descends to didacticism and sentimental cliché. The death of the angelic little Paul Dombey, which is actually attended by angels, represents, they feel, a shameless mining of sentiment that seems unworthy, vulgar, almost subliterary in its intense but uncomplicated emotionality. The mercilessly intricate anatomy of the ligatures of masochism, dread, shame, arrogance, and self-hatred that tie Paul Dombey *père* to Edith Granger, on the other hand, is commonly thought by the literary elite to represent Dickens at his very finest. How to describe the difference? Is it merely that in the one case Dickens submits to the canons of popular taste while in the other he upholds high artistic standards? Or that in the one case he produces the gratifying cheesecake and in the other he perversely withholds it? Or might a Darwinian criticism find other ways to discriminate between these two forms of pleasure, perhaps by linking Dickens at his "worst" to a desire, natural and perhaps instinctual—whether an adaptation or a byproduct of adaptation, it makes little difference—for immediate pleasure, and Dickens at his "best" to the more evolutionarily useful capacity of humans to transcend animal instinct and to confront, intellectually and emotionally, the deeper complexities or dissonances of existence. An argument such as this would have the effect of refuting Pinker's argument that the intellectual elite denies our evolutionary interests by aligning the judgments of literary merit made by that elite with our deeper evolutionary needs.

Such arguments would provide a scientific basis for value judgments, since the denial of dissonance through the generation of pleasurable fantasies appears to be, from the evolutionary perspective, not just bad art but a maladaptive rejection of the very conditions of our existence, a turning-away from reality that would, if pursued by one and all, spell our end as a species. "Deeper" truths are difficult or dissonant, generating their full share of negative wave modulations, because our own freakish existence represents a dissonance in nature. The pleasure that characterizes the art that we think of as great is complex, because it is an adaptive response that registers and helps us understand our complex selves and our complex position in the world. The most momentary and meaningless of private sensations, the path of pleasure actually leads, in the context of evolution, directly to an understanding of literature, and of the human condition. Much more can be said about this, and literature professors should be among those saying it.

>>><<<

Teachers and scholars at every level could, then, do much worse than to concentrate their attention on pleasure, which is at once the most obvious fact about literary experience and a lamp shining into as yet unknown facts about literature and the evolved human brain. Pleasure is both deeply characteristic of literature and a link—a sturdy lifeline—between literary study and other disciplines with powerful new technologies and conceptual tools at their disposal. A focus on pleasure could help to reclaim for the humanities the subject of the human, which has been the object of scientific research in a number of disciplines while literary theory has been committing itself first to antihumanism and then to an antiscientific emphasis on the social construction of the category of the human. Pleasure also joins the interests of undergraduates with those of the professoriate. Under the aegis of pleasure, literary study suddenly makes sense. A discipline centered on the tasks of eliciting, exploring, and analyzing pleasure would not be declining and falling but rising and rising, cheered on by the brain, the species, and everything in between.

5

Gold Mines in Parnassus: Thoughts on the Integration of Liberal and Professional Education

This chapter was originally a talk given at the University of Richmond in October 2008 to a group of faculty, administrators, and students charged with deliberating on how best to integrate the liberal arts with professional education programs, including the Jepson School of Leadership Studies.

Some ideas are so generally useful that, once established, they become very difficult to dislodge. The arrangement of the world itself supports them and makes them seem as if they were mere descriptions of fact rather than arguments that had at one point contended with and prevailed over adversaries, which they left bleeding in the dust. In the wake of their triumph, they assume a regal sense of inevitability—until the world rearranges itself, leaving the idea stranded and defenseless against new adversaries, which are often the old adversaries revived. Such is the career of the idea that the end of liberal education is the formation of character rather than preparation for any specific trade or occupation. This belief, which informs the humanities in particular, went almost without saying from the first stirrings of liberal education in the mid-nineteenth century until the last third of the twentieth century, when M.B.A. programs began a period of inexorable growth in prestige, alumni support, and enrollments, to the point where today, more than one in every five undergraduates is majoring in Business—more than twice the majors of any other course of study—while the humanities have lost ground.[1]

Many colleges and universities, this one among them, are now struggling to find some unifying principle, or at least some common goals, that will productively integrate the "liberal" and the "professional" components of their curricula, which may be another way of saying that they would like somehow to save liberal education from being swallowed whole by Business. I gather that my role here is to stimulate your deliberations. In order to do so, I would like to give you a sense of how I see the issues you have to negotiate. Of course, I am not disinterested: I speak as a humanist, and as you know, humanists are enamored of questions and suspicious of answers. To a humanist, a good phrasing of a question is a more profound accomplishment than any mere answer could possibly be. When humanists gather to ponder an issue, the questions are formulated, referred to first principles and ultimate causes, and duly *problematized*; and when questions, causes, principles, qualifications, alternatives, doubts, and points of order are all thronging in the air, like a juggler with seven balls—the session concludes, with immense satisfaction all around, except among those who have been affronted somewhere along the line, which may be everyone. This is our idea of real work, as well as our idea of a good time. I take it that while this "liberal" spirit of free inquiry and skeptical critique will be respected in this group, it will be as it were crossed by a "professional" drive to achieve a workable program. In other words, the mission of this group contains the problem in a nutshell—how to integrate the speculative, probing, exploratory, critical spirit of the liberal arts with the more worldly, results-driven orientation of professional education. And then, of course, to persuade all constituencies that the proposed solution does not degrade, dilute, or compromise the integrity of either the liberal arts or professional education, but actually realizes the full capacities of each in a way that neither could have achieved on its own.

As a humanist, I think it would be best to begin by backing up, by identifying and then critiquing the key premises behind the stated mission. Implicit in the idea that we need creative ways to integrate the liberal arts and professional education are three assumptions: first, that although the two are informed by different understandings of and approaches to education, they have common goals as well as common students; second, that the desired integration has not yet occurred; and third, that this failure of integration is a bad thing, and threatens the unity of the university. Why can't the university get, or keep, it together? What is the problem for which creative solutions are sought? And why do these solutions have to be so creative—why aren't there more obvious solutions? Why can't we all get along?

One reason for present disjunction is a long and remarkably durable tradition of opposition. It is worth recalling that challenges to liberal education predated liberal education itself. In "Some Thoughts concerning Education" (1693), John Locke declared himself astonished "that Men of Quality and Parts, should suffer themselves to be so far misled by Custom and Implicite Faith" that they would waste their time, not in the acquisition of "what might be useful to them when they come to be Men," but in having "their Heads stuff'd with a deal of trash, a great part whereof they usually never do ('tis certain they never need to) think on them again as long as they live; and so much of it as does stick by them, they are only the worse for." Strong words; but Locke is just warming up. An Oxford education, he says, is the first step of an academic Rake's Progress, for if the impressionable lad "gets once the Reputation of a Wit, I desire it may be considered, what Company and Places he is likely to spend his Time in, nay, and Estate too: For it is very seldom seen that any one discovers Mines of Gold or Silver in *Parnassus*." These are excellent points, and it is beginning to look bad for Oxford; but then Locke blunders, historically speaking, when he yokes his concept of utility to another concept, a father's right to determine his son's life. "Can there be any thing more ridiculous, than that a Father should waste his own Money, and his Son's time, in setting him to learn the *Roman Language*, when at the same time he designs him for a Trade.... [Why should a child be forced] to learn the Rudiments of a Language, which he is never to use in the Course of Life, that he is designed to; and neglect all the while the writing a good Hand, and casting Account, which are of great Advantage in all Conditions of Life, and to most Trades indispensably necessary?"[2]

In more enlightened times, this point came to be considered a weak point in the argument. By the mid-nineteenth century, Locke's concept of utility, like his theory that the brains of children were blank slates or empty cabinets, was out of favor, supplanted by the idea of "liberal education," which was premised on the belief that people are endowed with reason, and are therefore not necessarily confined to their stations or bound by the designs of their parents; they should rather be encouraged to explore the world on their own terms, and to deploy their various abilities to the fullest extent that they desire. In a sense, it was good for Locke that he lost the argument, since he is now remembered only because he lost it, and people now stuff their heads with useless trash like him rather than learning to write a good hand.

The most effective British advocate for the winning argument was undoubtedly John Henry Newman, whose 1852 book *The Idea of a University*[3] set many of the terms of liberal education in the Anglophone world for over a hundred years. For Newman, the goal of liberal education was the production of "gentlemen" who, having cultivated a liberal habit of mind, would be capable of navigating the world with ease, assurance, and appreciation. Throughout *Idea*, Newman defended this goal against other candidates, most particularly against "professional skill," which he regarded as a kind of inversion or even perversion of true knowledge because it is subordinated to other ends than its own, ends that may serve the individual in a limited or immediate sense but do not serve the community at large. Nor, Newman added, do these other ends even serve the individual in any real sense: they may advance the crafts, trades, or professions, but they actually insult the person by neglecting to develop the liberal habit of mind that would fit him to live a full and genuinely useful life.

Newman warmed most appreciably when he contemplated the end product of a liberal university education: a young man, "open-hearted, sympathetic, and observant, as young men are"; "at home in any society," this young man "has common ground with every class; he knows when to speak and when to be silent; he is able to converse, he is able to listen; he can ask a question pertinently, and gain a lesson seasonably, when he has nothing to impart himself; he is ever ready, yet never in the way." (105, 126). In such passages, we see emerging, like a Polaroid, an image of the grandfather, perhaps, of the figure who dominates the Harvard Redbook written nearly a century later, the "whole man" (see chapter 6). But there are differences. The whole man exemplifies a cold war democracy, whereas Newman's admirable young man is indelibly patrician and unmistakably nineteenth century. Moreover, the institution devoted to producing Newman's protégé bears little resemblance to today's institutions of higher learning. Newman's idea of a university had no room for either specialized or comprehensive knowledge, and the professors who taught there should, he fervently believed—it is the very first statement in the book—have nothing to do with research, an obsessive activity best conducted by those whose minds were too sadly contracted to engage in full life. Not that Newman believed that professors should devote themselves to teaching, however. He felt, on the contrary, that they should not be overly concerned with it, and at various points expressed an active hostility to the very idea of pedagogy, which he regarded as a poor substitute for the self-directed efforts of the independent mind, stimulated by the proximity of his similarly self-directed, open-hearted, sympathetic peers. For these and other reasons, Newman, too, has become a dead language, even though echoes of his core belief in a nonutilitarian liberal education continue to haunt the American scene in particular like a guilty conscience, preventing the resurgent descendants of Locke's hard-boiled paterfamilias from simply swooping in and throwing the weakened liberals out. Newman intuitively understood that the real threat to liberal education in his own time was not the shade of Locke but the spirit of research then crescent in Germany. By the end of the nineteenth century, the United States had begun to Germanize its academy, with some university faculties organizing themselves into departments that granted degrees that came to constitute credentials. With credentialing came professionalism, and with professionalism growth. President Lawrence Lowell of Harvard (1909–33) laid the foundation for Harvard's eminence as a research powerhouse by encouraging his faculty to think of themselves as professionals.[4] This meant adopting impersonal criteria of scholarly competence within each discipline, cultivating a spirit of empirical and methodological rigor, and coming to agreement about what would count as standards of achievement in a small, self-certifying group of mandarins

The new professionalism functioned as a way of insulating the university from extra-academic pressures by creating a separate world of academe that could be judged only by its own standards. But professionalism was accompanied by its dark familiars, partition and competition. A professionalized faculty was a faculty divided into units, each claiming considerable autonomy in matters of hiring and promotion, and competing with other units for salaries, students, office space, and prestige. Such competition naturally placed some stress on amity, and so while undergraduates were expected to enjoy four stress-free years in the groves of academe, the faculty in the same institutions were facing the prospect of going at it hammer and tong, competing with each other virtually face to face, for the rest of their lives.

The original division in the professionalized American college or university was between what would come to be called the humanities and the natural sciences. At first, the humanities seemed to have the upper hand, because the Departments of Literature,

History, Religion, and Philosophy could claim to represent the authentic continuation of the traditional religious mission of higher education, while mathematics and science were the latecomers, followed by the social sciences. As long as all these were considered among the "liberal arts," competition was fierce, but interdepartmental. The liberal arts discovered a common purpose and a collective identity when a common enemy—perhaps too strong a word, but anecdotal evidence suggests that there is some basis for it—arrived in the form of professional education, which began as a series of graduate programs but rapidly extended their snaky tentacles down into the undergraduate curriculum, making the liberal arts a part rather than the whole.

It is a point of curiosity that faculty salaries at many institutions reflect this sequence inversely. Among the liberal arts, humanists of all kinds are generally the lowest paid, scientists rank somewhat higher, and economists are almost invariably among the highest if not the highest paid. But not even economists compare with the most recent arrivals on the scene, the faculty in the fields of business, law, and medicine. In just a couple of decades, it seems, this distribution of resources has become so ingrained a fact in the modern university that it is rarely the subject of protest, much less civil disobedience. Even so, it has not gone unnoticed, nor have its effects on the collegial environment of higher education gone unremarked.

For those in the liberal arts, the fact that they fare so poorly in the competition for respect and money is a big and bitter pill to swallow, for they have not only history on their side—and a dismayingly weak ally it has proved to be—but also the deep-laid sense that they represent the essence, the heart and the soul, of the entire enterprise. The official rhetoric produced by the admissions office (prospective students are generically promised that they will enjoy "ample time for intellectual exploration," "a wide range of opportunities for critical thinking, intellectual inquiry, and individual expression") and then recycled at commencement addresses (Do Not Specialize Too Soon! Retain Your Youthful Curiosity! Empathize with Those Less Fortunate! Dare to Fail!)

underscores the conviction of liberal arts faculty that no matter how utterly wealth and the acquisition of wealth dominate the real agenda of higher education, many students—and their parents—still believe that the purpose of education is general enrichment of the kind that the liberal arts and the humanities in particular are well equipped to provide.

The research universities that appeared in the first decades of the nineteenth century in Germany had a double goal—to lead students to take an organized approach to knowledge, or *Wissenschaft*, and to develop moral character, or *Bildung*. Character, it was and is believed, is developed, exercised, and—to use a word one encounters again and again in reflections on the American undergraduate experience—*honed* by an exposure to the study of philosophy, literature, mathematics, natural science, and history. This honing, rather than the content of any course or major in particular, is often represented as the whole point. You go to college not to acquire knowledge as such, which you could do by any number of means, but to develop, in the course of interactions with professors and other students and perhaps even books, certain desirable skills, capacities, and habits. You (or your vexed parents) pay for the opportunity to stretch your range of responsiveness, sharpen your perceptions, deepen your understanding of things in general, and learn the art of discrimination. When students, having stuff'd their heads with John Locke and other detritus, ask, "When will I ever use X in my life?" they are always told, with a firmness intended to be final, "That's not the point—you're being honed."

As an English teacher, I take a certain pride in the fact that virtually all the novels and films that deal with universities focus on English teachers—their picturesque dissolution, their unsatisfying careers, their illicit relations with students and each other, their poor personal hygiene, their endearing human qualities. There is a reason for this focus. When alumni look back fondly at their undergraduate experience, they dwell, in general, not on the contributions made to their developing personalities by those who taught them differential equations, organic chemistry, intro to sociology, or computational finance, but rather on those color-ful, underpaid, out-of-control English teachers who managed to transmit, despite their impossible personal lives, a sense of the enduring greatness of Shakespeare, Milton, Dickens, Chaucer, Brontë, and Twain, and who also embodied the defiantly antiutil-itarian, antipractical, antiprofessional spirit of liberal education itself. They seem, to a retrospective gaze, to be demonstrations of what a life lived in closer contact with the spirit of great art than with the quotidian world might look like, and the sense they manifest of being slightly out of place in the world suggests the distance between things as they are and the actual reaches of the human imagination. These professors were not life models, the aging alumni reflect, but they did stick in the mind as exotic species, pure instances of their type, specimens not encountered elsewhere—in short, they were memorable, even inspiring.

An air of nostalgia clings to many of those fictional English teachers, however. It is as if they are all versions of Mr. Chips, slightly fuddled holdovers from some vanished time. Even in a film like *The Mirror Has Two Faces*, which is set in the mid-1990s at Columbia, Professor Streisand of the Comp. Lit. Department never seems pressed for time, never burdened by her departmen-tal or committee responsibilities, never wholly or even partly committed to research, publication, or even grading papers. She lives in a charmed and charming fictional space where she is paid to live her appealing, event-crowded life, dazzling students with her wit and charisma, even getting herself an extreme makeover (in an attempt to seduce a math professor). The message seems to be that professors are essentially self-creating individuals rather than employees, department members, or professionals. Their freedom is highly appealing, but leaves them seeming undevel-oped, unrealized, blocked in some way, in need of a makeover in order to compete. They have, in the popular mind, all the time in the world, but nothing of consequence to do. We might say that they represent an extreme form of the very spirit of liberal education. They enjoy their opportunities for critical thinking and individual expression, they dare to fail and often do; indeed, they are generally completely incompetent. They are curiosities. Compare them to John Houseman's Professor Kingsley in *The Paper Chase*, a professor of law who is stern, even sadistic, casually cruel, uncompromising, remote, intimidating. Students love Barbra Streisand—they love all their English teachers, at least in the movies—but they rightly fear Houseman, who is not only in the world but of it, and seems to bar their entry to it.

With some allowances and reservations, I think that popular culture actually manages to register some important features of the distinct intellectual culture of the liberal arts. In this culture, information is transmitted not for its own sake but as a way of accustoming a young mind to certain kinds of thinking, which it will deploy in postgraduate life. In a sense, the liberal arts are dedicated to unreality; or, to put it in a more positive light, the liberal arts train their attention not on the world as it is, not on what is demonstrably true, but rather on the world as it might be—the not-yet, not-obviously, or not-necessarily true. The essence of the liberal arts is that the imagination is engaged in the construction of a world not immediately present, a world yet to be encountered. The basic activities of liberal arts disciplines are critiquing, probing, testing, speculating—all undertaken in a spirit of skeptical distrust of the manifest or self-evident. In this respect, the liberal arts reflect the peculiar life circumstances of the undergraduate, who is exploring what he or she might become, trying on identities, suspending commitment while the work of maturation proceeds in silent, invisible, and indeed often utterly undetectable fashion. (I speak as the father of a current undergraduate.) In the ethos of the liberal arts, one must never presuppose, never assume, never jump to conclusions, never pronounce with perfect confidence, because the truth—like oneself, if one is an undergraduate—is always yet to be determined.

In the official rhetoric, at least, of the most prestigious colleges and universities, the undergraduate experience exists in an enchanted space, a precious bubble of time that exists for a charmed moment before the world closes in. In this country, higher education and the liberal arts in particular are conceived as preparation for a life that could lead in any of a number of directions, embracing a multitude of possibilities. This is especially the case in the humanities, where interpretation, evaluation, judgment are particularly important. The situation is apparently, but only apparently, different elsewhere in the liberal arts. Social science disciplines have often sought to produce hard data that could be used, for example, to influence public policy, and the natural sciences have, not altogether willingly in some cases, become identified with positive results proceeding from certain knowledge. In science, research is now linked to technology to industry to production to economic growth and finally to wealth and well-being, in an unbroken chain that forms the main justification for scientific research in a wide range of fields. But when social science is decoupled from policy, and when science is considered not as a chain that stretches from research to wealth and health but as part of the liberal arts, they, too, function as a set of disciplines devoted to questioning, interrogating, sowing doubt, revealing cracks in the edifice of the obvious and self-evident, introducing alternatives, delaying the rush to closure, opening up room for further inquiry, prolonging the discussion. The more liberal the art, the more protracted the discussion. Closure, decision, finality, certainty—these are, in the ethos of the liberal arts, synonyms for stupidity, or tyranny.

This ethos is all but explicitly moral and all but explicitly antiprofessional. It is moral because it is devoted to freedom, the condition of morality—freedom from the world as given, freedom from necessity or want, freedom to explore without commitment. With the liberal arts at its core, a college undergraduate experience represents a kind of free zone where the ordinary rules do not apply, and people can grow into themselves without being pressured, punished, or constrained. Despite the subprime moral character of undergraduate social existence, the undergraduate years are considered to be the time when character is forged, not in the crucible of responsibility and accountability, but in the absence of them. From the liberal arts perspective, professional training is properly reserved for graduate school, by which time a student's character has presumably been set, all impurities having been burned off in the fires of undergraduate life. That being the case, some traditionalists experience a jarring sense of wrongness when professional training in disciplines outside the liberal arts, such as, conspicuously, business, begin to offer majors and degrees, a development that seems to some like the entrance into the garden of the serpent.

The differences between the liberal arts and professional education can be financial and political as well as moral. Professional programs attract philanthropy more readily than English departments, in large part because more people who acquire wealth studied Milton Friedman than John Milton, and this fact registers in facilities, salaries, hiring lines, lecture series, research support, and the quality of the refreshments served at receptions. Perhaps reflecting their greater ease with money, the faculty in professional education are often politically to the right of those in the liberal arts, especially at places where the boomer generation is hanging on in the liberal arts. But the deeper and potentially more stubborn differences concern the very conception of the faculty. In the liberal arts, rewards are based on performance in three main areas of activity—research, teaching, and service. If the faculty in professional programs do not seem to have the same reward system or priorities as the liberal arts faculty, if tenure and promotion and rewards and goals do not reflect the same criteria or even the same values across the university, if professional education faculty seem more interested in consulting, professional practice, or running profitable weekend seminars than in the enlightenment of young minds, the unity of the university is called into question.

Faculty in professional programs, who in good times enjoy the feeling that they are providing skills necessary to flourishing, and in bad times that they are providing skills necessary to avoid disaster, may not be ready to make nice. They may see themselves as the only realists in town, the only ones in touch with the world as it is, not as a fantastic structure of possibilities, all deferred, but as a system of hard and definite things. They may feel that the primary mission of life is not to cultivate one's sensibility or to hone oneself but to get on with it, to develop one's competitive strengths in measurable ways. They may see their job as providing students with real as opposed to abstract value, and may regard the liberal arts as a fetish of the leisure class, a holdover from Newman's Oxford now become an anachronism like the shiny top hat worn by the Monopoly guy, or even an albatross. How, they might demand, can we justify incarcerating students for four years in a protracted limbo where they are sheltered from any awareness of what the world is really like, then loosing them on the world with little understanding and sloppy work habits, equipped only with knowledge that was never intended to be used? Why should the liberal arts have protected status? Why aren't the English teachers treated as the marginal ones, the ornaments rather than the tree?

When we contemplate the sources of potential tension, distrust, and misunderstanding, the chances for creative collaboration may seem slim. As so often happens, however, a closer look reveals a more complicated and, I believe, more hopeful picture.

To begin with, the differences are not as absolute as they seem. As we have seen, the liberal arts faculty itself was brought into being by the desire to professionalize knowledge. This same desire was also responsible for the creation of graduate degree programs, which constitute professional training. And for the past half century, the needs of professional training have played a role in determining the undergraduate curriculum, encouraging undergraduate research, offering courses in theory and methodology. In many ways, the faculty have fully embraced the concept of professionalization, compensating for their relative lack of status and prestige in a corporatized university—compensating for their compensation, as it were—by cultivating, even obsessing about, their own professional status. They have proliferated organizations, conferences, and publications, measuring their success not by the number of young minds awakened but by books published, nonspecialists mystified, honoraria reaped, awards won, bourgeoisies outraged, and plane tickets paid for. This form of professional self-awareness does not always make a favorable impression on those outside the college or university, and one of the most common criticisms heard about higher education today is that the faculty—by which is meant the liberal arts faculty and especially the humanities and especially English teachers—is not only too politicized but too worldly, too specialized, too pragmatic and careerist, too secure in their little self-confirming enclaves. In a word, too professionalized.

I would urge this group to consider the glass half-full. For if the liberal arts are already professionalized, then the intrusion of professional education into the curriculum does not constitute a second fall of man, and a productive collaboration may be feasible without either side's having to capitulate. There are several possibilities you may wish to consider.

One can, as the well-known Duke literary scholar Fredric Jameson once said, always historicize. Actually, what he said was, "Always historicize," in the imperative mood. What he did not say was that by doing so, you can convert anything at all into history. As the pragmatist philosopher William James said, in order to make a discipline "liberal," all you need to do is add history, as in "the history of civil engineering," or "the history of water management policy." And as one of the most famous philosophers in the world said to me recently in an eminently pragmatic spirit, "Garbage is garbage. But the history of garbage is scholarship." Similarly, we could say that professions are professions, but the history of professions falls into the domain of the liberal arts. Knowledge of the law equips you to teach or practice law; knowledge of the history of the law *hones* you.

One can also philosophize. There is medicine, and there is a rich tradition of discourse on bodily illness and healing; the former is a profession but the latter falls into the liberal arts, and to my humanistic ears sounds like material for fascinating collaborative efforts that could, like the historical program sketched above, provide useful employment for scholars in many disciplines, including philosophers, historians, psychologists, biologists, and physicians.

I can also imagine a course, a symposium, an ongoing multi-dimensional project that took as its object the ways in which the professions were represented, both by themselves and by others. How, such a project might ask, do professionals understand and represent themselves? How do others understand and represent them? How do professionals in one discipline distinguish themselves from professionals in others, both within the university and beyond? How have such representations changed over time? What ideological or cultural forces determine them? Such questions would open up the professions to the kinds of questions that the liberal arts ask about their subjects.

A lot of good work can be done in the general field of representations and self-representations. One of the most popular and genuinely instructive courses I taught in my thirty years in the classroom studied the university from this perspective. Called "Fictions of the University," it began as a kind of joke. I had my students studying the ways in which the university represented itself, looking at official self-descriptions put out by, for example, the Office of Student Life, or Advising, and comparing the official discourse with the actual experience of staff members and students, whom my students interviewed, with results ranging from the farcical to the deeply disturbing. My students found out what a department head, a dean, a provost, a president actually do by following them around; the students then compared the activities of these august personages—which turned out to be mostly meetings, meals, ceremonies, and receptions—with the memos and communiqués that issued from their offices, which were mostly heroic in tone. They learned how financial aid is portioned out, how the crime rate fluctuates, how many students attempt to take their lives, how eating disorders are reported and dealt with. They looked into the finances of the athletic programs, insofar as they could, and learned why that was not very far. They studied the very admissions brochures that had lured them there. And they read novels and saw films—most of them about English teachers, as you would expect, but also *The Paper Chase* and others.

A comparable course, offered in a law school, might have students study, not only the ways law schools and law firms represent the practice of the law, but also fictional representations of legal practice in Grisham, Dickens, Melville, Chekov, and Kafka, and cinematic representations such as *A Man for all Seasons*, *To Kill a Mockingbird*, *The Caine Mutiny*, *Twelve Angry Men*, *Double Indemnity*, *Anatomy of a Murder*, and *Inherit the Wind*. The premise of "Fictions of the Law" would be that, in order to be effective, a lawyer must understand how the law has been perceived and represented by those inside and outside the profession. Other courses might take up the history, the philosophy, or the psychology of the law.

In recent years, a new area of potential collaborative pedagogy and scholarship has emerged under the aegis of the concept of leadership, a phenomenon by which literature, psychology, history, and cinema have always been utterly bewitched. Perhaps you've heard of this development. Leadership seems to me to be inherently ambiguous with respect to the liberal arts/professional education divide. It might be considered the province of professional education, inasmuch as every professional school is implicitly committed to turning out leaders in their fields. But leadership can also be claimed by the liberal arts, in a very traditional sense. One of the primary goals of traditional liberal arts education was the cultivation of leadership. Liberal arts faculty sought, as Laurence Veysey put it, to inculcate future leaders "with a moral viewpoint that sought to rise above materialism."[5] There was a time when those aspiring to leadership studied Churchill or Lincoln, which they could only do in the liberal arts, specifically in the humanities. Leadership that rises above materialism, pragmatism grounded in the imagination—here is the very point of contact between the liberal arts and professional education.

Like the liberal arts disciplines, leadership of this kind focuses on the not-yet, not-obviously, or not-necessarily true. It has a probing, hypothesis-testing, and speculative aspect. One of the primary tasks of a leader of any organization is to envision and prepare for a future that will be different from today. Leadership is always countercyclical, turning away from the immediate or self-evident: in good times, a leader must prepare his or her colleagues for the inevitable downturn; in bad times, a leader must fortify them by assuring them that their fortunes will eventually improve. The essence of leadership is vision, as the first President Bush discovered to his regret when his casual dismissal of "the vision thing" was taken as a revealing glimpse of his flawed understanding of leadership. Leaders are known by their visions, or dreams. Perhaps the two most famous sentences that Bobby Kennedy ever uttered were "There are those that look at things the way they are, and ask why? I dream of things that never were, and ask why not?" This quotation became famous, I think, because it demonstrated that he grasped, and grasped the importance of, this fundamental characteristic of leadership, a characteristic shared by effective leaders of all political persuasions.

Can the capacity to dream of things that never were and to encourage others to dream the same dreams be taught? It is certainly tempting to think so, partly because literature and film have provided so many memorable examples. Shakespeare is an especially rich field of such examples, a fact marked in a series of recent books with titles such as *Shakespeare on Management*, *Power Plays*, or *Shakespeare in Charge*. For the past decade or so, an outfit called Movers and Shakespeares has been culling bardic management precepts in professional training sessions for such clients as Northrop Grumman, the American Red Cross, Foote Cone and Belding, the U.S. Air Force, the Aspen Institute, General Dynamics, Merrill Lynch, the Kennedy School of Government, and the Wharton School. A two-person mom-and-pop company, Movers and Shakespeares is founded on the premise that in order to be a good leader, one must understand people, and that Shakespeare understood people better than anyone. More important in the present context, it is also based on the conviction that professional education can be conducted using materials drawn from the domain of the liberal arts.

In a Movers and Shakespeares session, a few of the better-known plays are mined for insights into such subjects as risk taking, the damaging effects of discrimination and prejudice (*The Merchant of Venice*), and settling disputes within the team (that would be, of course, *Julius Caesar*). The most serviceable play of all is *Henry V*, which teaches the importance of team building and rousing support for a project. This play, as one of the principals says, "is suited to leadership training and can be easily taught without participants having to prepare or know Shakespeare at all."[6]

As it turns out, nonknowledge of Shakespeare is not just tolerated but absolutely required in order to glean the desired leadership precepts from this play. For as Shakespeare takes pains to establish, Henry was manipulated by his nobles, who saw in him a desire they could exploit, to prove to the world that he was not the disorderly and drunken youth that everyone took him to be and that in fact he was. They fabricated obscure legal grounds for declaring war on France that the young king accepted without question, perhaps recalling the advice of his dying father Henry IV, who told him (in *Henry IV Part II*) that in order to consolidate his shaky grasp on power, he should "busy giddy minds with foreign quarrels." The quarrel started by the son did produce short-term gains—Henry gained the throne of France and married the French king's daughter, even giving her some *charmante* English lessons—but the occupation of France proved to be grueling and costly, and awakened a dormant French nationalism. When Henry died, just two years after assuming the French throne, Katherine could only speak a few words of English, England was virtually bankrupt, and the French, inspired by Joan of Arc, threw the invaders out, with prejudice. Humiliated and weakened, England fell into civil war, culminating in the Wars of the Roses.

In short, Henry V's leadership, based as it was on fear, insecurity, arrogance, a heedless indifference to consequences, and the desire of a profligate son to impress his kingly father, was radically and disastrously shortsighted, resulting in massive suffering for the people of two nations, suffering that stretched out for nearly a century. Thank God those benighted times are past!

The genius of the play, from a humanist perspective, is not simply that it holds a mirror to the brilliance of Henry V, but that it discloses the dark and tangled roots of Henry's leadership, the naïve, politically ignorant, and even sinister currents that feed into his character and animate his entire rein. The founders of Movers and Shakespeares, who may know all this, do not go there in their seminars, preferring to underscore, as they say, issues of "leadership and ethics," as demonstrated primarily by Henry's extraordinarily inspirational rhetoric. We few, we happy few; once more into the breach, dear friends—that sort of thing. At one seminar held in the Department of Defense, a lieutenant general summed up the wisdom he had acquired with a question whose affirmative answer was plainly implied: "This idea of being a good leader—does it mean that your heart is pure?"[7]

By now, you may not be altogether astonished to hear that the principals of Movers and Shakespeares identify themselves with the conservative movement. Carol Adelman is a senior fellow at the corporate-funded, deeply conservative Hudson Institute (and—full disclosure—a high school classmate of mine) specializing in international aid; her husband Kenneth Adelman was a member of the hawkish Defense Policy Board and a highly visible advocate for the 2003 invasion of Iraq: he it was who famously predicted that the invasion would be "a cakewalk." When no cakewalk materialized, and when George Tenet was given the Presidential Medal of Freedom, he became disaffected from longtime friends of the family Dick Cheney, Paul Wolfowitz, and Donald Rumsfeld. He did not attend Rumsfeld's Christmas party in 2006, and in a 2007 interview reported in *Vanity Fair*, he pronounced himself shocked and appalled at the poor quality of leadership exhibited during the Iraq war and in the Bush administration generally.[8] On October 20, 2008, he endorsed Barack Obama for president, further limiting his viability in the Republican Party. But Movers and Shakespeares has thrived, commanding up to $30,000 to put executives, including many of our military leaders, in tight pants and codpieces.

You may also have surmised by now that I do not recommend

their seminars as a model for collaborations between professional education and the liberal arts. What has gone wrong in this instance is that the apparent form of cooperation, using great art to illuminate real-world issues in management, conceals the fact of domination, with Shakespeare's play being treated as a quiet well from which executives might draw anodyne lessons flattering to themselves, and to their pure hearts. The perceived goal of professional education, to instill in leaders an emphatically "conservative" conviction of their own excellence and purity of heart, has been permitted to override the "liberal arts" reading of *Henry V*, which would stress equivocation, doubt, skeptical analysis, and complication. This is cooptation, not collaboration.

It seems almost too obvious a point, but I will nevertheless insist on it: genuine collaboration, whether in an academic program or in the political domain, must be based on mutual respect, shared responsibility, and compromise. If the liberal arts and professional education are to make common cause, both must be permitted to retain their integrity and their identity. As an example of a more genuine form of collaboration, we might imagine a seminar on leadership that would use *Henry V* to entirely different purposes. This new and improved seminar I am proposing would begin by noting Henry's extraordinary gift for rousing his troops by giving them an assessment of their current situation that makes sense, a coherent account of the history that brought them to this point, and dreams to dream in the forms of reachable goals and a leader to believe in. This seminar would also reveal the various tactics Henry uses to establish the bonds of solidarity and authority with the men whom he is asking to risk their lives in a preemptive war of choice. It would point out, as well, the tactical nature of these tactics. But the seminar would not stop there. It would also dive more deeply into the play to note how Henry is both deceived and self-deceived. It would reach back before the action of the play to note the determining influence of Henry's father, a regicide; and it would note what happened after the action of the play concludes, the long-term effects of Henry's foreign quarrels. It would ask why Shakespeare would choose to limit his play to this particular sequence of events, which give such a misleading picture when studied apart from their context; it would ask, too, why English readers, guided by this play, still regard Henry V as one of the greatest sovereigns in their history. This seminar would thus consider leadership, not in a way that would encourage leaders or would-be leaders to think well of themselves, but in a way that awakened the larger, darker, and more complex questions of context and character that always haunt even the most pure-hearted exercises of power.

Such a seminar would not encourage the veneration of leaders, nor would it support the view that leadership is either a transferable skill or a divine gift. But the educational system that risked such a result in the service of the truth would be seen as fearless, confident, and open to the future. It would be one in which the goal of knowledge was understood to be the strengthening of the student's capacity for reflection and the deepening of the student's understanding of the real forces at work in the world, and in the human heart. A program organized around such seminars would be disinterested in partisan politics, but deeply interested in the larger question of the political. It would produce moral effects, but not directly or predictably. In such a program, the liberal arts would be seen not as an expensive form of dilettantism but as a way of understanding the world that engaged the critical intellect as well as the moral and artistic imagination. And professional education would be construed not as a sadly necessary vulgarity but as a valuable component in an educational system that included among its goals the preparation of some people to assume leadership positions in the professions.

Many today are pessimistic about the prospects for a successful integration of liberal and professional education. When they look at colleges and universities today, they see massive imbalances and a disturbing trend line that places the rhetoric of higher education at odds with the reality, and in a number of cases has transformed the rhetoric to bring it into line with the new reality. This is dangerous, because dominance of one side—either side—by the other threatens both. While Locke and Newman would have despised each other, we cannot afford the luxury of contempt, but must, for our own survival, discover new ways of merging principle and pragmatism. I believe that this can be accomplished. There is certainly incentive to do so. An educational system that managed to broker imaginative and intellectually serious partnerships between the liberal arts and professional education would be the envy of the world. It would also be profoundly American in the very best sense. At a recent conference in Denmark, I heard a young Danish scholar urging his European colleagues to refashion their system of higher education on the model of the American system. He was particularly impressed by that distinctively American invention, the liberal arts college or university, which has been so central to the development of liberal education in this country. What impressed him was the ability of Americans to devise a system that addressed both worldly and what he called "educational" needs. In Europe, he noted, the humanities, the core of liberal education, "are mostly discussed in their narrow relevance to the business sector strangely separated" from broader educational issues, while in America the humanities are "mostly debated in terms of their educational accountability."⁹ For this and other reasons, he thought that Europeans might learn a great deal from the American system, which, at its best, "facilitates a breadth of cultivation, what some consider being true *Bildung*, it is relevant for life rather than just for work, it has a broader agenda than *Wissenschaft* alone, and it includes ethics, civic engagement, and the instilling of a global outlook in its students" (ibid., 324). Coming at the end of a trip during which I had heard countless anti-American comments, this remark, and the applause that followed, was, as you can well imagine, deeply refreshing, even inspiring, and affirmed for me that the system of higher education that we have developed is one area in which America can and must continue to lead the world.

6

Melancholy in the Midst of Abundance: How America Invented the Humanities

I must study Politicks and War that my sons may have liberty to study Mathematicks and Philosophy. My sons ought to study Mathematicks and Philosophy, Geography, natural History, Naval Architecture, navigation, Commerce and Agriculture, in order to give their Children a right to study Painting, Poetry, Musick, Architecture, Statuary, Tapestry and Porcelaine.

«JOHN ADAMS, 1780»

What would Adams have made of the state of the nation two hundred and thirty years on? We are still studying politics and war, but have not gotten better at them. Wars are fought for causes that cannot be clearly articulated against enemies who cannot be located, for goals that cannot be articulated, and with allies who do not stand with us. And despite an intense culturewide obsession with politics, we cannot claim to have improved on the practices of Adams and his contemporaries. The sums of money expended on each would have been inconceivable even a generation ago. And meanwhile, the study of poetry, music, tapestry, and porcelain has been pushed beyond the margins of concern. Adams's vision for his progeny, in which they evolved from warriors into dilettantes, no longer provides a template for the progress of the nation.

Still, it is worth recalling that once upon a time the ruling class—which had also been the revolutionary class—imagined that they were risking their lives, their fortunes, and their sacred honor in behalf of a futurity where what would come to be called the humanities would dominate the concerns of the citizenry. The humanities, they felt, would represent the crowning achievement of a nation that, having prevailed in war, would build its new society on a foundation of such economic, political, military, and social security that citizens could enrich their lives by turning their attention to the study and appreciation of material and textual artifacts. Animating this vision was a specific understanding—growing out of the classical tradition, biblical influences, and the recent Enlightenment, all inflected by the memory of the American Revolution and the institution of democratic governance—of the ends of human existence, a clearly defined view of the human condition. Adams, Jefferson, and others believed that a general concern for the humanities represented not only the best possible future for the new nation but also the natural progression of mankind, if freed from fear and want. This double investment in the character of the nation on the one hand and the destiny of humanity on the other determined the development of liberal education in the United States, and had the effect, once upon a time, of placing the humanities at the center of American self-understanding.

To Adams, an active interest in the humanities was the culmination of and reward for successful nation-building.[1] After years of toil, with education always subordinated to the urgencies of the moment, there would, he felt, come a time when people could turn their minds to higher things, delighting in knowledge pursued for its own sake without any utilitarian end; indeed, education's claim to being "higher" depended on the distinction between its own goals and those of practical or professional training. The study of past human cultures manifestly served no immediate purpose beyond itself, and so an education devoted to the cultural archive of the past could be achieved only in a society that enjoyed security, prosperity, and freedom. The goal toward which the entire nation strove, therefore, was a state of tranquility in which immediate needs had been met, internal opposition calmed, and external threats held at bay—a society whose citizens might explore at leisure the record of the past (especially the Greeks and Romans), seek fulfillment on their own terms, and enjoy in a disinterested spirit the pleasures of the arts. An interest in the humanities would be rewarding to those who shared it, and would also serve as an advertisement to the world of the advanced state of American culture—a large-scale example of what Thorstein Veblen labeled conspicuous consumption.

By the end of the nineteenth century, when Veblen was publishing *The Theory of the Leisure Class* (1899), most of the prestigious colleges and universities in the country had implicitly endorsed a moderately democratized version of this national self-understanding and the patriarchal narrative that informed it. The traumas of the first half of the twentieth century had not brought Adams's vision of an American society distinguished for its superior civilization any closer to realization, but they had made that vision even more compelling as a distant goal. After World War II, conditions finally seemed right for Adams's grandchildren.

The term *humanities* did not appear for the first time in the United States, and it is now found all over the world, with humanities centers, departments, schools, and programs in such countries as Russia, Korea, Kenya, Chile, India, and Egypt. But as I remarked in the introduction, the modern concept of the humanities is truly native only to the United States, where the term acquired a meaning and a peculiar cultural force that it does not have elsewhere. In no other nation are the humanities discussed with such urgency or fervor; in no other nation do the humanities mean what they do, or as much as they do, in the United States; in no other nation do the humanities excite such passionate advocacy, denunciation, or public concern. Insofar as the global humanities have an agenda, that agenda is set in the United States. Movements originating or coming into prominence in the United

States are followed closely by academics in other countries, many of whom were trained in American institutions. The reverse is not true: movements originating in the humanities outside the United States do not, in general, attract many American followers, despite the pronounced receptivity of American academics to such non-humanistic and even antihumanistic movements as French-based structuralism and poststructuralism, social-sciences-oriented British cultural studies, various European forms of Marxism, and *Annales* historiography.

I cannot undertake here a comprehensive comparative study of the global humanities, but there is no shortage of examples of the humbling of the humanities outside the United States before paradigms of utility and forms of assessment that are altogether inappropriate to them. In 2004, the University of Hamburg instituted a "reform" resulting in a severe cutback in resources, including half its staff, for the humanities, reductions based on a simple analysis of what the business sector would demand of its employees in 2012. If a given discipline involved trade, it might survive; language study would survive if the language was used by potential trading partners. In response, the American philosopher Richard Rorty was provoked to ask if the Germans knew what universities were for.[2] The following year, the Danish Ministry of Science, Technology, and Innovation, which is responsible for overseeing the universities, issued a report whose affinities with Hamburg were immediately apparent in that the humanities were described almost exclusively as a set of disciplines in which the central issue was the manipulation of meanings, a skill the report deemed useful in business. The Danish report defended the humanities in what it probably presumed was the only way possible in the political environment, not by insisting that the humanities were a collection of ways of encountering the record of human creative activity in all its richness, a project that was valuable in itself, but by claiming that "human qualities" were misunderstood as "soft competencies": in fact, the report says, they are as "hard" and "formal" as anything in science, and can be transferred just as technology can be transferred.[3]

The emphasis on "transference" has been reaffirmed in Great Britain, where the primary government funding agency for the humanities, the Arts and Humanities Research Council, has openly committed itself to an "impact agenda"[4] based on what it describes as a "knowledge transfer (KT) strategy," defined as "the processes by which new knowledge is co-produced through interactions between academic and non-academic individuals and communities." The success of the KT strategy will be measured by the degree to which it promotes "global economic performance, and specifically the economic performance of the UK." The overall mission of the AHRC is to "advance understanding of arts and humanities research as an innovation driver," and to "deliver a step change in the social, economic and policy impact from arts and humanities research across key technology areas."[5] The "impact indicators" identified by the other source of research support in England, the Higher Education Funding Council for England, include "has value to user communities (such as research income)," "clear evidence of progress toward positive outcomes (such as the take-up or application of new products, policy advice, medical interventions, and so on)," "commercializing new products or processes," and improving "social welfare, social cohesion, or national security."[6] John Adams would undoubtedly have recoiled from such a misguided, illiberal, philistine, and antihumanistic program, and would have been horrified by the thought that his grandchildren's education might fall into the hands of people with such a shriveled understanding. He might, however, have taken a grim satisfaction from knowing that the descendants of the British against whom he rebelled would, two hundred and thirty years later, be reduced to such a sorry state.

Not all those descendants are happy with the situation. In 2009, the *Times Literary Supplement* published an impassioned protest by one of the leading humanists in the country, Stefan Collini, who invited his readers to consider the hypothetical example of three researchers who were doing, by traditional measures, excellent work in the history of Anglo-Saxon England.[7] When they submit their work to the review panel, they all receive an "impact score" of zero. In response, the first scholar throws himself into the task of marketing his scholarship to museum curators and TV producers, a process that, together with the annual reports he is required to file, leaves little time for his actual work. Equally fearful for his future, the second scholar "ghostwrites the *King Alfred Book of Bread and Cakes*," the popular success of which eventually leads to his becoming the university's Director of Research Strategy (Humanities). In the third instance, the scholar "simply cannot stand any more of this idiocy: he takes a post at an American university and goes on to do 'highly innovative' and 'groundbreaking' (but impact-free) research which changes the way scholars all over the world think about the field" (ibid., 19).

As this third example suggests, the humanities in the United States have, despite terrific pressures, resisted to a far greater degree than elsewhere the drive to reduce education to training and credentialing, making universities feeder schools for the professions. At most American research universities and liberal arts colleges, the humanities are still thought to be central to the educational experience—even at MIT, students must take eight courses in humanities, arts, and social sciences to graduate—and education is still regarded as a process not merely of KT but of forming, over the course of four years of maturation and exploration, the character that one will carry throughout life. To the extent that higher education in the United States remains "liberal" in spirit, most of the credit must go to the beleaguered, devalued, and marginalized humanities, which have provided the only brakes on the advance of corporatization, professionalization, and instrumentalization. The dismay, even revulsion that an American feels reading about the AHRC agenda registers a perhaps residual and contested but still palpable respect for the idea that the contribution of the humanities cannot be measured in solely economic terms, and must be considered as well in terms of a less definable or quantifiable but very real effect, if not "impact," on individuals and, more broadly, on society. The display of indifference to immediate threats represented by an interest in the humanities may well reflect and perhaps encourage a feeling of security about the future, just as the savorless, officious prose of the AHRC may register the desperation widely felt in Britain today with respect to its competitiveness in the twenty-first century.

As it enters the second decade of the twenty-first century, the United States is not as secure or as dominant as it might wish to be, but as economic, ecological, military, and political anxieties have increased around the world, the American educational system has continued to inspire emulation and admiration. Even in those countries where the needs of the nation dictate that universities devote themselves primarily to developing skills in management, technology, health care, computer science, agriculture, or engineering, the kind of liberal education that is delivered by the American system of higher education exerts a powerful appeal. Some developing nations have actually begun to worry that they are producing a generation of technically and managerially competent but unimaginative people, and are rethinking their educational priorities. Singapore is moving rapidly to strengthen the liberal arts;[8] and even China, whose universities are known for being massive, impersonal institutions largely dedicated to rote teaching in the areas of technology, engineering, and political education, is now beginning to institute programs designed to inspire creativity through intimate classes, a broader range of electives, and more intimate residential environments, mimicking some of the features of the American liberal arts college.[9] Some Western observers have been impressed by the formidable traditional strengths of the Chinese system—the work ethic and discipline of its students and teachers, the systemwide commitment to success—but the Chinese themselves now fear that these strengths may be linked with a weakness. As one observer put it in 2006, "Asian higher education is long on discipline but short on creativity . . . the very strengths of their system may prevent the fostering of a versatile, innovative style of intelligence that will be the key to future economic advancement."[10]

They fear, in short, that the liberal arts approach, which places a high value on flexibility, general competence, independence of mind, and innovation, gives the United States a huge structural competitive advantage over them. Concerns of this kind have been responsible for the dissemination of the concept of the humanities around the world. Humanists ought, I think, to be wary of such developments, because they imply a direct link between an academic program in the humanities and a general creativity or wisdom of a kind that will be cashed out in terms of economic performance. This link, to be blunt, cannot be demonstrated.[11] But other connections, as between an engagement with the humanities and a general sense of well-being, of groundedness, of meaningfulness, of depth or richness of experience, and of the feeling of power that accompanies a capacity to take critical or reflective distance on the problems of life, have been attested to by many. Even more important, the capacity to sympathize, empathize, or otherwise inhabit the experience of others—the kind of capacity that is developed by an education that includes the humanities—is clearly essential to democratic citizenship, especially in a pluralistic society predicated on respect for the individual. A society comprising individuals who both value their own lives and have the capacity to value the lives of others will in all probability be more creative, dynamic, and responsible than a society of managers, technicians, and engineers, as valuable as those professions are. And so the humanities, or at least the discourse of the humanities, has been appropriated globally in the same way, and for some of the same reasons, as the English language, the dollar, rock and roll, and American movies. And still, it remains an American discourse arising from an American context.

In support of this claim, I want to consider several different kinds of this discourse, underscoring the uniquely American component in each. The first kind consists of official pronouncements made by high-level committees or commissions, beginning with what is, in effect, the Declaration of Independence of the humanities, the Harvard "Redbook" of 1945. The prose of committees or commissions can be tedious, as distinguished citizens who have little to gain from originality, much less controversy, strive to deliver authoritative pronouncements in language that represents the lowest common denominator of consensus and the highest level of generality. But committee prose can also be deeply revealing both in the way it tries to create the impression of inevitability and in the way that it accommodates the occasional resistant voice by permitting it momentary expression. The second kind of discourse I will consider is the discourse of private philanthropy, my example being an essay by Richard J. Franke, a leader in philanthropic support of the humanities. And the third is the discourse of humanities scholarship as it sees or rather dreams itself, approached by way of Andrew Delbanco's *The Real American Dream*.

General Education in a Free Society: *The Harvard "Redbook," 1945*

The single most important document in the history of "the humanities" is *General Education in a Free Society*, produced by a committee of eminent Harvard professors convened in the spring of 1943 by university president James Bryant Conant.[12] The group worked for two years as World War II was being waged and won, and submitted its report in 1945. The Redbook, as it became known because of its distinctive cover, is a wartime document, undertaken with the purpose of re-envisioning American education from the secondary to the graduate levels, in a postwar context. Conant understood that with hundreds of thousands of soldiers returning home and looking for the education guaranteed them by the G.I. Bill of 1944, nothing could remain as before, at Harvard or anywhere else. The challenge was to create an educational system that made available to vastly expanded numbers of people the cultural advantages hitherto available only to a few. The fundamental idea was a democratization of culture and education. In his charge to the committee, Conant had stated, "The primary concern of American education today is not the development of the appreciation of the 'good life' in young gentlemen born to the purple. It is the infusion of the liberal and humane tradition into our entire educational system. Our purpose is to cultivate in the largest possible number of our future citizens an appreciation of both the responsibilities and the benefits which come to them because they are American and are free" (Redbook, xv). At the time Conant wrote these words, freedom was not assured; but by the time they appeared at the front of the Redbook, it had been, and the Redbook itself, announcing the mission of American education, became, as one writer put it, "the national symbol of renewal" in American culture after World War II.[13]

The Redbook was produced with the intention of establishing leadership on multiple levels: at Harvard, the curriculum would be shaped by the recommendations of this presidential committee; in the American educational system, the agenda would be set by Harvard; in the nation, the leadership class would be formed by the educational program outlined in the report; and in the world, America would prevail because of the superiority of its educational and social philosophy. The committee fully understood that the United States was about to become a global power, a dominant but far from unopposed nation whose fundamental principles were about to be tested in the same way as its military capabilities had been tested in the war. As Daniel Bell put it twenty-one years later, "Such problems as 'why we fight,' the principles of a free society, the need to provide a consistent image of the American experience, the definition of democracy in a world of totalitarianism, the effort to fortify Western civilization, and the need to provide a 'common learning' as a foundation of national unity, were the factors that shaped the thinking of the Redbook."[14] The war itself instructed the committee about what would be required of the educational system; as the members noted, "War is the great educator" (Redbook, 266).

In the view of the Redbook, education serves the interests of the nation by calling out and fortifying those attributes most essential to political, economic, and ideological success. These attributes are not American inventions, nor do they serve America directly or exclusively. They are, rather, broadly human attributes that had become associated with the great age of Athenian democracy, and have been subsequently refined by the "Western" tradition, of which the United States was, in the postwar era, claiming to be the leading contemporary representative. The pertinence of the classical tradition to contemporary American circumstances is established immediately with two epigraphs placed at the beginning of the book. The first is from Thucydides, a speech in which Pericles states plainly the position of an exultant new superpower eagerly awaiting a global expansion of its ambitions: "We need no Homer to praise us. Rather, we have opened the whole earth and sea to our enterprise and raised everywhere living memorials to our fortune." In the second epigraph, from *The Republic*, youth is described as "the time when the character is being molded and easily takes any impress one may wish to stamp on it" (quoted in Redbook, 3). The two taken together establish a context in which the goal of education is seen as the formation of a nation fitted to the task of ruling the world.

The most obvious deficiency in the current system, from the perspective of the national interest, was the lack of coherence in the curriculum. The introduction in the 1870s of the free elective system, combined with the decline of the influence of religion over the curriculum, had produced a chaos of options that were restricted only by the necessity of selecting a major course of study. Students were using this freedom, the committee noted, to select courses based on a principle of "vocationalism," as preparation for a job rather than for life in a free and enlightened society (Redbook, 38). As an antivocational "Jeffersonian" counter to the "Jacksonian" tendencies of the free elective system, the committee proposed a "core curriculum" that would expose each student to essential knowledge. Over time, it felt, the core would establish itself as a "common discipline" reflecting a "common view of life"—a kind of American *Volkgeist*, or "common spirit," although this connection was not stressed (39).

In proposing a principle of unity in the curriculum, the Redbook did not break new ground. The innovation was rather in the explicitness of its geopolitical rationale. When the committee members asked themselves what should serve as the central organizing principle of the curriculum, they considered and rejected several alternatives, including "Western culture as embodied in the great writings of the European and American past," before settling on "the character of the American society" (Redbook, 39). The new core curriculum, they said, was designed to "embody certain intangibles of the American spirit" (41). Anchored by the core curriculum, education would be dedicated to the making of Americans through the inculcation of "heritage." (It is perhaps not coincidental that *American Heritage* magazine was launched in 1947.) The Redbook concludes with the emphatic statement that "in general education the greatest incentive comes from the whole man's awareness of his share in the common fate, of his part in the joint undertaking" (267).

This phrase, the "whole man," signals another of the Redbook's distinctive features, the normative vision of humanity that education is to serve. The authors devoted a good deal of attention to the whole man, whose development, they said, is "the aim of liberal education" (Redbook, 74). This exemplary figure possesses "poise" and "firmness," but also enjoys a rich emotional, spiritual, and even instinctual life. Whole men are reflective, curious, and appreciative of art, but they are also "gregarious" and at home in the world. They are committed to intelligent and principled action, and are "full-blooded human beings as well as trained minds" (75). They embrace ideals of both virtue and citizenship, and differ decisively from the partial men of the totalitarian states against which America had just waged war by being fully realized individuals as well as citizens. Again and again, the Redbook's authors stressed that the American heritage honors equally the dignity and freedom of the individual and the needs of the common weal; democracy, they insisted, is "a *community of free men*" (76).[15] The whole man is at once characteristically American and optimally human. Combining their understandings of the national interest, the national heritage, and the national character, the authors declared, in language that echoes, as we will see, down to the present day, that the aim of education is "mastery of life, and since living is an art, wisdom is the indispensable means to this end" (75). It is the job of the American educational system to create a nation of whole men by awakening, cultivating, and strengthening that singular combination of attributes that has served the nation so well in its recent wars, and will now be required to prevail in a vigilant peacetime.

In the context of this new postwar national self-understanding, "the humanities" emerge as the central element of "general education." It is in the humanities classroom that students are inspired, that the emotions as well as the rational intellect are engaged, that abstract values are shown being tested in action; and it is in the historical and literary texts studied in the humanities that students encounter instructive images of mastery and wisdom. While the Redbook never explicitly identifies the humanities as the first among equals in the divisions of knowledge, their primacy is strongly implied, not least by the fact that whenever the divisions of knowledge are treated serially, the sequence is humanities, social studies, and science and mathematics. And within the humanities, it is English that invariably sets the tone as "the central humanistic study," offering "peculiar opportunities for achieving the goals" of general education (Redbook, 107).

Considering the elevated and generalizing tone of the entirety, the section on English in secondary education (Redbook, 107–19) has a striking particularity. In fact, it presents an account of literature and literary study that was highly controversial and edgy in its time. This section, like the references to the "whole man," "wisdom," and "the art of living," betrays the undoubted influence of I. A. Richards, the British literary critic who came to Harvard in 1944 from Cambridge University, where he had been a pioneer in the new field of English literature.[16] The author of *The Foundations of Aesthetics* (1922; coauthored with C. K. Ogden and James Woods), *Principles of Literary Criticism* (1924), and most important, *Practical Criticism* (1929), Richards was also deeply committed to promoting "Basic English," a plan for making English into an international auxiliary language by such means as eliminating verbs and reducing the vocabulary to a bare minimum of eight hundred and fifty words. Unlike his fellow committee members, most of whom were distinguished professors with administrative positions at Harvard, Richards was an iconoclast and a polemicist, not to mention a newcomer to the country and the committee. Before he arrived at Harvard, his work in criticism, which emphasized a discipline of close reading that focused on the language and formal features of the text to the exclusion of extratextual sources such as biography or history, had exerted a profound influence on many who subsequently became important critics, including F. R. Leavis and William Empson; once in America, Richards continued to be a compelling voice, influencing the "New Criticism," whose adherents included John Crowe Ransom, W. K. Wimsatt, Monroe Beardsley, and Cleanth Brooks.[17]

Perhaps the most striking feature of Richards's approach to literary study was its scientific-empirical character. Richards had at one point planned to become a psychoanalyst, and in *Practical Criticism*, he proposed a method of teaching poetry whose rationale closely resembled Freud's psychopathology of everyday life—what John Forrester has called a "psychopathology of everyday reading."[18] By giving his students printed sheets of poems without the authors' names and inviting them to comment on the poems, Richards deliberately induced his students to make "errors": contempt for the meretriciousness of a Shakespeare sonnet, wild misunderstandings of literal sense, substitutions of "stock responses" for genuine engagement. Richards would then identify and diagnose their mistakes in class—and in print—and train them to adopt a more alive, alert, and sensitive approach, just as the patient in the clinic, once properly diagnosed, could be encouraged to correct his own neuroses. In effect, *Practical Criticism* taught others how to develop their critical capacities by abandoning their neuroses and partialities and becoming whole men.

Richards was apparently a highly effective advocate within the committee, because the treatment of English—the core of the humanistic core of the core curriculum—so perfectly contradicts the rest of the Redbook that it appears he composed it without either opposition or assistance. It is written like no other section in the book in that it specifies an orthodoxy, beginning with a list of "prevailing trends" that are to be firmly discouraged:

> Stress on factual content as divorced from design . . .
> Emphasis on literary history, on generalizations as to periods . . . in
>   place of deeper familiarity with the texts. . . .
> Strained correlation with civics, social studies. . . .
> Didacticism: lessons in behavior too closely sought. . . .
> Irresponsible attitude to the implications of what is being read. (Red-
>   book, 110–11)

Approved trends are specified with equal detail:

> That ethical results of literature are not to be seen as obedience to a
>   body of precepts, but come in quickened imagination, heightened
>   delight, and clearer perspective . . . (111).

And finally, there is a list of things to be stressed, including

> intensive, close study of well-written paragraphs and poems which are
>   saying important things compactly. . . .
> the normal ingredients of full meaning: the literal sense, the meta-
>   phoric implications, the writer's (or speaker's) mood, his tone, his
>   intent, his attitudes toward his point, his reader, himself, his work,
>   and other people and things. . . .
> the utility, almost the necessity, of metaphor. (112)

Presented as "the consensus on the art and science of teaching English, a middle-of-the-road policy," these lists constitute in fact a compressed version of the multidimensional program that the ambitious and determined Richards had been promoting in Britain for over twenty years (113). And in its radical exclusion of the extratextual, this program of course perfectly contradicts the emphasis on "heritage," much less on a particular national heritage, that the Redbook insistently places at the center of the entire concept of general education.

The committee may have been willing to tolerate such a striking deviation from its message because it found congenial the overall moralism and individualism of Richards's approach, which emphasized the importance of charismatic teaching on the Socratic model, informed by Matthew Arnold's evangelical zeal for the disinterested appreciation of culture. To Richards, who early in his career had to collect fees directly from his Cambridge students as they entered the classroom because the university would not commit itself to supporting the new discipline of English, a certain kind of teaching was a professional necessity, and he built into the Redbook an impassioned evocation of the power of the pedagogue: "The best way to infect the student with the zest for intellectual integrity is to put him near a teacher who is himself selflessly devoted to the truth; so that a spark from the teacher will, so to speak, leap across the desk into the classroom, kindling within the student the flame of intellectual integrity, which will thereafter sustain itself" (Redbook, 72). Derived directly from Arnold, this account of teaching also had roots in an American tradition of pedagogical fervor. "The whole secret of the teacher's force," Ralph Waldo Emerson wrote in his journal, "lies in the conviction that men are convertible. And they are. They want awakening. Get the soul out of bed, out of her deep habitual sleep."[19] In the eyes of the other Redbook authors, who had committed themselves to an account of the American heritage that underscored the nobility of the individual and the necessity of teaching virtue in addition to citizenship, Richards's understanding of the mission of the teacher may have seemed deeply consonant with the best traditions of the American Cambridge.

Some may find it curious that a book so explicitly devoted to awakening an appreciation in citizens of "the benefits which come to them because they are Americans and are free" should include at its very center such an explicitly prescriptive passage written by an Englishman with his own agenda. Others might find interesting the suspension of history in the core discipline of a curriculum ostensibly devoted to heritage. Still others might wonder how electrifying classroom experiences would accomplish the job of transmitting a common tradition. But perhaps the most strikingly incongruous fact about the Redbook is that most of its recommendations were eventually rejected by the Harvard faculty, including the idea of requiring a course on the humanities, the course Richards himself had been teaching as an elective: Humanities 1A, "Sources of Our Common Thought: Homer, The Old Testament, and Plato." This was a defeat at Harvard for the advocates of the core curriculum, but it meant that the reputation and influence of the Redbook were free to flourish unencumbered by any record of its actual effect in practice.

The most durable but also the most problematic contribution of the Redbook was its conviction that a curriculum required some principle of coherence, some identification of the knowledge essential to citizenship. With citizenship as the issue, the burden of providing curricular coherence naturally fell to the humanities. Only the humanities, the authors felt, could produce the sense of a common heritage that would form whole men of the right kind—"alert and aggressive" individuals with a sense of obligation toward each other, fully individuated and free and yet bound in mutual obligation (Redbook, 77). Only in the humanities was the individual given opportunity and space to explore his own identity and the larger mysteries and responsibilities of the human condition. Only through the humanities could people learn that their freedoms had been secured not by the passive handing-down of tradition alone but also by armed conflict undertaken for certain principles and for the preservation of inalienable rights. And only the humanities resisted the alienating tendencies of modernity. A wartime document, the Redbook defines the humanities as the curricular means by which students could achieve full human being, and links the humanities with national identity and security.

Higher Education for American Democracy:
The "Truman Report," 1947

The Redbook may have failed at Harvard, but it immediately became national policy in the form of a six-volume report from

President Truman's Commission on Higher Education, which was convened in the year following the Redbook's publication. *Higher Education for American Democracy*, or the Truman Report, covers all areas of education, making its most noteworthy recommendations in the area of what its authors called "community colleges," which were proposed as a way of accommodating the vast numbers of new students in the wake of the war. The Truman Report establishes education as a national priority worthy of federal support, and goes much farther than the Redbook in detailing how this would happen. But it repeats without significant alteration the analysis and many of the recommendations formulated at Harvard, including the need for a "core of unity" achieved through "general education." The Commission on Higher Education deplored specialization, fragmentation, and instrumentalization in terms that would have been warmly, even wholly endorsed by Conant's committee. The emphasis on credentials comes, it said, at the cost of preparation for full citizenship: "Too often [the graduate] is 'educated' in that he has acquired competence in some particular occupation, yet falls short of that human wholeness and civic conscience which the cooperative activities of citizenship require." To counteract this tendency, it proposed "a unified general education for American youth," one that would involve "the transmission of a common cultural heritage toward a common citizenship" in a "free society." Education, it argued, is not an end in itself, but a "means to a more abundant personal life and a stronger, freer social order."[20] In each phrase, the commission relayed the message of the Redbook in its own report—except that its mention of common citizenship was not a mere phrase, as it had been in the Redbook, for it was accompanied by a direct and emphatic rejection of the quotas that had restricted the access of Jews and Negroes to higher education.

The Truman Report does not pay much attention to the humanities, but it does establish the sign under which subsequent discussion of the humanities was to proceed. Reflecting on the new postwar world, at once more interconnected and more dangerous than any that had preceded it, the commission described the present as, in the title of one section, "A Time of Crisis." This crisis, in which the security of the nation depended in part on the effectiveness of the educational system in providing the common heritage that would bind in solidarity a free society, was, at the time the Truman Report was issued, situated in the world at large, a "worldwide crisis of mankind."[21] But just a few years later, the crisis would become associated with the humanities themselves. In 1964, the first of dozens of publications with *Crisis in the Humanities* in their title was published, a collection of dyspeptic essays edited by the historian J. H. Plumb that complained about specialization, incoherence, jargon, and a sense of drifting purposelessness.[22] Oddly, at the same moment, a new document was issued, the *Report of the Commission on the Humanities*, sponsored by the American Council of Learned Societies (ACLS), the Council of Graduate Schools in the United States, and Phi Beta Kappa; this document led directly to the creation the following year of the National Endowment for the Humanities. It was the best of times, it was the worst of times, for at the very moment that the humanities were said to be in disarray, the federal government was determining that the national interest required a new federal agency devoted to their support.

Report of the Commission on the Humanities, *ACLS, 1964*

Somehow, the distinguished twenty-member Commission on the Humanities, which included five active humanities scholars, had not heard of any crisis in the discipline. In the context of the Soviet launch of Sputnik and the threat of a "missile gap" between the United States and a crescent Soviet Union, and in the immediate aftermath of the Kennedy assassination, it was, however, highly aware of a more general crisis, in which the humanities might, it thought, play a useful role if only they did not have their own crisis to deal with. "The state of the humanities today creates a crisis for national leadership," the commission reported[23]—not because the humanities had fallen into disrepair, but because they were scandalously underfunded by comparison with science, which had been the beneficiary of a massive postwar effort inaugurated by Vannevar Bush's 1945 report to President Truman: *Science—The Endless Frontier.*[24] In order to move the Congress to action and establish what it saw as an appropriate balance, the commission voiced its concerns in the most oracular terms possible, defining the humanities as nothing less than the guardian of human being, the nurturer of human existence, a set of academic practices that not only represent the essence and highest aspirations of humanity but drive human progress:

> The humanities are the study of what is most human. Throughout man's conscious past they have played an essential role in forming, preserving, and transforming the social, moral, and aesthetic values of every man in every age. One cannot speak of history or culture apart from the humanities. They not only record our lives; our lives are the very substance they are made of. Their subject is every man. We propose, therefore, a program for all our people, a program to meet a need no less serious than that for national defense. We speak, in truth, for what is being defended—our beliefs, our ideals, our highest achievements. (*Report*, 1)

Even by the lofty standards of the Redbook and the Truman Report, this was idealism of an impressively unembarrassed sort.

The ACLS Commission's report faithfully retains the Redbook's identification of humankind in the abstract, with the United States in particular: "All men require that a vision be held before them, an ideal toward which they may strive. Americans need such a vision today as never before in their history" (*Report*, 4). It retains, too, the double insistence on the individual considered in himself, as a man—at this point the subject of the humanities was still determinedly masculine—who is, on the one hand, a private person capable of independent judgment and entitled to seek intellectual enrichment and emotional fulfillment, and on the other hand a responsible citizen with obligations to the social totality. And it repeats the Redbook's emphasis on "wisdom," a term it invokes, with a glancing reference to Matthew Arnold, in the context of a darkly threatening world:

> Democracy demands wisdom of the average man. Without the exercise of wisdom free institutions and personal liberty are inevitably imperiled. To know the best that has been thought and said in former times can make us wiser than we otherwise might be, and in this respect the humanities are not merely our, but the world's best hope. (Ibid.)

This report does contribute something new to the discourse of the humanities: a tone of grave aristocratic alarm, and the sense that *only* the humanities can save us from external threats and from our own folly. With the fate of mankind hanging in the balance, the commission declared, the United States cannot afford to be "second best" in the humanities (ibid.). We begin to see signs that "the humanities," a recent addition to the academic lexicon, is becoming entangled with the culture's most extravagant hopes and fears.

In its report, the Commission on the Humanities placed an immense burden on humanistic scholars, who alone, it seems, hold the keys to survival: "It is both the dignity and the duty of humanists to offer their fellow-countrymen whatever understanding can be attained by fallible humanity of such enduring values as justice, freedom, virtue, beauty, and truth. Only thus do we join ourselves to the heritage of our nation and our human kind" (*Report*, 4). Without the humanities—or, rather, without increased funding for the humanities—people would be utterly isolated, sunk in primitive delusions, the prey of whatever barbarity is sweeping around the world. Indeed, one prescient passage seems to take note of the incipient spirit of the 1960s: "When men and women find nothing within themselves but emptiness they turn to trivial and narcotic amusements, and the society of which they are a part becomes socially delinquent and potentially unstable" (5). From the perspective of the twenty-first century, the entire scenario seems to be populated with luridly iconic figures drawn both from the "heritage" and popular culture, with the humanist scholar leading Socrates, Sir Gawain, and Superman in an epic struggle against hippies, delinquents, and communists.

The vastly higher stakes and the hugely inflated mission for scholarship those stakes entail represent, then, one distinctive feature of the 1964 report. Another is a linkage, which has since become NEH boilerplate, of a puritan antimaterialism and the "softer" qualities associated with the aesthetic:

> World leadership of the kind which has come upon the United States cannot rest solely upon superior force, vast wealth, or preponderant technology. Only the elevation of its goals and the excellence of its conduct entitle one nation to ask others to follow its lead. These are things of the spirit. If we appear to discourage creativity, to demean the fanciful and the beautiful, to have no concern for man's ultimate destiny—if, in short, we ignore the humanities—then both our goals and our efforts to attain them will be measured with suspicion. (*Report*, 5)

The Redbook's moralized virility has, a generation later, evolved into an emphasis on the spiritual, the creative, even the "fanciful." All the passages that have been cited so far occur in the report's first five pages, which, with an efficiency that bespeaks assurance, tie the humanities into a dense mesh of concepts, including spiritual elevation, the sensual appreciation of beauty, creativity and the imagination, civic virtue, and world leadership.

The distance between the rhetoric and the reality of humanistic scholarship became, in the 1964 report, vast and seemingly unbridgeable. Nevertheless, it was bridged: the language in the legislation creating the National Endowment for the Humanities was taken almost directly from this report.[25] With the establishment of the NEH, support for humanistic scholarship and teaching began to flow from Washington. That flow was imperiled in the 1990s, when successive NEH chairs William Bennett (1981–85) and Lynne V. Cheney (1986–93) argued before a committee of Congress that humanistic scholars had so lost touch with the rhetoric of ennoblement, virtue, and the verities, and had become so "politicized" in their scholarship and teaching, that the NEH should be abolished rather than continue to enable them. Their attacks revealed an even deeper paradox in the American conception of the humanities. Conceived as an expression of the "American spirit," the humanities were also predicated on individual self-realization. In other words, the humanities were understood as a state-supported form of independence from, even resistance to statism that, in a further paradox, would nevertheless redound to the glory of the state. When Bennett, Cheney, and other conservatives[26] did not see among the professoriate sufficient signs of patriotic fervor, they felt betrayed.

The potential for such a misunderstanding was created by the procedures of the NEH, procedures that reflected a particular and distinctive understanding of the relationship between the state and scholarship. Unlike state agencies in other countries that supported scholarship, the NEH did not merely allocate funds according to certain formulae, but sponsored peer-reviewed competitions under a range of programs. In other words, the world of scholarship was treated as self-regulating and autonomous even as it received state funding. This made sense as long as the state was committed to a view of itself as the guarantor of individual liberty, and individual freedom served the highest interests of the state. But it was inevitable that from time to time the distance between the interests of the state, or at least the administration, and the behavior of scholars would seem to some to be too great to warrant continued state support.

Periodic attacks notwithstanding, a diminished trickle of support has continued to flow from the NEH, which still explains "What We Do" with the language of 1964: "Because democracy demands wisdom, the National Endowment for the Humanities serves and strengthens our Republic by promoting excellence in the humanities and conveying the lessons of history to all Americans."[27] In 2005, the endowment celebrated its fortieth birthday by issuing a coffee-table book whose title recalls its origins in the cold war era, when American geopolitical interests were first tied to education and scholarship: *Fearless and Free*.

The Humanities in American Life: The Report of the Commission on the Humanities, *1980*

The ACLS Report's fine phrases, and the recommendations that accompanied them, had a bracing straightforwardness, even a kind of innocence, that became difficult to sustain in the years that followed, as it became increasingly clear that many of the nation's cultural, military, and political problems could not be usefully addressed by a government agency supporting scholarship, museums, libraries, and outreach programs. Indeed, the very moment when this report was issued may have been the last occasion when the humanities could plausibly be advanced as the instrument of the national will or the expression of the national character. If one wished to identify a single moment when such a vision became untenable, it might be August 1964, when the Mississippi Freedom Democratic Party was denied a seat at the Democratic National Convention, and the Gulf of Tonkin resolution was passed by Congress; at that moment, Todd Gitlin argues, the vision of the Great Society morphed into the nightmare of Vietnam.[28]

By the late 1970s, many Americans were experiencing a new kind of crisis, which President Jimmy Carter characterized in a speech delivered on July 15, 1979, as a "Crisis of Confidence." In this famous address, Carter identified two threats to the nation's security. The first was dependence on foreign energy sources, and the second, which acquired the name of malaise (a word that does not occur in the speech), was more abstract but deeper and, as Carter said, "nearly invisible in ordinary ways." This was a crisis afflicting "the very heart and soul and spirit of our national will. We can see this crisis in the growing doubt about the meaning of our own lives and in the loss of a unity of purpose for our nation." The most obvious sign that something had gone awry was the widespread tendency "to worship self-indulgence and consumption.... But we've discovered that owning things and consuming things ... cannot fill the emptiness of lives which have no confidence or purpose."[29] An engineer by training but soon to become a novelist and historian (following his defeat at the hands of Ronald Reagan in 1980), Carter was reaffirming, in the throes of a present crisis and in a somewhat more melancholic tone, the analysis of the threats to America's cultural and political health that had informed the discourse of the humanities since the Redbook, and even before, when "the humanities" referred to the inspiriting example of the classics as set against the alienations of modernity.

Carter's speech and the crisis it registered provided an immediate context for the last of the official pronouncements to be considered here, a substantive and thorough 180-page publication sponsored by the Rockefeller Foundation under the title *The Humanities in American Life*.[30] The product of a thirty-two member commission chaired by Richard Lyman, president of Stanford University, the report begins by announcing its own malaise, a "profound disquiet about the state of the humanities in our culture" (*Humanities*, xi). For the most part, it defers to its distinguished predecessors. Like the Redbook, it invokes "wisdom," "mastery," and "heritage." And it simply repeats without comment much of the 1964 ACLS Report's analysis: the identification of the humanities with critical judgment, aesthetic appreciation, and moral decision making; the claim that the humanities represent "things of the spirit" arrayed against the corrosive force of "materialism"; and the insistence that the fate of the nation is bound up with humanistic scholarship: "We must," the authors said, "stress how limited our sense of national purpose is, indeed how imperiled our civilization is, if the humanities are exiled to a peripheral role of irrelevance" (109).

The worried tone was justified, for at the time these words were written, the project of a morally prescriptive and implicitly nationalistic program in higher education had virtually no credibility with scholars themselves. Over the course of the previous decades, three factors had conspired to weaken the connection between the humanities and the state. First and most important, the vast numbers of students entering postsecondary education after World War II had changed the nature of higher education

from the bottom up. A larger and more diverse student population demanded a less prescriptive and more practical approach
to the business of preparing for life, and the humanities as traditionally conceived were not necessarily at the top of everyone's
list of priorities. Second, the disciplines themselves had enlarged
their self-understanding. The classical tradition was no longer
considered the sole source of or best model for contemporary
civilization. New disciplines and subdisciplines arose that did not
take the nation, with its "interests" and "purposes," as their frame
of reference, and scholarship became increasingly global in its
orientation. And third, the increasing domination by research—
fueled by the National Science Foundation, the National Institutes of Health, and, yes, the National Endowment for the
Humanities—of the agenda for higher education meant that all
disciplines were becoming more professionalized, with a growing
emphasis on research and the creation of new knowledge.

For the sciences, this emphasis on research meant that science, once considered a shining instance of a purely intellectual
pursuit undertaken for its own sake, was increasingly dedicated
to specific industrial or commercial ends, to the point where, as
one scholar put it, there is "an unbroken chain connecting knowledge to science to research to technology to industry to production to economic growth and finally to wealth and well-being,"
a chain that "forms the main justification for research."[31] The
humanities have not been able to connect themselves so directly
to wealth and well-being—not even their own—but by 1980 it
was perfectly clear that they were able to dedicate themselves to
research, along with its concomitants, a pronounced receptivity
to theory and a de-emphasis on primary texts. The result was
that, especially over the course of the 1970s, liberal education at
many leading institutions came to be focused less on values and
heritage and more on skills or expertise. The "core curriculum"
adapted at Harvard in the 1970s, for example, omits any mention
of a common tradition and substitutes an emphasis on "moral
reasoning," "quantitative reasoning," and "social analysis."

None of these three developments—the democratization of higher education, the globalization of knowledge, and the consensus that the function of the university was research—served the kinds of ends outlined in the Redbook or in the 1964 ACLS Report, and if the Rockefeller Commission seemed determined, in the spirit of tradition but against the tide of history, to hold on to those ends, it did at least register an alarmed sense that the relation of the humanities to the national purpose was badly stressed.

Perhaps the most traditional aspect of the Rockefeller Report is the combination of an extraordinary portentousness—the fate of the nation and of civilization itself as well as people's access to their own humanity are said to be at stake—and the highly specific proposals for increased funding (all but six of the thirty-one recommendations involve money). By 1980, this combination was beginning to seem suspect, even vulgar, to humanists themselves, who deplored the necessity of making absurdly inflated claims in order to get even modest funding. In a review of the report published just as William Bennett was settling in at the NEH, Mel A. Topf described as a "litany" the series of vacuities that had become part of the standard defense of the humanities. "Why," he asked, "does the litany dominate?" The only reason, he argued, was that it "provides valuable service"; that is, it secures funding by "[pitting] the humanities against an otherwise lost, inhuman world."[32] Topf's review was among the first to suggest that the official discourse of the humanities was a tissue of false consciousness and bad faith, a mere rhetorical construct devised to obtain funding. The very word *humanities*, he suggested, "signifies a recent bastard notion of doubtful definition. . . . The term 'humanities' is like Milton's Death without shape or substance, obsessed with and often assaulting the sciences from which it was born. . . . Those who talk of the traditions embodied in the humanities are engaging in futile nostalgia" (ibid., 469). The value of the humanities was no longer unchallenged.

But the Rockefeller Report was not all litany. Embedded in

what sometimes seems like a matrix of cliché were three new elements. First, the crisis in the humanities announced in Plumb's 1964 book is now recognized, and situated not only in the funding of the humanities but in the practice of the humanities disciplines themselves. The world of scholarship, the report's authors said, has not escaped the general loss of purpose Carter noted: "Many would argue that the humanities are in crisis and would describe this crisis as symptomatic of a general weakening of our vision and resolve" (*Humanities*, 3). During the "culture wars" of the 1990s, the humanities would actually be saddled with responsibility for that weakening, but in 1980 they were merely part of the milieu. Second, while the ACLS Report mentions "the fanciful and the beautiful," the Rockefeller Report dives much further into the sanctuary of the inner life, where, it asserts, the humanities also live. At the end of a section titled "Culture and Citizenship," the authors noted that "there are other values besides civic ones, and they are often found in privacy, intimacy, and distance from civic life. The humanities sustain this second conception of individuality, as deeply rooted as the other in our cultural inheritance. . . . The humanities offer intensely personal insights into the recesses of experience" (12–13). This passage seems to bear the stamp of Rockefeller Commission member Helen Vendler, the noted Boston University (soon to go to Harvard) scholar and critic of poetry who would, in 2005, publish a book called *Invisible Listeners: Lyric Intimacy in Herbert, Whitman, and Ashbery*.[33] And while it is consistent with the "softening" or devirilizing trend of official pronouncements already noted in the discussion of the 1964 report, it also marks a moment of genuine dissensus on the commission, when the discourse of entirely private reflection and sensibility, an interior zone of secrecy and inner experience untouched by the external world, becomes, if only momentarily, detached from the discourse of public civic virtue.

The third and perhaps most interesting contribution to the discourse of the humanities made by the Rockefeller Report is the prominent mention given to private support for the humanities. Philanthropic support from corporations, foundations, and individuals provides "multiple centers of initiative and response, and often attaches fewer political and bureaucratic strings to grants. It can allow more freedom for innovative and controversial projects" (*Humanities*, 151). This new element represents an even more decisively American contribution to the concept of the humanities than the rhetoric of national identity and security, because it represents the perspective of the entrepreneurial individual operating in a free market.

The Rockefeller Report was sponsored, not by a university or by a consortium of academic institutions, but by a private foundation endowed by such an individual, a foundation that, moreover, saw itself and its peers as bearing some responsibility for alleviating the crisis and restoring health to the humanities and the nation. At that time, the Rockefeller and other foundations also saw themselves as the natural sponsors of cutting-edge humanistic scholarship that might be controversial if it drew on taxpayer support. And they understood that the federal government alone could not be depended on either to provide all necessary support or to make the most powerful arguments for the humanities as the torch illuminating "the recesses of experience." In the years since the Rockefeller Report, foundation commitment to scholarship in the humanities has diminished, with the exception, among the major foundations, of the Andrew W. Mellon Foundation. The Rockefeller Commission Report has not been succeeded by any further reports with comparable scope, credentials, or ambitions.[34] After the appearance of *The Humanities in American Life*, distinguished national committees producing substantial statements about the humanities disappeared from the scene. With sharply reduced government support and a shrinking list of committed foundations, the humanities have become vulnerable to ideological attack. They have not, however, lacked altogether for defenders, among the most vigorous of whom have been the private citizens celebrated in the discourse of the humanities since the Redbook.

Private Thoughts: Richard J. Franke on the Humanities, 2009

One of the most distinctive features of the humanities in the United States is the involvement of private individuals who have supported scholarship through philanthropy, often through private foundations. The connection between the humanities and private philanthropy in America has been deep and determining, if not as broad-based as many might wish.[35] Humanists work in buildings, including libraries, named for the individuals who built them; their salaries, research expenses, conference travel expenses, and sabbatical salaries are drawn at least in part from endowments contributed by individuals. The presses and journals that publish their work may be supported by grants from individuals or foundations, and the very colleges and universities that employ them are, of course, supported by massive development operations that train their sights on individual donors. It is shocking how imperfectly most American scholars grasp the fact that their work is at every level and every point supported by private gifts. Even some of those fortunate enough to hold endowed chairs are oblivious to the perspective or the life history of the donor of the gift that pays their salary. On the principle that one ought to know one's friends, I would like now to consider, as an instance of the philanthropic perspective, a recent essay by one of the most generous funders of the humanities in the United States, Richard J. Franke, former chair of the John Nuveen Company and the founder of the Chicago Humanities Festival, as well as of the Franke Center for the Humanities at the University of Chicago. His essay "The Power of the Humanities and a Challenge to Humanists"[36] appeared in the winter 2009 issue of *Daedalus*, a collection of twelve essays on the humanities gathered by the American Academy of Arts and Sciences.

Franke's essay is the only one in the collection written by someone who is not either a distinguished scholar or a senior administrator at the Andrew W. Mellon Foundation. Franke is in the group, but not of it. He does not write or think like a scholar, and his frame of reference, grounded in his experiences in the world beyond the campus, is very different from that of his co-contributors. And yet, he is completely at home in the discourse of the humanities that I have been considering so far, even more so than his cocontributors. He shares with that discourse a familiar set of convictions: that "the humanities protect and give life to our most enduring values"; that they prepare people for life, especially moral decision making; that they "relate to robust and prosperous citizenship"; that they have "suffered neglect over the last few decades"; and that, despite all these quite obvious points, humanists themselves have not succeeded in explaining the value of their work (Franke, 13, 22, 13). Given this broad agreement with a series of distinguished commissions, it is not at all surprising that Franke begins his essay with a reference to "general education," by way of the *Report of the Task Force on General Education* produced at Harvard in 2007, which sought to create a curriculum that would enable today's whole men and women of Harvard to put the learning they would acquire "in the context of the people they will be and the lives they will lead after college."[37]

These lives, rather than the lives led inside the academy, are Franke's primary, indeed his only concern. The value of the humanities is in their application, not in themselves. Lorenzo Valla's scholarly exposé of the fraudulent *Donation of Constantine* by philological examination of the language of the text, for example, represents a triumph of scholarly method and an early instance of "what we might today call close reading" or "critical thinking," but its value is as an example of how the humanities can serve the public interest (Franke, 15). Franke concedes that science, exemplified by Bacon and Leonardo da Vinci, also employs critical thinking, but distinguishes between humanistic and scientific instances by noting that in the humanities, "our emotions and values are always at play," so that "instead of setting our feelings and assumptions aside as is done in the sciences, humanistic critical inquiry requires that we explicitly acknowledge our own personal bias and emotional investment" (17). Business depends on having good judgment, and since unacknowledged biases can interfere with judgment, the humanities can contribute to good business practice. Indeed, the staff seminars led by professors that Franke organized at Nuveen were "crucial to Nuveen's success" (19). The humanities, like the arts, can also help by producing vivid representations. Public policy, for example, would benefit immensely if it were informed by the work of artists and writers who could help us understand in concrete terms the horrific effects of natural or manmade disasters. To his credit, Franke also respects the traditional distance of liberal education from considerations of immediate utility. He notes, for example, that great works of art pose "fundamental questions about the nature and purpose of life. We read," he says decisively, "to pursue answers to those questions" (21). For all these reasons, Franke concludes, the humanities are "vital to public life; they help us imagine the consequence of our actions and give us the tools to make informed policy decisions. Even more, the moral, aesthetic, and spiritual discoveries of the humanities reveal what is common to the human experience and provide the foundation for a successful and fulfilling life" (18). In short, he almost says, the humanities make us whole men.

It is difficult to imagine a clearer statement. Its lucidity reflects the confidence generated by a long tradition of discourse and by Franke's own success in corporate life. But in style and substance, it is remote from the ordinary practice of the scholars whose work it purports to describe. Franke betrays, at least in this brief essay, little interest in the discipline of humanistic scholarship, and while his grasp of art is more sophisticated than that of William Bennett or Lynne V. Cheney, he does not consider the study of the human cultural archive as an end in itself, to be pursued out of a simple desire for learning, but rather as an aid to "a successful life." He seems uninterested in whether the current paradigm in humanistic scholarship is New-Critical, deconstructionist, feminist, psychoanalytic, Marxist, historicist, or culturalist. He does not restrict his references to a particular field, genre, period, or methodology. He scarcely mentions the academy, except as the place where teaching happens. The entire conception of the humanities is wrapped tightly in a coil of utility that circles round to profits, which he construes in a quite literal way: seemingly oblivious to the "critical" or "resistant" posture of much humanistic scholarship, Franke says directly that you can make money with this stuff, and that he himself has done so. His essay seems almost designed to produce in scholars an acute sense of discomfiture, even embarrassment.

Why is Franke's essay so cringe-inducing in those whom it wishes to praise? It cannot be because he expresses untrue or unworthy thoughts. How could anyone reject the proposition that the humanities help people lead successful lives? (Would a humanist rather believe that the humanities make no contribution to such lives, or that they contribute to unsuccessful lives?) No, the reason is that Franke has a completely different orientation to the humanities from that of most scholars. Franke is unrepentantly liberal (as in liberal arts) in his approach: his understanding of the humanities is drawn not from professional scholarship but from a lifetime of amateur enthusiasm. Scholars are different: the credentialing process beats such enthusiasm out of them. New graduate students may begin with a love of their subject and a desire to do the world some good. But as the 2007 Harvard Task Force noted, graduate training has a "de-liberalizing" effect on students, structuring their thinking, disciplining their mode of expression, and professionalizing their relationship to their chosen fields (*Report of the Task Force*, 2). They become not just concerned with other issues than the ones Franke raises, but trained to reject any calculation of the applied worldly benefits of their work. A loose comment made by a graduate student to the effect that studying *Antigone* really helps people understand the nature of morality, or that Saul Bellow's *Herzog* illustrates the value of "emotional honesty," would be considered a sign of professional immaturity (Franke, 19, 21). The image Franke presents of the humanities is a professional embarrassment, like a baby picture shown to one's grownup friends.

What should we make of the fact that the humanities depend on the support of people like Franke, whose outlook, attitudes, and life experiences are so at variance with those whose work he supports? Does the relationship necessarily involve misplaced idealism, bad faith, and cynical pragmatism? Or is there some other way of thinking about the matter that might enable academics to seek and accept philanthropic support with a good conscience?

We can make a beginning on this other way of thinking by setting Franke's essay alongside another essay in the same issue of *Daedalus*, one that issues from the heart of the professional study of the humanities. In "A World without Literature?"[38] Michael Wood of Princeton University answers Franke's "challenge to humanists" to explain themselves to the public by attempting to identify the specific value of his field, literary criticism. Other disciplines are concerned with knowledge, he begins, but literary criticism is "rather different." In a luminous passage that deserves to be quoted at length, Wood probes what it is that we know when we know literature:

> Literature . . . does not deal in information or announcement. Literature is embodiment, a mode of action; it works over time on the hearts and minds of its readers or hearers. Its result in us, when we are receptive or lucky, is the activation of personal knowledge: knowledge of others and ourselves; knowledge of stubborn, slippery, or forgotten facts; knowledge of old and new possibilities—a knowledge that is often so intimate and so immediate that it scarcely feels like knowledge at all because it feels like something we have always known. (Ibid., 62)

This passage is the ripened fruit of a lifetime's immersion in the study of literature. But from a professional perspective, it is perhaps even more jarring than Franke's cheerful utilitarianism, because it translates Franke's message—the underpinning of the "strictly intellectual life" by "serious reflection and emotional honesty"—into terms that command academic respect. Wood's perspective is larger, his view longer, and his eloquence greater than Franke's; but all that is simply Wood's job, as running Nuveen—and having a successful life, and supporting the humanities—are Franke's. The differences are superficial, but the compatibilities are deep.

One difference concerns scale. While Franke thinks in terms of individual lives and corporations, Wood thinks of the species. But this difference aside, the points they are arguing are similar. Wood links literature to the idea of "the classic," suggestively defined by J. M. Coetzee as "the human; or, at least, it is what survives of the human."[39] This survival depends, Wood says, on a cultural habit of concern for, or "non-indifference" to, other minds and lives (Wood, 65). A classic, in this account, is a work that we return to voluntarily in a state of non-indifference, not as a repository of "answers," as Franke infelicitously puts it, but as a possible "model"—Coetzee's term—of human thought or action in which we might recognize or come to understand ourselves. When we allow literature to work on our hearts and minds, we recognize and honor our investment in the world, which becomes valuable. Franke's understanding of investment and value may be more limited and specific than Wood's, but it is not fundamentally different. When Franke ran seminars in which young leaders of the Nuveen staff read literature so that they might "broaden their imagination and sharpen the critical faculties so necessary for their success," he was encouraging them in effect to adopt a posture of "non-indifference" to other minds and lives, to exercise the capacity to participate imaginatively in experiences not their own, a capacity that he thought would serve them well (Franke, 19). At this point, Franke seems close to Léon's excited account to Emma Bovary of how, when reading, "your thought, blending with the fiction . . . mingles with the characters, and it seems you are living their lives, that your own heart beats in their breast" (see chapter 1). But he is also close to Wood, far closer than either is to the perspective of those for whom literature is merely the object of professional concern.[40]

If Franke betrays some of the secrets of the professionalized humanities—that they are not disinterested or completely objective in their approach to their subject, that their way of knowing involves acts of judgment that cannot be fully rationalized, that they give a distinct kind of pleasure, that they are irreducibly "first-person" as well as "third-person" in their orientation, and that they are really good for you—Wood reveals the secret of Franke's secret: that the ultimate stakes of the humanities, and literature in particular, are not prosperity or success, marvelous though these may be, but the survival of the species in a form we can recognize and value.

While Franke and Wood might be far removed in terms of taste, stylistic elegance, and intellectual sophistication, they are located on the same line, and it is a line leading away from the idea that the humanities can be reduced to knowledge in a quantifiable or cumulative sense, and toward the idea that the humanities represent the deepest interests of human beings—whole men and women—who must grasp the world intellectually, emotionally, and morally. To be sure, the humanities, including literary studies, offer forms of positive knowledge that can safely be learned without risking a total upheaval of the soul. But the unique kernel of the humanities, what they have that other disciplines do not, is the "activation of personal knowledge," the experience of simultaneous self-surrender and self-discovery through a sympathetic imaginative encounter with a text or artifact that somehow manages to register our own half-formulated thoughts or feelings and yet also to offer us different ways of thinking or feeling that give us a perspective on our own lives and the lives of others, and thereby a sense of power over circumstances and freedom from mere contingency. Engaging with the products of past cultures in a spirit of non-indifference, as if they might somehow contain a model for us, as if our identity were somehow at stake—as if something of us were somehow in there— we indirectly but effectively learn to imagine a life for ourselves that is at least slightly and perhaps fundamentally different from the life we currently lead. We are released from specificity and invited to think of shared experience and general categories. In its most benign and productive forms, this kind of imagining constitutes an emancipation from actuality that opens onto a free futurity.

I have been arguing that the perspective of the humanities is at once deeply literary, deeply American, and deeply philanthropic. It rests on a belief in the human capacity for transformation, metamorphosis, and creation, a belief most conspicuously shared by artists, inventors, pioneers, reformers, and by those who create wealth where none had existed. Such people are driven by an aggravated discontent with the given, an appetite or even a yearning for what is not, or not yet. Literature stimulates and feeds this yearning, which is, of course, also an element in American self-understanding. Ralph Waldo Emerson described literature as "a point outside of our hodiernal [present-day] circle through which a new one may be described. The use of literature is to afford us a platform whence we may command a view of our present life, a purchase by which we may move it."[41] This passage captures the literary experience in terms that also apply to the philanthropist: a person who has, through the exercise of the imagination, commanded, who has moved, who has created a new reality, and who now wishes to give others the opportunity to get their own "purchase" on life by underwriting those academic practices most supportive to the enterprise. Some of these individuals support the business school; others, with a broader, richer, and deeper understanding, support the humanities.

Most scholars today do not describe their work as the heart and soul of the university, or the moral center of higher education; nor do they rally themselves with the thought that the humanities are where the educational system addresses the deepest needs of the nation or the species, much less the corporation. Scholars generally reject as a vulgar misunderstanding the idea that their work amounts to helping people increase their happiness or improve their chances for success. Most see themselves as specialists, professionals engaged in a self-certifying disciplinary practice founded, many believe, on a critique of received ideas, common sense, or habitual responses, especially those that can be traced to the machinations of capital. Defending their discipline against charges of "softness," some insist that the humanities offer disciplinary knowledge on the same order as that of the natural or social sciences. But such a defense risks everything by failing to grasp or appropriately value the genuine difference of the humanities, a difference that reaches a point of maximal differentiation in the undergraduate or nonprofessional experience of reading literature. An insistence that the humanities are just like other disciplines does not secure their place in the university; it eliminates it.

At this point, an irony appears. Philanthropists hold the humanities in great esteem: they understand how money is made, and they understand in particular the notion of market share; they value the humanities in part for their distinctiveness. Above all, they understand that the goal of wise investing is long-term gains. This understanding can lead them to an appreciation of what the educational reformer Abraham Flexner described as "the usefulness of useless knowledge,"[42] knowledge, that is, that produces no immediate benefit but may result in some distant but more enduring reward. Taking the long view, philanthropists such as Franke place their bets on the proposition that the humanities represent a particularly useful—and pleasurable, and worthy, and instructive—form of useless knowledge. Moreover, while many are politically conservative, they support the academy in the full understanding that most professors are politically liberal; they are willing to look beyond politics even if the professoriate cannot seem to imagine anything beyond politics. In short, the (diminishing number of) capitalist-philanthropists are the idealists, and the (increasingly dependent) scholars are the cynics. The situation may call for a rethink on the part of the scholars.

The Humanities as the American Dream

So far I have focused on two kinds of discourse about the humanities, official statements of committees and commissions, and the discourse of philanthropy. Most scholars regard both discourses as being detached from what they actually do. I would like to close, then, by considering an instance of a scholarly discourse on the humanities, Andrew Delbanco's 1999 book *The Real American Dream*.[43] This is not a book about the humanities but an uncategorizable combination of history, polemic, sermon, and personal testament, a wide-ranging meditation on the fantasy life of America. But since the humanities are part of that fantasy life—and the part in which Delbanco himself has invested his entire career—his book can be read as an angled account of the humanities in America; indeed, one reading of Delbanco's book is as a reaffirmation of the case first made by John Adams, that the humanities themselves are the real American dream. A frequent critic of certain tendencies in the humanities as well as a widely recognized scholar—trained at the same institution that produced the Redbook and a longtime faculty member at an institution famous for its commitment to the humanities, Columbia University—Delbanco is admirably positioned to make such a case.

The Real American Dream begins, not with a discussion of the ways Americans have dreamed their dream, but with an analysis of the reason people dream at all, which is, in Delbanco's account, to escape the persistent feeling that life lacks purpose, form, meaning, or pattern.[44] People tell stories, Delbanco says, as a way of turning their attention away from this disturbing intuition.[45] Stories that are repeated, read, or listened to eventually become "culture"; and culture gives us the hope on which Delbanco meditates. This basic response to existential terror is a species characteristic, but Americans have experienced it with particular intensity, beginning with the Puritans, who told themselves stories about a vengeful and omnipotent God, stories that, while threatening people with everlasting torment after death, helped them escape "the hell of loneliness" while alive (Delbanco, 117). When, over the course of the nineteenth century, such stories lost their suasive power, Americans turned to stories about the Nation; after the 1960s, these stories were replaced with tales of the Self. Thus American history can be divided very roughly into epochs of God, Nation, and Self—"two phases of coherent belief followed by a third phase of incoherence and nervous waiting" (111).

A "meditation on hope," *The Real American Dream* is, then, more immediately about hopelessness. The term Delbanco prefers, and the one that hovers over the entire book, is *melancholy*, whose first theorist in an American context was Alexis de Tocqueville, who identified it as an attribute of democracy itself. In a passage Delbanco cites at the very beginning of his book, de Tocqueville said that in a democracy, "men easily attain a certain equality of condition, but they can never attain as much as they desire. It perpetually retires from before them, yet without hiding itself from their sight, and in retiring draws them on.... That is the reason for the strange melancholy that haunts inhabitants of democratic countries in the midst of abundance."[46] Democracy creates fantasies of a state of perfect wholeness and integration. With promises of abundance, and enough actual abundance to encourage the illusion that those promises might one day be redeemed, America is in fact the most melancholy of nations. And so, Delbanco says, his meditation on hope can also be considered "a theory of melancholy in its particular American form" (Delbanco, 2).

Delbanco is particularly melancholic about our own era, which seems to him a time of singular emptiness when compared to its predecessors. The Puritan God was horrifying but impressive; and the Nation, especially as articulated by such titans as Jefferson, Whitman, Lincoln, and Melville, could be inspiring.[47] But the current phase is, in Delbanco's account, simply pathetic. We slipped into incoherence, he says, in the mid-1960s, when—just as the NEH was getting started—something gave way in American society. The dream of Nation collapsed into a daydream of personal gratification, and the notion of a common destiny worth tears and sacrifice was abandoned in favor of a meretricious fantasy of consumption; the very Self that dreamed of fulfillment through acquisition was emptied of content. Delbanco finds reasons for despair everywhere—in overflowing prisons, rising rates of depression, society given over to a virtual carnival of self-interest engineered by corporations that manipulated the feeble fantasies of consumers, an unprecedented national fixation on money. (And this was in 1998!) And so now, there we sit, miserable amid our possessions. The whole abysmal situation brings out the puritan moralist, or perhaps the Jimmy Carter, in Delbanco: "And what," he cries, "does the plenty avail us?" (Delbanco, 106).

In response, Delbanco proposes that we take action, overthrowing Self after a brief reign and moving on to World. He anticipates a time when, as William James put it, "the outlines of the confining selfhood melt down,"[48] so that "human beings will no longer construct their identities within the symbolic and functional structure of the nation-state," but will identify themselves with mankind in general. Delbanco may want to move on, but clearly one of the great appeals of World for him is that it represents a restoration of the most exalted aspects of Nation. The "real" American dream, he says, "has always been a global dream.... To be really American has always meant to see something beyond America" (Delbanco, 117). With this breathtaking vision, a globalized version of the green light at the end of Jay Gatsby's dock, Delbanco virtually declares his affiliation with the sensibility informing the Redbook and the subsequent discourse of the humanities.

That affiliation is deep and multidimensional. It is based on a common investment in the belief that the goal of education is the creation of what might be called moral citizenship, and on the notion that a humanistic education prominently including literary study is capable of promoting both individual self-realization and the sense of a cultural heritage. Delbanco's vernacular style and loosely interdisciplinary, even antidisciplinary approach suggest that he is addressing an audience not of professional scholars but of concerned citizens, and that he is offering them not knowledge but wisdom. He is most thoroughly humanistic in the sense I have been developing, however, in his understanding of the responsibilities and benefits that come to Americans because they are American and because they are free. He quotes, with a palpable thrill, the passage from Melville's *White-Jacket* in which the manifest destiny of America is announced:

> We Americans are the peculiar, chosen people—the Israel of our time; we bear the ark of the Liberties of the world. . . . God has predestinated, mankind expects, great things from our race; and great things we feel in our souls. . . . And let us always remember that with ourselves, almost for the first time in the history of earth, national selfishness is unbounded philanthropy; for we can not do a good to America but we give alms to the world.[49]

For Melville, Americans represent a privileged instance of humanity at large in that their system of government encourages them to explore without hindrance the full range of the human condition. It is in this sense that the interests of the United States and the human race are identical, and "national selfishness is unbounded philanthropy."

The mention of philanthropy brings us back to our previous theme, and enables us to grasp together a distinctively American nexus: a "dream" of ultimate human fulfillment achieved through liberal education, the humanities as the central element in such an education, and private support for scholarship, a point on which Delbanco's book is exemplary as well as descriptively acute. Delivered by the Julian Clarence Levy Professor in the Humanities (Delbanco's title at Columbia) at the William E. Massey, Sr. Lectures in the History of American Civilization at Harvard, the talks that comprise the book were underwritten by philanthropy, and are, in style and substance, entirely consistent with the "love of humanity" or "love of people" that defines philanthropy.

Most revealingly, Delbanco has also put a name—melancholy, signifying lack or incompletion—to something that is generally only obliquely implied. As we have seen, the discourse of the humanities is dominated by images of enrichment, repletion, and almost spiritual satisfaction. The humanities are represented as the answer to our prayers, the way out of crisis, the key to success and survival. A deep and persistent sense of longing, a melancholic yearning, haunts the humanities, which have always, in the United States, signified not only a set of academic disciplines but also a phantasmatic elsewhere, a utopian place where we can be made whole and complete—an "America" of the academy.

In some respects, *The Real American Dream* is an American response to Max Weber's *The Protestant Ethic and the Spirit of Capitalism* of 1904.[50] Weber identified the "unprecedented inner loneliness" of the modern capitalist, the sense of being driven by the profit motive away from an identification with a larger social or cultural group (ibid., 169). Weber was a German social scientist and knew nothing about the humanities or about philanthropy, but if he had been American, he might have been able to glimpse, in the philanthropic activities of, for example, Andrew Carnegie or Andrew W. Mellon, ways in which modern capitalists could relieve their melancholy and reconnect with a larger purpose. Like many of their cohort of capitalists, Carnegie and Mellon devoted themselves in later life to philanthropy, supporting a wide range of causes, including what we now call the humanities. That the humanities could be supported by men who dedicated their lives to the profitable production of steel (Carnegie) or the profitable production of profit (Mellon, through banking) makes sense, perhaps, only when one considers that the humanities themselves have been conceived essentially as a form of philanthropy for the human race, a more-than-merely academic practice that will give Americans—and through Americans, the world—free access to a vivifying tradition, a moral framework, and an ennobling experience of beauty that can help to create whole people and situate them in a whole culture and a whole world. Humanistic scholarship in America is not just supported by philanthropy, and not just brushed by the spirit of philanthropy; it is the academic form of philanthropy.

That the United States is founded on concepts of individual rights, beginning with life, liberty, and the pursuit of happiness, goes a long way toward explaining the distinctive place long occupied by the humanities in American higher education; it may also help explain why the concept of the humanities has spread across the globe, traveling on the same winds as the English language, the dollar, rock and roll, baseball, and American movies: the concept speaks to the longing for freedom, self-realization, and belonging, and holds out the tantalizing suggestion that these may be learned at school. And lastly, it may provide some understanding of why leadership in humanistic scholarship tends to be centered in America: it is not that Americans are smarter than anybody else, but that the humanities are an American discourse whose deepest assumptions and implications resist translation into other cultural settings.

>>><<<

If a very short story could be told about the humanities, it might go something like this. In the beginning, there was philology, a master discourse that combined elements of what would become science and what would become the humanities. Philology focused on the origins of linguistic forms, languages, races, and the human species. Focused initially on classical literature, it flourished for over a century, and when the influence of religion over the curriculum began to wane, philology served to anchor the curriculum in many colleges and universities in Europe and the United States. By the beginning of the twentieth century, however, both the pedagogical and the scientific credentials of philology were being questioned. As a way of studying literature, philology could not compete with the livelier pedagogy of the critics and generalists who had broken off from it; and as a science, philology could not stand comparison with the natural sciences that had once looked to it as a model of taxonomic rigor. Eventually, the postreligious yearning that drove the philological quest for the origins of humankind settled, in the United States, on the concept of the humanities, which also emphasized culture and heritage. By the mid-twentieth century, the term *the humanities*, firmly identified with notions of personal fulfillment, creativity, and freedom, had emerged as the core of the liberal arts, the center of "general education," the means of establishing a common culture, and the academic expression of the American national character: curious, open-minded, unburdened by fear and want, and eager to explore in a disinterested spirit the full range of opportunities inherent in the human condition. Support for the humanities, whether public or private, was seen as a form of enlightened patriotism. With higher education growing at an extraordinary rate after World War II, the humanities entered into a golden age of robust confidence and prestige.

With the end of the cold war era, however, the humanities lost something of their reason for being, the legitimating crisis in which they were to have played so necessary a part. Moreover, as the humanities, like other academic disciplines, became professionalized, they became insular—self-validating, self-legitimating, self-referring, self-interested. The link between the humanities and the state on the one hand and the individual on the other became attenuated. Detached from its rationale and isolated from its supporters, the humanities, conceived as a response to various crises, themselves fell into crisis; and as higher education took a pragmatic, scientific, research-oriented, and vocational turn, other sectors of the university, particularly the sciences and professional education, came to command more attention, resources, and prestige.

If this short story is to take a happier turn, humanists today must find ways to reactivate the links between their practice and the larger interests of a society based on individual freedom and self-realization. They must insist and demonstrate that it makes sense for both the state and individuals to support what they do. They must resist any temptation to refashion their discipline along the lines of the natural or social sciences, and accept utopian unreality as one of the conditions of their work. They must remind the larger culture that the humanities were made in America as an image of American aspirations, and that we ignore, marginalize, or denigrate the humanities at the cost of those aspirations. Some features of our traditional national self-understanding might be relinquished without loss; indeed, it could be argued that some ought to be erased, beginning with the presumption that Americans enjoy privileged access to the fullness of the human condition. But the aspiration to personal fulfillment and self-enrichment achieved on a mass scale through education cannot be abandoned without immense cost to American self-understanding. We must also take very seriously the philanthropic mission that has been central to that understanding: as the most thoroughly "globalized" nation, the United States has the ability and the responsibility to lead the world in the study of human creative achievement, with leadership construed not as domination but exemplification.

The concept of the humanities truly makes sense only in a society in which authority is mobile; where what one can do is not limited by who one is; where the parameters are never set; where one must figure out for oneself how to navigate a social world peopled by others with their own motives, drives, and incentives. Humanistic study trains people to participate in a world in which solutions are not simply matched with predetermined problems, because both problem and solution must be defined; a world that requires and rewards imagination and character as well as intellect. The humanities flourish in flux, the extreme form of which is crisis. Humanists should understand their work, not as a set of professional practices unfortunately afflicted with crises, but as part of the way we think of and in crisis. To imagine a social, moral, or political crisis, we might say, is to imagine the humanities.

The humanities cannot give us everything we seek or lack; they cannot make us whole. Their mission in that respect will always be impossible. Still, some kinds of learning are best obtained in just such an environment, in which what Michael Wood calls "personal knowledge" is permitted to break through other, more impacted, objective, and impersonal forms of knowledge, an environment in which knowledge of the world provokes or activates knowledge of oneself. The last chapter of this book is offered as a single example of the kind of breakthrough possible in the impossible environment of the humanities.

7

The Depths of the Heights: Reading Conrad with America's Military

For one who has spent his entire adult life in academic settings, a trip to Colorado Springs, Colorado, seems like an inverted *Heart of Darkness* where, instead of going deeper in toward the horror, you ascend to space and light. The skies are open above you; and the air, while there's not much of it at six thousand feet, is clean and clear. You find yourself constantly looking up, thinking large thoughts, or no thoughts at all. To the west are the Garden of the Gods and the immensity of Pike's Peak. Just to the north is the campus of James Dobson's vast Focus on the Family, a corporate headquarters, gift shop, and museum of its own history. A couple of miles north from there is the New Life Church founded by the now-disgraced and departed Ted Haggard, both mall and amusement park, the halls crowded with youth groups on their way to another large room, another inspiring message delivered by a guy in blue jeans who once was lost but now is found. And just over there, at the end of that road that winds toward the Rockies, and below the spot where those tiny figures are gently descending to earth (no matter when you happen to glance up), that's the gleaming, geometrical U.S. Air Force Academy, where I had been invited to lead a seminar—on *Heart of Darkness*, as it happens—with faculty from humanities departments.

Going up Academy Boulevard was like traveling to some primal nexus of mystic patriotism, military service, and evangelical Christianity. I found myself worrying that the seminar I was about to lead—one week long, nearly twenty hours on one text—might create cognitive dissonance in this place, despite the fact that they, not I, had chosen the text. The Air Force Academy is not known for its dedication to literary study; what it has become known for over the past few years are a series of metastasizing scandals concerning religious harassment by evangelicals, cheating, and unpunished sexual assault. All this might put it in the same category as Brussels as represented in Conrad's book, a city that makes Marlow think of a "whited sepulchre," a phrase from the Gospel according to Matthew that applies to Pharisees, who "appear beautiful outward, but are within full of dead men's bones, and of all uncleanness."

The more I reflected on the upcoming seminar, the more starkly its Conradian implications stood out. Of course, to a Conradian, all situations are Conradian, but still, it cannot be denied that *Heart of Darkness* has an exceptional representational plasticity. So primal is the situation, so elemental the narrative form (up the river, down the river), so compellingly does the text capture the general theme of modernity-and-its-other, that there are, it sometimes seems, more metaphorical hearts of darkness in the world than any other body parts, or hearts of any other hue. Modernity generates hearts of darkness with an efficiency, and on a scale, that could only be called modern. Google "Heart of Darkness" and "Joseph Conrad" and you get fewer than four hundred thousand entries; leave off Conrad so that you are looking not for a text but a concept, and you get nearly 2 million. And the characters in the text are so iconic, and are presented with such hyperreal clarity—one at a time, with each occupying a segment of the text—that they seem almost allegories of some aspect of selfhood, like figures in *Pilgrim's Progress*. No matter who you are, you should be able to find yourself somewhere in *Heart of Darkness*.

In fact, you can probably find yourself in several places. Depending on the circumstances, you can float from one icon to another. One moment, you can feel yourself to be an African mistress, wild and free and full-bodied; but then, you discover, the kaleidoscope has turned a tiny bit, and you are actually the Intended—desiccated, deceived, betrayed, and pathetic. Or you could approach a given task in an uncommitted Marlovian spirit as a job involving a bit of adventure, with no historical or ideological burden at all—but then find that you are Kurtz, the exemplar of the horrors of modernity laid bare. This actually happens to Marlow, who finds, to his deep discomfiture, that he is insistently linked with Kurtz: the two of them, he hears, are both considered part of "the new gang—the gang of virtue."[1] Everything in the text has, it seems, a "heart" that both negates and expresses it.

So what was I at this moment, and what was my heart? I was an academic going to lead a seminar. An innocent undertaking—but what, precisely, was my job, in its deepest essence? Specifically, what was my relation to the war in which the nation, with the assistance of the Air Force Academy, was currently engaged? Was my real assignment to "humanize" the military, at a time when the conduct of the war was widely seen as degrading the nation that undertaken it? Which of us was the agent of enlightenment—the military that was hard at work creating the conditions of democracy in a distant land, or me? Was I supposed to "darken" the imperial mission by introducing doubt, fiction, language, and the exposure of ideology into a scene of unreflective patriotism? Did my small mission have a colonial character of its own? If so, how could I accomplish, excuse, or refuse it? Had this mission really been thought through? It seemed the best thing to do was just to keep driving up that road to the hotel, and go to bed.

And so, the following morning at 8:30 a.m. on a crystal-clear day in July, with questions thronging in my head, I took my seat in a clean but windowless room, along with eighteen members of the Academy faculty. They ranged from a sixty-eight-year-old senior professor, a civilian who had spent most of his distinguished career at Dartmouth and the University of Maryland, to an undergraduate cadet, with colonels, lieutenant colonels, majors, captains, and some civilian professors in between. They were in the unfamiliar but, for them, refreshing situation of being the "students," while I was in the unfamiliar and discomfiting situation of being addressed as "Sir" by uniformed personnel. Dissonance all around.

But a seminar is a seminar and so we began. This book, I said, is about someone who leaves the familiar world and ventures into the unknown. Conrad himself had done this, not just by going up the Congo River on a steamer, but by leaving Poland as a teenager and joining the French merchant marine. What, I asked, might motivate someone to do that?

In an American undergraduate classroom, this question might merely have served to get people talking, but since most people in the room would have chosen to go down the expected path, from one protected environment to another, the answers themselves might not have been particularly productive. The question would not have been understood as an invitation to talk about oneself. Here at the Academy, the question provoked a dozen or more narratives whose writers attempted to map Conrad's and Marlow's experiences onto their own decisions to join the military. Each one of the stories that unfurled had its own strikingly individual trajectory. The military might be a subculture in which "the individual" is regarded as an impediment to "trust" or "discipline," something to be broken down rather than fortified, but each person in the room had come to the military in his or her own way. The Academy had, for them, represented an honorable solution to some difficult problems, a bracing summons to patriotic duty, a way of carrying on a family tradition, a gateway to the world, a life of order and clarity, a way of experiencing managed risk, an opportunity to take pride in oneself, or simply a decent job. "I know exactly why I'm here," one said. "If I hadn't joined the military, I'd be driving a milk truck in Auburn, California." The seminar included those who themselves had graduated from the Academy, as well as those who had joined out of college, during the first Gulf War, at the invasion of Afghanistan, and more recently. Not all were from small towns, not all were escaping grinding poverty or lack of opportunity. In fact, the lone cadet in the seminar was a rogue debutante from North Carolina who had astonished her family by foregoing an easier life in favor of military service. All seemed to assume that *Heart of Darkness* was written by a man, Conrad, whom they could understand and who understood them; a man who escaped from unpromising circumstances by joining an institution with an honorable tradition of discipline and service; a man who, as a boy, had wanted to see the world. It was also, more pointedly, about a man, Marlow, who finds himself caught up in a much larger and different narrative than any he had foreseen. It was also about a man, Kurtz, whose commitment to discipline—"the discipline that makes the soldiers of a free country reliable in battle," as the inscription on the dormitory at the Academy reads—had failed. And it was about an imperial power pursuing an unworthy mission that is justified with rhetoric appealing to the highest universal values.

Like Conrad and Marlow, the members of the seminar were acutely aware of their own marginal status within the institution they had joined. As humanist professors, they represented the "academy" part of "military academy," Athens rather than Sparta, their task being to teach not engineering, aeronautics, or military strategy but literature, history, and philosophy. But their position on the edge of the main mission gave a certain edge to their comments. Professionally sensitive both to rhetoric and to danger, they were, I noticed, keenly aware of the powerful link between idealistic pronouncements made by high officials and violence visited on others, including themselves. The Norton edition we were using included a passage of soaring rhetoric attributed to Leopold II, the Belgian sovereign who administered the Congo as a personal possession, with an eye to maximum profit from ivory regardless of the human cost borne by Congolese natives.

In a passage titled "The Sacred Mission of Civilization," Leopold contended that "if, in view of this desirable spread of civilization, we count upon the means of action which confer upon us dominion and the sanction of right, it is not less true that our ultimate end is a work of peace" (119). A connection was immediately drawn to President Bush's 2003 Christmas message to American troops: "You are confronting terrorists abroad so that . . . people around the world can live in peace."² When military people hear talk of world peace, they prepare for deployment. "As Walter Benjamin said," a uniformed colonel commented (from out of the clear blue, it seemed to me), "there is no document of civilization that is not also a document of barbarism." In general, I began to realize, the participants in this seminar had a highly developed capacity for detecting connections between civilization and barbarism, idealism and violence. Again on the first day, someone asked what a gifted man like Kurtz was doing in the jungle. Someone else mentioned "the Intended," his fiancée back in Brussels; another noted the piano in her apartment, with its ivory keys. After a pause, one young captain, who had been entirely silent until then, ventured her first comment, and it was startling and decisive: "She killed him."

Having taught Conrad many times before, I found myself constantly bumped off balance by comments indicating, for example, considerable sympathy for Marlow as a man who finds himself on a mission more problematic than the one he had signed up for and who has to decide whether this new mission still commanded his loyalty; and even for Kurtz as a man sorely tested by extreme isolation and by the deep corruptness of the task he has been assigned. There was less sympathy for Edward Said or Chinua Achebe, authors of two critical texts also included in the Norton edition, texts that have been so firmly attached to Conrad's in American teaching practice that they almost seem part of it. Said had charged Conrad with an inability to imagine a state of affairs in which Europeans were not dominating Africans; Conrad, he said, could not "grant the natives their freedom."³ In American colleges and universities, this argument generally sweeps all opposition aside; here, it met resistance. "The natives don't want 'freedom,'" a captain said; "they just want the Belgians to go away. And freedom wouldn't be Conrad's to grant anyway." This critique seemed to be clinched when it was aligned with President Bush's description of liberty as "God's gift to humanity," a gift America was divinely charged with delivering.[4] Achebe's famous accusation that Conrad was racist[5] received a respectful hearing, but was ultimately dismissed on the grounds that "racism" in the modern sense did not exist in Conrad's day. It appeared that, from the seminar's point of view, both Said, a Palestinian, and Achebe, a Nigerian, were "too American" in their perspectives.

Shortly after we reached this comfortable affirmation of the superiority of creative artists over critics, however, we hit a snag. I had wanted to talk about how Marlow insistently turns things inside out. The first instance occurs in his very first words, when he gestures upriver toward the English heartland and says, "This, too, has been one of the dark places of the earth." Again and again, I noted, Marlow casually offers his listeners a thought-experiment involving a total reversal of present circumstances. Another example would be his explanation of the curious fact that his party encountered no natives on their two-hundred-mile tramp to the Central Station. I read the passage: "Well if a lot of mysterious niggers armed with all kinds of fearful weapons suddenly took to traveling on the road between Deal and Gravesend catching the yokels right and left to carry heavy loads for them, I fancy every farm and cottage thereabouts would get empty very soon."[6] On this day, Wednesday, we had another participant, a young black woman who was only able to attend this one session. She had been looking attentively at me, but at this point she stared down at the book and did not look up for another hour, until the session ended. Two days later, I spotted her at the end of a hallway during one of our breaks, but wasn't able to make contact, and never saw her again. Conrad presents such difficulties. Once, some years ago, I was phoning the university bookstore, ordering that semester's texts, including *The Nigger of the "Narcissus."* "The ... Nigger ... of ... the ... 'Narcissus,'" the bookstore employee repeated very slowly as she wrote it down, with, I thought, a certain accusatory emphasis.

The distance between the past horrors of the Congo Free State and the enlightened politics of the present day in America had in a sense made things easy for us. The morality of the case may have troubled Marlow, but after a century of universal condemnation of Leopold's administration, it did not trouble us: the issue was settled. The pastness of the past, and the consolidation of history's judgment, can have an anesthetic effect on discussion. On the last day, however, the anesthesia wore off as we took up Coppola's *Apocalypse Now*, which translates *Heart of Darkness* into terms that American military people could understand immediately. On this day, the conversation, which had been so free, candid, and direct, became stressed and troubled. In an undergraduate classroom, the discussion might center on Brando's Kurtz; here, it fastened immediately and almost exclusively on Robert Duvall's Lieutenant Colonel Kilgore, an Army officer (First Squadron, Ninth Cavalry) who, in a famous scene, leads a helicopter attack on a Vietnamese beach village, with speakers blaring Wagner's *Ride of the Valkyries*. Weathering Viet Cong mortars and machine gun fire, he wipes out the village and lands Willard (Martin Sheen) on the river so he can hunt Kurtz down. Mission accomplished, Kilgore adds a gratuitous napalm strike ("I love the smell of napalm in the morning") that improves the surfing. The helicopters, like the playing cards Kilgore places on the corpses of his victims, bear the motto "Death from Above."

In ways the participants appreciated, Kilgore is an excellent officer. He has, as Willard notes, a "weird light around him. You just knew he wasn't gonna get so much as a scratch here." He is devoted to his men and has earned their trust. Under him, they feel motivated and safe. And yet, as one of the women in the seminar pointed out, he deliberately chooses to land at a place he knows to be defended in preference to another location where there is no surfing, and loses both men and equipment as a consequence. And while he is a passionate surfer, he kills with a disturbing indifference. Is there a problem? The nation is at war, and some of the Vietnamese, at least—hard to tell which—have the means and the motivation to kill Americans. What did we think of Kilgore?

As a way of approaching, or avoiding, this question, we took up the issue of "Death from Above," which is, after all, what the Air Force is all about. In one sense, a colonel said, death from above is easier and cleaner to inflict than "grime on the ground" (the Army's job), because there is greater distance between one's action, in a plane or a missile silo, and its consequences. A young female captain noted that more imagination is required for the airman to grasp what he or she is doing—but, she seemed to imply, because of the increased risk, almost a certainty in some cases, of civilian casualties, there is a greater shock to the conscience for those who do grasp it. That kind of shock is not good: you can, as one put it, lose your mojo and become tentative, doubtful, or uncommitted, placing yourself and others at greater risk.

About one-third of all Air Force personnel have been to Iraq in recent years, but I was reluctant to ask whether any in the room had actually dropped or launched weapons. When they spoke, they focused on training missions. A lieutenant colonel recalled being trained to turn the key that would launch a missile from a silo. When she subsequently visited Moscow, it struck her that if that training session had been real and the target had been Moscow, everything around her would be toxic rubble. A captain to her left noted that the key used in training was not spring-loaded like the real key, and had a different feel—no tension to it. There was a pause while people considered the difference. Another recalled sending a man whose wife had just given birth to twins on a dangerous assignment because he had been ordered to send "the most qualified person available," a decision that still troubled him over twenty years later. He did not say whether the man returned, but he did note that the officer who took his place in that decision-making position committed suicide two months after returning home.

Diverted into channels of personal reflections, the conversation seemed to be losing its way, in search of the main current. There were longer pauses between comments—greater depth but sluggish progress, albeit with moments of sudden clarity emerging from the fog. After nearly an hour circling around Kilgore, a lieutenant colonel with a Ph.D. in English from the University of Michigan (dissertation on Seamus Heaney's treatment of violence) and a refugee from the milk trucks of Auburn, California, broke the silence by saying—as I recall—the following: "I wear this uniform because I believe that, in the end, our way of life is better than any other at defending the *sanctity of the individual.* My understanding of history teaches me that violence is always going to be part of human existence, and my moral sense says that managed violence, in the service of the right principles, is better than the alternatives. What we try to do here . . . is train . . . *reluctant killers.* We teach them how to do things that will haunt them for the rest of their lives. That's what we do. We stand there in front of our cadets, and we train them to do things they would never do if the nation didn't ask it of them. And even though the nation asks it, and no matter how disciplined they are, they will still be haunted by what they've done. And they have to be. If they aren't, then we've only trained Kilgores, murderers without a conscience."

After a long silence during which we all stared at the table, we took a break.

The humanities have been the subject of an immense quantity of elevated rhetoric. Distinguished people have described and defended the need for a national investment in teaching and research in literary studies, history, philosophy, and the arts. I have read many of these testimonials and have written some myself. I do not recall seeing this particular approach taken before. But this statement grasped the nettle with a boldness that grew in the mind during that long silence, and thereafter.

What are the humanities about if not the cultivation of an informed conscience, a habit of reflection in which the flow of thoughtless action and means-end calculation is interrupted by a consideration of historical contexts and ethical concerns, by an imaginative awareness of the character and consequences of action, by a deep investment in the human condition and its possibilities? If those with such knowledge and such capacities do not assume some kind of responsibility for worldly action, including the management of violence, then that responsibility passes to the Kilgores, and the Kurtzes, of the world.

Even those who serve in the military do not always, much less naturally, think in these terms. Hard training is required in order to achieve an understanding so deeply counterintuitive. What this training inculcates is not simply competence in destruction but the proper attitude to have toward it. The stated mission of the English Department at the Air Force Academy includes instilling in cadets "an appreciation for the culture they've promised to defend,"[7] even as they carry out the violence that culture occasionally requires. Insofar as humanistic study imbues people with a moral imagination, the real burden of the humanities, as opposed to their manifold pleasures and benefits, does not fall on professors, students, or the culture-loving population in general. That burden is allocated to those whom society charges with the conscience-testing task of sanctioned killing. In a democracy with a volunteer military, the weight falls on that small number of people who have chosen to bear it by enlisting. For them it is, as Marlow puts it, always "a choice of nightmares." For the rest of us, the key is never spring-loaded, the flights are all simulated.

We had spent a good deal of time over the course of the week talking about the ways that honorable people get ensnared in and somehow committed to large patterns of action that they would not, if given the option, choose or approve of. Marlow continually remarks on how insistently he is identified with the ivory trade, Belgian rapacity, and Kurtz. It struck me on this final day that despite never having worn a uniform, I was now part of the American military mission, part of homeland defense, even of Operation Iraqi Freedom. My honorarium had been approved by the Pentagon (I was a very small unit in the Wide Area Workflow), which expected me to provide professional development for those whose job was, in a sense, to produce warriors who would kill with an attitude worthy of a morally enlightened democracy committed to the principle of the sanctity of the individual. This mission was implicitly informed by the conviction that a conscience with the capacity to be deeply disturbed, even traumatized, is a precious thing, an indicator of democratic principles and ethical values.

In a culture whose commitment to the freedom of the individual often seems to begin with the freedom from guilt, the military perspective on the humanities is well worth pondering.

Postscript

After I had written this piece, one of the seminar participants, Lieutenant Colonel Thomas C. McGuire of Auburn, California, wrote his own account of the seminar, "War, Literature, the Constitution, and Fostering Reluctant Killers."[8] In it, he speaks of how, in teaching his own courses in the Air Force Academy, he invariably seeks to show how war both squanders human beings and draws from them, or some of them, "palliative and redemptive works of wartime art." He does so by tracking, for example, the "formal and stylistic innovations inspired by the experience of trench warfare" in the work of Wilfred Owen in order to enable the cadets in his class "to know and appreciate the ingenuity and resourcefulness of human beings *in extremis*, ordinary people caught up in deadly conflict who find ways to enlist creativity in the service of survival and transcendence" (ibid., 28). McGuire recalls words spoken by Major General John Borling, a six-year Vietnam POW, who, when asked to name the most important courses he had taken as an Air Force Academy cadet, said without hesitation, "Humanities courses—art history, music appreciation, literature, introductory philosophy." These, Borling said, were the courses that "cultivated seeds of hope and put [one] in touch with the centuries-long development of an intellectual tradition that contains essential, life-giving wisdom—a body of knowledge that provided a reason to persevere and survive the hell of captivity and torture. And so," McGuire concludes in words that will also provide my conclusion, "I strive in my teaching and research to share with cadets the rich trove of existential and moral insight offered by the humanities. The humanities keep us honest and human, reminding us of our capacity for committing unspeakable violence and of our ability to outface brutality through the transformative power of art" (29).

Notes

INTRODUCTION

1. See Geoffrey Green, *Literary Criticism and the Structures of History: Erich Auerbach and Leo Spitzer* (Lincoln: University of Nebraska Press, 1983).

2. On "comparative literature," see Emily Apter, *The Translation Zone: A New Comparative Literature* (Princeton, NJ: Princeton University Press, 2006), chapter 3, "Global Translation: The 'Invention' of Comparative Literature, Istanbul, 1933," 41–64. For a closer focus on Spitzer, see chapter 2 of Apter, "The Human and the Humanities," 25–40.

3. Steven Marcus, "Humanities from Classics to Cultural Studies: Notes Toward the History of an Idea," *Daedalus* 135, no. 2 (Spring 2006): 15–21; quotation is from p. 19.

4. Literary study's claim to being the "purest" or most humanistic of the humanities disciplines rests on the fact that it is the discipline most strongly committed to the mixing of human labor—judgment, evaluation, and interpretation—with the object. But there can be no question of purity or priority in the discipline: all the humanistic disciplines are either dependent on the others or on empirical methods most often associated with the sciences.

5. Francis Oakley, *Community of Learning: The American College and the Liberal Arts Tradition* (New York: Oxford University Press, 1992). See especially 39–72.

6. Bruce Kimball, *Orators and Philosophers: A History of the Idea of Higher Education* (New York: Teachers College Press, 1986).

7. Vannevar Bush, *Science—The Endless Frontier. A Report to the President by Vannevar Bush, Director of the Office of Scientific Research and Development, July 1945*, online at http://www.nsf.gov/about/history/vbush1945.htm (accessed April 21, 2010). Bush's epic report laid the foundation for "endless," i.e., peacetime, federal funding of scientific research as a national priority, thereby shifting responsibility for research from the military to the universities.

8. Matthew Arnold, *Culture and Anarchy: An Essay in Political and Social Criticism* (New York: Macmillan, 1883), chapter 1, pp. 6–7; quoted in Oakley, *Community of Learning*, 57–58.

9. Matthew Arnold, "Literature and Science," in *Discourses in America* (New York: Macmillan, 1902), 72–137; quotation is from p. 129.

10. John Henry Newman, *The Idea of the University*, ed. Frank M. Turner (New Haven, CT: Yale University Press, 1996), 3.

11. A. L. Rowse, *All Souls in My Time* (London: Duckworth, 1993), 44; quoted in Henk Wesseling, "The Idea of an Institute for Advanced Study: Reflections on Science, Art, and Education," Uhlenbeck Lecture 20, given June 14, 2002 (Wassenaar: The Netherlands Institute for Advanced Study in the Humanities and Social Sciences, 2002), 14.

12. For an account of the division within literary studies between "scholars" and "critics," see Gerald Graff, *Professing Literature: An Institutional History* (Chicago: University of Chicago Press, 1987), 121–44; for a more detailed account of the "Chicago Plan" instituted by Robert Maynard Hutchins and Mortimer Adler, see 163–67.

13. Patricia Beesley, *The Revival of the Humanities in American Education* (New York: Columbia University Press, 1940), 3.

14. Marcus, "Humanities from Classics to Cultural Studies," 17.

15. Norman Foerster, ed., *Humanism and America: Essays on the Outlook of Modern Civilisation* (Port Washington, NY: Kennikat Press, 1930). See also J. David Hoeveler, *The New Humanism: A Critique of Modern America, 1900–1940* (Charlottesville: University of Virginia Press, 1977).

16. David A. Hollinger, introduction to *The Humanities and the Dynamics of Inclusion since World War II*, ed. David A. Hollinger (Baltimore: Johns Hopkins University Press, 2006), 1–22; quotation is from p. 5. For an account of the era following World War I, see Graff, *Professing Literature*, 128–32. And for a probing account of "The Humanities Revolution"—actually two revolutions, one toward disinterestedness and disciplinarity and a second toward multiculturalism and interdisciplinarity—following the end of WWII, see Louis Menand, *The Mar-*

ketplace of Ideas: Reform and Resistance in the American University (New York: W. W. Norton, 2010), 59–92.

17. As far back as 1938, one commentator bemoaned the fact that "the humanities are attacked everywhere . . . they are losing ground every day." Gilbert Chinard, "Literature and the Humanities," in *The Meaning of the Humanities: Five Essays*, by Ralph Barton Perry, August Charles Krey, Erwin Panofsky, Robert Lowry Calhoun, and Gilbert Chinard; edited by Theodore Meyer Greene (Princeton, NJ: Princeton University Press, 1938), 151–70; quotation is from p. 153.

CHAPTER 1

1. Louis Menand, "The Marketplace of Ideas," American Council of Learned Societies Occasional Paper, no. 49 (2001); http://www.acls.org/op49.htm (accessed April 24, 2010).

2. Commission on the Humanities in American Life, *The Humanities in American Life* (Berkeley and Los Angeles: University of California Press, 1980), 2.

3. Richard Lanham, *The Electronic Word: Democracy, Technology, and the Arts* (Chicago: University of Chicago Press, 1993), 228.

4. Carla Hesse, "Humanities and the Library in the Digital Age," in *What's Happened to the Humanities?* ed. Alvin Kernan (Princeton, NJ: Princeton University Press, 1997), 107–21; quotation is from p. 112 (hereafter cited in text).

5. Quoted in *The Humanities in American Life*, 2.

6. The authors of *The Humanities in American Life* note that, traditionally, the humanities were defined as "languages and literatures, history, and philosophy." But the 1964 report by the Commission on the Humanities added the arts as well as "the history and comparison of religion and the law" and "those aspects of the social sciences which have humanistic content and employ humanistic methods." When the National Endowment for the Humanities was created in 1965, on the plan laid out in this report, the legislation authorizing it added linguistics, archeology, and ethics (p. 2).

7. Michael Ondaatje, *The English Patient* (New York: Vintage, 1992), 192.

8. Arnold Davidson, ed., *Foucault and His Interlocutors* (Chicago: University of Chicago Press, 1997), 107–45 (hereafter cited in text).

9. Ernst Cassirer, *An Essay on Man* (New Haven, CT: Yale University Press, 1944), 62.

10. Gustave Flaubert, *Madame Bovary*, ed. and trans. Paul de Man (New York: W. W. Norton, 1965), 59 (hereafter cited in text).

11. Gustave Flaubert, quoted in *De l'intelligence*, by Hippolyte Taine, 2 vols. (1870); quoted in Roger Shattuck, "'Think Like a Demigod,'" *New York Review of Books*, June 13, 2002, 27.

CHAPTER 2

1. Edward Said, *Humanism and Democratic Criticism* (New York: Columbia University Press, 2004), 61 (citations hereafter *HDC* and given in text); de Man, "The Return to Philology," in *The Resistance to Theory*, Theory and History of Literature, vol. 33 (Minneapolis: University of Minnesota Press, 1986), 3–26; quotation is from p. 23 (citations hereafter *RP* and given in text).

2. See Edward Said, *Beginnings: Intention and Method* (Baltimore: Johns Hopkins University Press, 1978), 6–8, 68–70, 366–67. On other occasions, Said attacked the discipline, especially as practiced in the nineteenth century, for its orientalizing ideology. See Edward Said, *Orientalism*, 2nd ed. (New York: Vintage Books, 1994), 130–48, and "Islam, Philology, and French Culture: Renan and Massignon," in *The World, the Text, and the Critic* (Cambridge, MA: Harvard University Press, 1983), 268–89. For an informative discussion of Said and philology, see Tim Brennan, "Places of Mind, Occupied Lands: Edward Said and Philology," in *Edward Said: A Critical Reader*, ed. Michael Sprinker (Oxford: Blackwell, 1992), 74–95.

3. For a detailed account of Wolf's debt to J. G. Eichhorn's work on the Old Testament, see Anthony Grafton, Glen W. Most, and James E. G. Zetzel, introduction to *F. A. Wolf: Prolegomena to Homer, 1795, Translated, with Introduction and Notes*, trans. Anthony Grafton, Glen W. Most, and James E. G. Zetzel (Princeton, NJ: Princeton University Press, 1985), 18–26.

4. As James Engell and Anthony Dangerfield note, "In Germany . . . it was the humanities and not the sciences that first introduced, in the earlier nineteenth century, rigorous empirical methods." *Saving Higher Education in the Age of Money* (Charlottesville: University of Virginia Press, 2005), 97.

5. Roy Harris, "History and Comparative Philology," in *Language and History: Integrationist Perspectives*, ed. Nigel Love (London: Routledge, 2006), 41–59; quotation is from p. 57. For a history of academic asceticism stressing the charisma of Wolf and the discipline of philology,

see William Clark, *Academic Charisma and the Origins of the Research University* (Chicago: University of Chicago Press, 2006).

6. Ihor Ševcenko, quoted in Jan Ziolkowski, "'What is Philology?' Introduction," in *What is Philology?* ed. Jan Ziolkowski (University Park: Penn State University Press, 1990), 6.

7. See Gerald Graff, *Professing Literature: An Institutional History* (Chicago: University of Chicago Press, 1987), 28–41, 67–69.

8. Friedrich Nietzsche, preface to *Daybreak: Thoughts on the Prejudices of Morality*, ed. Maudemarie Clark and Brian Leiter, Cambridge Texts in the History of Philosophy, no. 5 (Cambridge: Cambridge University Press, 1997), 5. See also Friedrich Nietzsche, "We Philologists," in "Nietzsche: Notes for 'We Philologists,'" ed. and trans. William Arrowsmith, *Arion*, n.s., 1/2 (1973/74): 279–380; quotation is from p. 281; and Friedrich Nietzsche, "Homer and Classical Philology," in *On the Future of Our Educational Institutions/Homer and Classical Philology*, trans. J. M. Kennedy (Edinburgh: T. N. Foulis, 1909), 145–70; online at http://www.gutenberg.org/etext/18188 (accessed April 24, 2010). See also William Arrowsmith, "Nietzsche on Classics and Classicists (Part II)," *Arion* 2 (1963): 5–27.

9. Walter Rüegg details the contribution of the neohumanist movement to the development of the "human sciences" in Germany, pointing out that Germans sought to retrieve Greek civilization in part as a deliberate contrast with the French fascination with ancient Rome. "Rhetoric and Anti-Rhetoric in the Nineteenth- and Twentieth-Century Human Sciences in Germany," in *Persuasive Discourse and Disciplinarity in the Human Sciences*, ed. R. H. Roberts and J. M. M. Good (Charlottesville: University of Virginia Press, 1993), 87–100.

10. Lionel Gossman, "Philhellenism and Antisemitism: Matthew Arnold and His German Models," *Comparative Literature* 46, no. 1 (1994): 1–39; quotation is from p. 13; see also Suzanne L. Marchand, *Down from Olympus: Archeology and Philhellenism in German* (Princeton, NJ: Princeton University Press, 2003), and Nicholas Rand, "The Political Truth of Heidegger's 'Logos': Hiding in Translation," *PMLA* 105 (1990): 437–47.

11. Grafton, Most, and Zetzel, *F. A. Wolf*, 45–46.

12. Ibid., 233; emphasis in the original.

13. Wilhelm von Humboldt, *On Language: On the Diversity of Human Language Construction and Its Influence on the Mental Development of the Human Species*, ed. Michael Losensky, trans. Peter Heath

(Cambridge: Cambridge University Press, 1999), 21. For an authoritative account of the "languages and nations project" of the eighteenth and nineteenth centuries, an attempt to discover the deep history of nations through the genealogies of their languages, see Thomas R. Trautman, *Aryans and British India* (Berkeley and Los Angeles: University of California Press, 1997).

14. Ernest Renan, *The Future of Science* (Boston: Roberts Brothers, 1891), 131, 128; emphasis in the original. Originally published as *L'Avenir de la science: Pensées de 1848* (Paris: Calmann-Lévy).

15. Said, *Orientalism*, 131, 132.

16. Max Müller, *Lectures on the Science of Language*, 2 vols. (1864; London: Routledge/Thoemmes Press, 1994), 2:14. Unless otherwise noted, subsequent citations are to this edition.

17. "The History of Modern Philology," *New Englander and Yale Review* 16, no. 63 (1858): 465–510; quotation is from p. 506; online at http://memory.loc.gov/cgi-bin/query/r?ammem/ncps:@field(DOCID +@lit(ABQ0722-0016-75)) (accessed April 24, 2010). In addition to scientific exhibits, museums also held the treasures of imperial conquest, a fact that was occasionally noted in the discourse of philology. In one of the most telling moments in his discussion of Renan in *Orientalism*, Said noted that philology placed the scholar in the position of the European expert delivering to a European audience the exotic fruits of foreign adventures, surveying "as if from a peculiarly suited vantage point the passive, seminal, feminine, even silent and supine East, then going on to *articulate* the East, making the Orient deliver up its secrets" (138; emphasis in the original).

18. Sir William Jones, "Third Anniversary Discourse of the President of the Royal Asiatick Society ('On the Hindus')," in *On Language: Plato to von Humboldt*, ed. E. Peter A. Salus (New York: Holt, Rinehart, and Winston, 1969), 167–72.

19. Tomoko Masuzawa, *The Invention of World Religions; Or, How European Universalism Was Preserved in the Language of Pluralism* (Chicago: University of Chicago Press, 2005), 147–48.

20. Franz Bopp, *A Comparative Grammar of the Sanskrit, Zend, Greek, Latin, Lithuanian, Gothic, German and Sclavonic Languages*, trans. Lt. Edward B. Eastwick, vol. 1 (n.p.: Bopp Press, 2007); originally published in Berlin, 1833.

21. Gossman, "Philhellenism and Antisemitism," 6–8.

22. Friedrich Schlegel, *On the Language and Wisdom of the Indians*,

in *The Aesthetic and Miscellaneous Works of Friedrich von Schlegel*, ed. and trans. E. J. Millington (1808; London: Henry G. Bohn, 1849), 451.

23. "Early Writings of Charles Darwin," in H. E. Gruber, *Darwin on Man: A Psychological Study of Scientific Creativity; Together with Darwin's Early and Unpublished Notebooks*, ed. H. E. Gruber, transcribed and annotated by Paul H. Barrett, with a foreword by Jean Piaget (London: Wildwood House, 1974), 383.

24. Others were also urging Darwin to think of linguistic analogies. His cousin Hensleigh Wedgwood wrote to him in 1857, saying, "I have often thought that there is much resemblance between language & geology in another way. We all consider English a very mixed language because we can trace the elements into Latin, German &c. but I see much the same sort of thing in Latin itself & I believe that if we were but acquainted with the previous state of things we should find all languages made up of the debris of former tongues just as every geological formation is the grinding down of former continents"; "To Darwin from Hensleigh Wedgwood, before September 29, 1857," in *The Correspondence of Charles Darwin*, vol. 6, 1856–1857, ed. Frederick Burckhardt and Sydney Smith (Cambridge: Cambridge University Press, 1990), 458.

25. Charles Darwin, *On the Origin of Species by Means of Natural Selection* (New York: P. F. Collier and Son, 1909), 53, 459. For an illuminating account of the roughly simultaneous emergence of evolutionary thinking in linguistics (Schleicher) and in biology (Darwin), see Robert J. Richards, "The Linguistic Creation of Man: Charles Darwin, August Schleicher, Ernst Haeckel, and the Missing Link in 19th-Century Evolutionary Theory," in *Experimenting in Tongues: Studies in Science and Language*, ed. Matthew Dörries (Stanford, CA: Stanford University Press, 2002), 21–48; and, particularly, Stephen G. Alter, *Darwinism and the Linguistic Image: Language, Race, and Natural Theology in the Nineteenth Century* (Baltimore: Johns Hopkins University Press, 1999), a commanding and efficient discussion of a complex phenomenon.

26. Charles Darwin, *The Descent of Man and Selection in Relation to Sex*, 2nd ed. (New York: D. Appleton & Co., 1909), 92.

27. August Schleicher, *Die Darwinsche Theorie und die Sprachwissenschaft* (Weimar: Böhlau, 1863). On Schleicher, see Liba Taub, "Evolutionary Ideas and Empirical Methods: The Analogy between Language and Species in Works by Lyell and Schleicher," *British Journal for the History of Science* 26 (1993): 171–93; Alter, *Darwinism and the Linguistic*

Image, 73–79; and Robert J. Richards, *The Meaning of Evolution: The Morphological Construction and Ideological Reconstruction of Darwin's Theory* (Chicago: University of Chicago Press, 1992).

28. Max Müller, *Lectures on the Science of Language*, 1st ser. (London: Green, Longman, and Roberts, 1861), 368; emphasis in the original. To be sure, Müller, a devout Christian, had his limits, and regarded Darwinism as both ally and threat. Preempting the argument that Darwin would make in *The Descent of Man*, Müller wrote in 1863 that "it is not any accidental variety that survives and perpetuates itself," but "the individual which comes nearest to the original intention of its creator, or what is best calculated to accomplish the ends for which the type or species to which it belongs was called into being, that conquers in the great struggle for life." *Lectures on the Science of Language Delivered at the Royal Institute of Great Britain in February, March, April, and May 1863*, 2nd ser. (New York: Charles Scribner's Sons, 1890; originally published 1864), 323. Müller drew an even more emphatically bright line where the evolution of humanity from primates was concerned, using language as proof of its impossibility. "Language is our Rubicon," he declared in a memorable phrase, "and no brute will dare to cross it." Ibid., 340.

29. Alter, *Darwinism and the Linguistic Image*, 7.

30. Ernst Haeckel, *The History of Creation*, trans. Sir E. Ray Lankester, 2 vols. (New York: Appleton, 1925; originally published 1868).

31. "Man-like Apes," ibid., 2:398; "highest authorities," 2:408; "real and principal," 2:410.

32. Ernst Haeckel, *The Evolution of Man*, 2 vols. (New York: D. Appleton and Company, 1896; originally published 1874), 2:20.

33. Haeckel, *History of Creation*, 2:429.

34. See Stefan Arvidsson, *Aryan Idols: The Indo-European Mythology as Science and Ideology* (Chicago: University of Chicago Press, 2006); Leon Poliakov, *The Aryan Myth: A History of Racist and Nationalistic Ideas in Europe* (1974; reprint, New York: Barnes and Noble Books, 1996); Thomas R. Trautman, ed., *The Aryan Debate* (New Delhi: Oxford University Press, 2005); and Kenneth A. R. Kennedy, *God-Apes and Fossil Men: Paleoanthropology of South Asia* (Ann Arbor: University of Michigan Press, 2000), 80–85. The thesis, articulated by Müller and other philologists, of an "Aryan invasion" of India around 1500 BC has recently been contested on the basis of the discovery of a genetic similarity between the darker inhabitants of southern India and the more light-skinned (presumably "Aryan") inhabitants of northern India. For

a review of genetic evidence that the Central Asian "invasion" happened much earlier than philological evidence would suggest, around 9000 BC, see S. Sahoo et al., "A Prehistory of Indian Y Chromosomes: Evaluating Demic Diffusion Scenarios," *PNAS* [*Proceedings of the National Academy of Sciences of the United States of America*] 103, no. 4 (2006): 843–48; and T. Kivisild et al., "Deep Common Ancestry of Indian and Western-Eurasian Mitochondrial DNA Lineages," *Current Biology* 9, no. 22 (1999): 1331–34. For an authoritative, indeed perhaps final, demonstration that the Proto-Indo-European language originated on the steppes of Central Asia, see David W. Anthony, *The Horse, the Wheel, and Language: How Bronze-Age Riders from the Eurasian Steppes Shaped the Modern World* (Princeton, NJ: Princeton University Press, 2008).

35. Bruce Lincoln, *Theorizing Myth: Narrative, Ideology, and Scholarship* (Chicago: University of Chicago Press, 1999), 95.

36. Joseph Arthur Comte de Gobineau, *The Inequality of Human Races* (1853–55; New York: Howard Fertig, 1999), 182–204.

37. See Müller, *Lectures*, 1:329–78, especially 327 for the "original pair."

38. Ibid., 1:12. An illustration that approximates Müller's description, and may have been the original of the image to which he referred, is in Josiah Clark Nott and George R. Gliddon, *Types of Mankind; or, Ethnological Researches, Based upon the Ancient Monuments, Paintings, Sculptures, and Crania of Races, Based on the inedited papers of Samuel George Morton*, 8th ed. (1854; Philadelphia: Lippincott & Co., 1857), 459, where the "Hottentot" is placed suggestively next to the "orang-outan" in a series of images of human (and animal) "types." In the text, the authors argue that the Negro stands at the lowest margin of humanity, just above the primates. This book may have come to Müller's attention because, in the course of arguing for ineradicable racial differences at the origin of humankind, the authors complain bitterly about the efforts of philologists to trace existing languages back to a single *Ursprache*, insisting on "that radical diversity of languages which philology has not yet been able to overcome" (285). For them, the decisive evidence of fundamental difference was that while the Negro might learn many languages, he still "preserves that peculiar, unmistakeably-*Negro*, intonation, which no culture can eradicate" (282; emphasis in the original). Among his other accomplishments, Nott translated Gobineau's *Essay* into English.

39. For a detailed account of W. D. Whitney's sustained and largely

successful assault on Müller's credentials as a linguist, see Linda Dowling, "Victorian Oxford and the Science of Language," *PMLA* 97, no. 2 (1982): 160–78.

40. See Maurice Olender, *The Languages of Paradise: Race, Religion, and Philology in the Nineteenth Century*, trans. Arthur Goldhammer (Cambridge, MA: Harvard University Press, 1992); on Müller in particular, see 82–105 passim, especially 88–92. Müller rejected the theory of the evolution of humankind from primates, declaring that "language is our Rubicon, and no brute will dare to cross it" (*Lectures*, 1:340). Still, he corresponded with Darwin (see *Darwin Correspondence Project*, online at http://www.darwinproject.ac.uk/darwins-letters [accessed April 24, 2010]), and on several occasions in his *Lectures on the Science of Language*, he accounted for linguistic change by referring to Darwinian principles. The fact that ancient languages display a superabundance of synonyms when compared to more modern languages, for example, seemed to him evidence of "natural selection" or a "*struggle for life* . . . which led to the destruction of the less strong, the less happy, the less fertile words, and ended in the triumph of *one*, as the recognised and proper name for every object in every language" (*Lectures*, 1:368; emphasis in the original). Müller rejected not natural selection or competition but rather the idea that these forces might result in a transformed species, an idea that in fact played a large role in the subsequent development of "scientific racism." See Ivan Hannaford, *Race: The History of an Idea in the West* (Baltimore: Woodrow Wilson Center Press, 1996), and Elazar Barkan, *The Retreat of Scientific Racism: Changing Concepts of Race in Britain and the United States between the World Wars* (New York: Cambridge University Press, 1992), 54–57, 137–76.

41. Max Müller, "Translator's Preface," *Immanuel Kant's "Critique of Pure Reason"* (London: Macmillan, 1881), v–lxii; quotations are from pp. lxi, lxii. Despite his enlightened views in many areas, Müller was a man of his times, capable of explaining, for example, German anti-Semitism as an understandable reaction to Jewish financial success. See Max Müller, *My Autobiography: A Fragment* (New York: Charles Scribner's Sons, 1901), 69–70.

42. Ernest Renan, *Till the Time of King David*, vol. 1 of *History of the People of Israel* (Boston: Roberts Brothers, 1892), 39, 13.

43. Ibid., 1:2–3. On one occasion at least, Renan conceded that a linguistic "mould" could improve the thoughts of lesser creatures who learned a second language. In his otherwise antidemocratic closet

drama *Caliban*, Renan has Ariel say to Caliban, "Prospero taught thee the Aryan language, and with that divine tongue the channel of reason has become inseparable from thee." Ernest Renan, *Caliban: A Philosophical Drama Continuing "The Tempest" of William Shakespeare*, trans. Eleanor Grant Vickery (New York: Shakespeare Press, 1896), 18.

44. Renan, *History*, 1:40.

45. Ibid., 21; Ernest Renan, *From the Time of Hezekiah Till the Return from Babylon*, vol. 3 of *History of the People of Israel* (Boston: Roberts Brothers, 1891), xiii; Renan, *From the Reign of David up to the Capture of Samaria*, vol. 2 of *History of the People of Israel* (Boston: Roberts Brothers, 1892), 444.

46. Renan, *History*, 1:7.

47. Renan, *History*, 3:xiii, 2:444; Ernest Renan, *Period of Jewish Independence and Judea under Roman Rule*, vol. 5 of *History of the People of Israel* (Boston: Roberts Brothers, 1895), 355.

48. See Olender, *Languages of Paradise*, 57–63. See Olender 55–81 for a full account of Renan's understanding of the distinction between Aryan and Semitic languages.

49. Ernest Renan, *Questions contemporaines*, vol. 1 of *Oeuvres complètes de Ernest Renan*, ed. Henriette Psichari (Paris: Calmann-Lévy, 1868), 390. My translation.

50. See Ernest Renan, *Dialogues philosophiques* (Paris: Calmann-Lévy, 1876), 117–20.

51. Matthew Arnold, *Culture and Anarchy*, ed. J. Dover Wilson (Cambridge: Cambridge University Press, 1969); online at http://www.library.utoronto.ca/utel/nonfiction_u/arnoldm_ca/ca_all.html (accessed April 24, 2010).

52. Matthew Arnold, "A Speech at Eton," in *The Complete Prose Works of Matthew Arnold*, ed. R. H. Super (Ann Arbor: University of Michigan Press, 1961), 9:28–29; quotation is from p. 29. See also Gossman, "Philhellenism and Antisemitism," 21.

53. Matthew Arnold, *On the Study of Celtic Literature* and *On Translating Homer* (New York: Macmillan, 1883); online at http://www.sacred-texts.com/neu/celt/scl/index.htm (accessed April 24, 2010).

54. See Müller, *Lectures*, 1:223–36.

55. Ernest Renan, *The Poetry of the Celtic Races and Other Studies* (Port Washington, NY: Kennikat Press, 1896), 4; online at http://www.bartleby.com/32/302.html (accessed April 24, 2010). Renan linked purity with femininity, describing the Celts as "an essentially feminine

race. . . . No other has conceived with more delicacy the ideal of woman, or been more fully dominated by it. It is a sort of intoxication, a madness, a vertigo" (8). Celts appeared particularly feminine when compared to the English, whose very language was, to some, the essence of manliness. "There is," the Danish linguist Otto Jesperson said, "one expression that continually comes to my mind whenever I think of the English language," namely, that it is "positively and expressly *masculine*." *Growth and Structure of the English Language* (1905; reprint, New York: Appleton and Company, 1931), 3.

56. Houston Stewart Chamberlain, *The Foundations of the Nineteenth Century*, 2nd ed. (London: Bodley Head, 1912); originally published as *Die Grundlagen des neuntzehnten Jahrhunderts* (Munich: F. Bruckmann A.-G., 1899).

57. Christopher M. Hutton, *Linguistics and the Third Reich: Mother-Tongue Fascism, Race, and the Science of Language* (London: Routledge, 1988). Hutton argues that while the 1933–45 period is generally taken as an aberration in the honorable history of philological scholarship, much of what was said and done in the fields of historical Indo-European philology as well as in descriptive "structuralist" linguistics during this period had its seed in earlier, well-respected and established disciplinary practice (260–61). Philology is not alone among scholarly disciplines in having been susceptible to ideological overdetermination, but it is distinctive in that many of its most distinguished figures can, from another perspective, be seen as mere ideologues who prostituted their discipline by subordinating it to external and, in retrospect, deeply sinister ends. One of the most poignant testimonies in this regard is that of Bruce Lincoln, who writes of his early training, when he encountered the work of a number of eminent and otherwise admirable scholars who were, as it happened, deeply involved with the Nazi movement.

To that side of their work, however, I was largely blind. Instead of dangerous ideologues, I saw talented linguists, erudite Orientalists (a word not yet suspect), and trailblazing students of myth. Whatever questions I had—and they were not many—were deftly deflected. The *"Aryan thesis"* was fundamentally sound, I was told, although Hitler and Co. had badly abused it. But no one spoke of *"Aryans"* anymore or located their (presumed) Urheimat in Scandinavia, Germany, or the North Pole. Rather, the postwar discourse dealt with Indo-Europeans, elided questions of race, and placed the origin of this sanitized people off to the east, on the Russian steppes. In the pages that follow, I hope to show that things are not that simple and the problems—moral and intellectual—that attend this discourse or discipline are not so easily resolved. (Emphasis in the original)

Bruce Lincoln, *Theorizing Myth: Narrative, Ideology, and Scholarship* (Chicago: University of Chicago Press, 1999), 48.

58. On the link between philology and psychoanalysis, see John Forrester, *Language and the Origins of Psychoanalysis* (New York: Columbia University Press, 1980).

59. Among those who took up Müller's work was Madame Blavatsky, founder of the theosophical movement. Dismissing most of Müller's conclusions, Blavatsky still relied on philology to define the relation between Aryans and Semites. In her system, Semites were the fifth root race evolved from an even more ancient people whose secrets were hidden in vast archives in Himalayan monasteries. Aryans and Semites were equally removed from this ancient race, but were related to each other: Semitic languages were the "bastard descendants" of "the eldest children of the early Sanskrit," and Semitic peoples were a branch of the Aryan line that had become "degenerate in spirituality and perfected in materiality." H. P. Blavatsky, *The Secret Doctrine: The Synthesis of Science, Religion, and Philosophy* (1888), 2:200; Theosophical University Press online edition at http://secretdoctrine.net/ (accessed April 24, 2010).

60. Ferdinand de Saussure, *Course in General Linguistics*, trans. Wade Baskin (New York, 1959), 1.

61. De Saussure, "Letter to Antoine Meillet," January 4, 1894, *Cahiers Ferdinand de Saussure* 21 (1964): 93–96; quoted by Calvert Watkins, "What Is Philology?" in *On Philology*, ed. Jan Ziolkowski (University Park: Penn State University Press, 1990), 21–25; quotation is from p. 23.

62. Benjamin Lee Whorf, "Decipherment of the Linguistic Portion of the Maya Hieroglyphs," in *Annual Report of the Board of Regents of the Smithsonian Institute, 1941*, ed. C. G. Abbott (Washington, DC: United States Government Printing Office, 1942), 479–502; quotation is from p. 482.

63. See Gerald Graff, *Professing Literature: An Institutional History* (Chicago: University of Chicago Press, 1987), 65–80. Graff suggests the importance of the philological emphasis on race in the formation of language and literature departments in the 1880s. "The very decision

to divide the new . . . departments along national lines was an implicit assertion of pride in 'the English speaking race'" (71).

64. Albert H. Smythe, "American Literature in the Classroom," *PMLA* 3 (1887): 239; quoted in ibid., 72.

65. René Wellek and Austin Warren, *Theory of Literature*, 3rd ed. (New York: Harcourt, Brace, and World, 1956), 38.

66. In addition to editing the special issue of *Speculum* 65 (1990), Nichols coedited the book version, *The New Medievalism*. See Kevin Brownlee, Marina S. Brownlee, and Stephen Nichols, eds., *The New Medievalism* (Baltimore: Johns Hopkins University Press, 1991). Of particular interest in the *Speculum* issue is Stephen G. Nichols, "Introduction: Philology in a Manuscript Culture," 1–10. Nichols and others have acknowledged the influence of Bernard Cerquiglini, *In Praise of the Variant: A Critical History of Philology*, trans. Betsy Wing (Baltimore: Johns Hopkins University Press, 1999); originally published as *Eloge de la variante* (Paris: Éditions du Seuil, 1989). See also R. Howard Bloch and Stephen G. Nichols, eds., *Medievalism and the Modernist Temper*, Parallax: Re-visions of Culture and Society (Baltimore: Johns Hopkins University Press, 1996). Contributors to this volume emphasize the historicity of medieval studies, particularly in the context of nineteenth-century nationalist conflicts and twentieth-century institutional ambitions. For an account of the impact of New Philology on medieval studies, see Jan Ziolkowski, "Metaphilology," *Journal of English and Germanic Philology* 104, no. 2 (2005): 239–72; the account is given on pp. 243–47.

67. Lee Patterson, "The Return to Philology," in *The Past and Future of Medieval Studies*, ed. John van Engen (Notre Dame, IN: University of Notre Dame Press, 1994), 231–44; quotation is from p. 241.

68. See Mieke Bal, "Virginity: Toward a Feminist Philology," *Dispositio: revista hispánica de semiótica literaria* 12 (1987): 30–82.

69. As one participant in this movement says, the "goal is to assess the realities involved in the multiple productions of a classical text so as to facilitate a literary philology alive to the fact of plurality. I call this a radical philology." Sean Alexander, *Iphigenias at Aulis: Textual Multiplicity, Radical Philology* (Ithaca, NY: Cornell University Press, 2005), x.

70. See Matthew Restall, "A History of the New Philology and the New Philology in History," *Latin American Research Review* 38, no. 1 (2003): 113–34.

71. See David J. A. Clines, "Philology and Power," in *On the Way to the*

Postmodern: Old Testament Essays, 1967–1998 (Sheffield, UK: Sheffield Academic Press, 1998), 2:613–30.

72. Hans Ulrich Gumbrecht, *The Powers of Philology: Dynamics of Textual Scholarship* (Champaign: University of Illinois Press, 2003); Seth Lerer, ed., *Literary History and the Challenge of Philology: The Legacy of Erich Auerbach* (Stanford, CA: Stanford University Press, 1996); Seth Lerer, *Error and the Academic Self: The Scholarly Imagination, Medieval to Modern* (New York: Columbia University Press, 2003). In "Metaphilology," Ziolkowski reviews Gumbrecht and Lerer's *Error and the Academic Self,* both of them harshly, if wittily.

73. Michael Holquist, "Why We Should Remember Philology," *Profession* (2002): 72–79; see also Holquist, "Forgetting Our Name, Remembering Our Mother," *PMLA* 115, no. 7 (2000): 1975–77.

74. Columbia's Department of French and Romance Philology might seem an exception, but according to its Web site, the department defines itself as "a thriving point of contact between American and European scholarship," distinguished not by its insistence on traditional methods but by its promotion of a "broad range of specializations" and "dedication to teaching." Many American departments of philology became departments of linguistics in the 1940s; others were converted into departments of comparative literature. Today, American philology is housed primarily in classics departments. Departments of philology remain in some universities in eastern and northern Europe, and Russia.

75. For the argument that contemporary accounts of cultural difference resurrect older arguments about race, see Walter Benn Michaels, *Our America: Nativism, Modernism, and Pluralism, Post-Contemporary Interventions* (Durham, NC: Duke University Press, 1997).

76. Nichols, "Introduction," 1.

77. Said, at least, was sensitive to the potential for philology-sponsored racism, but he did not display a similar sensitivity to philological anti-Semitism. While he mentioned, for example, the racial stereotypes that inform Renan's account of Semitic (Jewish and Muslim) languages and cultures, he lay far greater stress on what he saw as Renan's single-minded antipathy to Muslims than he did on Renan's prejudice against Jews. According to Said, Renan did his work "within the edifice we call Oriental studies"; and within that edifice, his "main project is to shut down Islam" ("Islam, Philology, and French Culture," 282, 288).

CHAPTER 3

1. These and all subsequent quotations from Cole are taken from his "Mississippi Gubernatorial Inaugural" speech of January 12, 2004; online at http://www.neh.gov/whoweare/speeches/01122004.html (accessed May 21, 2010).

2. Even stronger sentiments were expressed by the National Association of Scholars, which linked the attacks to the liberal academy's shameful abuse of our precious cultural heritage. Many commentators blamed aspects of American culture—homosexuals, sinners, feminists, corporations—for the 9/11 attacks, but Stephen H. Balch, president of the National Association of Scholars, placed the ultimate blame on professors, primarily those in the humanities. "Unfortunately," Balch said, "a great deal of academe lives in a cartoon world whose reigning assumption is that behavior has no consequences." Now, however, with the attacks having "shaken us out of our complacency," the time has come to stop "descanting on our nation's ills" and display more respect. See Stephen H. Balch, "The Shame of the Campuses," *NAS . . . Update* 12 (2001) 1: 2–3; quotation is from p. 3; online at http://www.nas.org/polArticles.cfm?doctype_code=Article&doc_id=330 (accessed May 21, 2010).

3. In a striking irony, an earlier generation of conservatives attacked the NEA for insufficient elitism. As Hilton Kramer reported in 1980, "the NEA spends millions of dollars yearly to fund programs and policies which are unconcerned in any way with enduring artistic accomplishments; the best of these projects do no more than fossilize the popular culture of the past, and the worst are little more than high-flown welfare and employment schemes." Kramer called for a categorical distinction to be made between "serious art" and "art for the sake of social service." Hilton Kramer, "Reagan Aides Discuss U.S. Role in Helping Arts And Humanities," *New York Times*, November 26, 1980.

4. See Antony Levi, *Renaissance and Reformation: The Intellectual Genesis* (New Haven, CT: Yale University Press, 2002), especially 71–94 and 259–84. See also Michael Allen Gillespie, *The Theological Origins of Modernity* (Chicago: University of Chicago Press, 2008), especially 44–100.

5. A. C. Crombie, *Augustine to Galileo* (Cambridge, MA: Harvard University Press, 1961), 2:103.

6. Matthew Arnold, preface to *Culture and Anarchy* (1882), no. 4; on-

line at http://www.library.utoronto.ca/utel/nonfiction_u/arnoldm_ca/ ca_titlepage.html (accessed April 24, 2010). Subsequent citations are given in the text.

7. The description is Arnold's. See ibid., chap. 3, no. 35.

8. Bill Readings, *The University in Ruins* (Cambridge, MA: Harvard University Press, 1996), 53. Readings details the difference between Fichte and Humboldt on the precise relationship between the university and the state, with Fichte insisting on a direct relationship between the two and Humboldt recommending a "liberal margin of tolerance" for an institution that was, at most, "in dialogue with the state" (68).

9. According to Richard E. Lee, "the turn to 'culture' as a major category of analysis was immediately occasioned by the geopolitical events of the cold war: Khrushchev's 'secret speech' exposing Stalinism, the compromise in Poland, the 10,000 casualties of the Hungarian revolution, and the British/French/Israeli conspiracy that was Suez. These events called into question the proud posturing of both the Communist, Stalinist, East, and the liberal, social democratic, West." See Richard E. Lee, "Cultural Studies as *Geisteswissenschaften*: Time, Objectivity, and the Future of Social Science," 1997; online at http://fbc.binghamton .edu/rlcs-gws.htm (accessed April 24, 2010).

10. Stuart Hall, "The Emergence of Cultural Studies and the Crisis in the Humanities," *October* 53 (Summer 1990): 11–23; quotation is from pp. 11–12.

11. See National Association of Scholars, "Bruce Cole Tapped for NEH Chairmanship," *NAS . . . Update* 12, no. 1 (2001); online at http:// www.nas.org/pdf/update/UpD_v12n1_2001.pdf (accessed May 21, 2010). Applauding the appointment of Cole to replace William Ferris, this article looks forward to the restoration of the notion of the humanities as "a body of national and international literature and art that transcends in meaning and significance the circumstances of its origin." This notion, which is explicitly attributed to Arnold, is contrasted with the view said to be held by Ferris and "the Women's Studies Program at SUNY New Paltz," that "all human thought [is] the expression of one regional cave or another" (4).

12. See Julie A. Reuben, *The Making of the Modern University: Intellectual Transformation and the Marginalization of Morality* (Chicago: University of Chicago Press, 1996), 211–29.

13. Mel A. Topf, "The NEH and the Crisis in the Humanities," *College English* 37, no. 3 (November 1975): 229–42; quotation is from p. 233.

14. J. H. Plumb, ed., *Crisis in the Humanities* (Baltimore: Penguin Books, 1964), 5.

15. Ernest Gellner, "The Crisis in the Humanities and the Main-stream of Philosophy," in ibid., 45–81; quotation is from p. 72 (hereafter cited in text).

16. *Report of the Commission on the Humanities* (New York: ACLS, 1964), 4.

17. Barry Bingham, "A Journalist Looks at the Humanities," in *The Humanities and the Understanding of Reality*, ed. Thomas B. Stroup (Lexington: University of Kentucky Press, 1966): 78–79; quoted in Topf, "The NEH and the Crisis in the Humanities," 231.

18. National Endowment for the Humanities, "Program Announce-ment," 1973–1974, 3; quoted in Topf, "The NEH and the Crisis in the Humanities," 230. Topf's article is an invaluable compendium of the rhetoric that gathered around the NEH in the early years. That rheto-ric was remarkably blunt in its nationalism, as can be seen in the an-nual reports issued by the NEH. The First Annual Report, for example, spoke of our "darkening problems of urbanization, of lacerating political and social division" as a context for the humanities, which are intended to "make us wise, and . . . lead us to apply our wisdom in ways which can heal both private and public life. . . . We are persuaded that 'being humanistic' . . . is necessary for solutions to our national anguishes, to maintain our leadership abroad, and to represent to the world what the quality of human life can be." National Endowment for the Humani-ties, *First Annual Report*, 1966 (Washington, DC: U.S. Government Printing Office, 1967); quoted in ibid., 236.

19. Hannah Arendt, *The Human Condition* (Garden City, NY: An-chor Books, 1959), 4.

20. The amount, to be sure, is not large. The NEA and the NEH together represent less than one one-hundredth of a percent of the fed-eral budget, or around 70¢ per person per year. Total funding, private *and* public, for "culture" amounts to just over $6 per person per year in the United States. In Great Britain the figure is $27, while Finland, the most cultured country in the world by this measure, expends $98 per person each year for "culture." For a more complete picture of relatively recent funding, see Cynthia Koch, "The Contest for American Culture: A Leadership Case Study on the NEA and NEH Funding Crisis," *Public Talk: Online Journal of Discourse Leadership*"; online at http://www.upenn.edu/pnc/ptkoch.html (accessed April 24, 2010).

21. Arts and Humanities Research Council Web site; online at http://www.ahrc.ac.uk/About/Pages/default.aspx (accessed April 24, 2010).

22. National Endowment for the Humanities Web site, "Who We Are"; online at http://www.neh.gov/whoweare/overview.html (accessed April 24, 2010).

23. See Thomas Greene, "Imitation and Anachronism," chap. 3 in *The Light in Troy: Imitation and Discovery in Renaissance Poetry* (New Haven, CT: Yale University Press, 1982), 28–53.

24. Perhaps the concept of society might serve as a less dubiously "transcendental" context for the university than culture—less heavily occulted, less suggestive of the nation or the ethnicity. For an argument that literary study could profit from an orientation toward the concept of society rather than culture, see Geoffrey Galt Harpham, *Shadows of Ethics: Criticism and the Just Society* (Durham, NC: Duke University Press, 1999), 1–17.

25. For a historical account of the ways in which religion and morality were supplanted in higher education by ideals of free inquiry and the advancement of knowledge, see Reuben, *The Making of the Modern University*.

CHAPTER 4

1. Peter M. Blau, *The Organization of Academic Work* (New York: Wiley, 1973), 5.

2. Louis Menand, *The Marketplace of Ideas: Reform and Resistance in the American University* (New York: W. W. Norton, 2010); citations are given in the text. Menand notes the difference in orientation between George Saintsbury's *A History of Criticism and Literary Taste in Europe, from the Earliest Texts to the Present Day* (1900–1904) and later books by René Wellek (*A History of Modern Criticism: 1750–1950* [1955–56]) and William K. Wimsatt and Cleanth Brooks (*Literary Criticism: A Short History* [1957]), comparing the essentially nonprofessional and nondisciplinary orientation of Saintsbury with the increasingly scientistic approaches of Wellek, Wimsatt, and Brooks. See Menand, *The Marketplace of Ideas*, 111–12.

3. Gerald Graff, *Professing Literature: An Institutional History* (Chicago: University of Chicago Press, 1987), 283n.

4. Michael Bérubé, *The Employment of English: Theory, Jobs, and the Future of Literary Studies* (New York: NYU Press, 1998), 4.

5. Stuart Hall, "The Emergence of Cultural Studies and the Crisis

of the Humanities," *October* 53 (Summer 1990): 11–23; quotation is from pp. 11–12.

6. See Stanley Fish, "Profession Despise Thyself: Fear and Loathing in Literary Studies," and "Anti-Professionalism," both in *Doing What Comes Naturally: Change, Rhetoric, and the Practice of Theory in Literary and Legal Studies* (Durham, NC: Duke University Press, 1999), 197–214, 215–46.

7. In Menand's somewhat less pugnacious version, professions do many good things, reinforcing standards and democratizing access to the occupation. But "since it is the system that ratifies the project . . . the most important function of the system is not the production of knowledge. It is the reproduction of the system" (*The Marketplace of Ideas*, 105).

8. This image is used by Donald Davie, "Criticism and the Academy," in *Criticism in the University*, ed. Gerald Graff and Reginald Gibbons (Evanston, IL: Northwestern University Press, 1985), 175.

9. Edward Said, *Representations of the Intellectual: The 1993 Reith Lectures* (New York: Vintage, 1996), 76.

10. In the past decade, the conversation on professionalism has taken a darker turn as the market for Ph.D.'s has shrunk drastically, with economic difficulties dictating the increased use of adjunct, that is, nontenure-track, faculty to teach undergraduate courses. A vast migrant workforce of helots with high teaching loads, low salaries, and often no benefits now staffs half of all courses in English in higher education. See Neil Gross and Solon Simmons, "The Social and Political Views of American Professors" (2007), working paper, at http://www.wjh.harvard.edu/~ngross/lounsbery_9–25.pdf (accessed April 24, 2010); cited in Menand, *The Marketplace of Ideas*, 134. The widely used phrase "the casualization of the workforce" does not capture the mood on the ground as well as the title of a 1997 book describing the situation: *Will Teach for Food*. See Cary Nelson, ed., *Will Teach for Food: Academic Labor in Crisis* (Minneapolis: University of Minnesota Press, 1997); see also Bérubé, *The Employment of English*. With no jobs waiting, the time to degree has been extended to nine years. The effect on the intellectual life of the graduate program is predictable: a demoralized conformism, driven by fear and anxiety. See Menand, "Why Do Professors All Think Alike?" in *The Marketplace of Ideas*, 129–55.

11. For a critical account of the premature professionalization of graduate students, see John Guillory, "Preprofessionalism: What Graduate Students Want," *Profession* (1996): 91–99.

12. William M. Chace, "The Decline of the English Department," *American Scholar* (Autumn 2009); online at http://www.the americanscholar.org/the-decline-of-the-english-department/ (accessed April 24, 2010).

13. Chace's conviction that there is simply too much research is widely shared. See for example Mark Bauerlein (also from Emory), "Professors on the Production Line, Students on Their Own" (2009), a report produced for the conservative American Enterprise Institute for Public Policy Research. Bauerlein, who has an extensive publication record of his own, argues that the saturation point of knowledge about literature has been reached, and that there can be no continued justification for more scholarship on any of the major authors. He recommends that some of the resources currently devoted to supporting scholarship be diverted to the support of teaching—as if scholarship were too generously supported! Online at http://www.aei.org/docLib/Bauerlein .pdf (accessed April 24, 2010). Bauerlein elaborates his views in "Diminishing Returns in Humanities Research," *Chronicle Review* (July 20, 2009); online at http://chronicle.com/article/Diminishing-Returns-in/ 47107/ (accessed April 24, 2010). See also Elizabeth Redden, "Unread Monographs, Uninspired Undergrads," *Inside Higher Education*, March 18, 2009; online at http://www.insidehighered.com/news/2009/ 03/18/production (accessed April 24, 2010).

14. Andrew Delbanco, "The Decline and Fall of Literature," *New York Review of Books* 46, no. 17 (November 4, 1999): 32–39; quotation is from p. 34. The quoted phrases are from Walter Pater.

15. Robert Louis Stevenson, "A Gossip on Romance," in *Memories and Portraits*, vol. 13 of *The Works of Robert Louis Stevenson* (New York: Scribner's, 1896), 327–43; quotation is from p. 327. Quoted in Barry Weller, "Pleasure and Self-Loss in Reading," *ADE Bulletin* 99 (Fall 1991): 8–12.

16. Weller, "Pleasure and Self-Loss in Reading," 8 (hereafter cited in text).

17. Nina Auerbach, "Engorging the Patriarchy," in *Historical Studies and Literary Criticism*, ed. Jerome J. McGann (Madison: University of Wisconsin Press, 1985), 229–39; all quotations taken from pp. 232–33.

18. *Formations of Pleasure* (London: Routledge and Kegan Paul, 1983).

19. Fredric Jameson, "Pleasure: A Political Issue," in ibid., 1–14; quotations are from pp. 10, 13.

20. Slavoj Žižek, *Enjoy Your Symptom!: Jacques Lacan in Hollywood and Out* (New York: Routledge, 2001); *For They Know Not What They Do: Enjoyment as a Political Factor* (London: Verso, 1991); and *The Metastases of Enjoyment: Six Essays on Woman and Causality* (London: Verso, 1994).

21. Philip Davis, "Syntax and Pathways," *Interdisciplinary Science Reviews* 33, no. 4 (2008): 265–77; quotation is from p. 265. Subsequent citations are given in the text.

22. See Lisa Zunshine, "Fiction and Theory of Mind: An Exchange," *Philosophy and Literature* 31, no. 1 (April 2007): 189–96; quotation is from p. 189. See also Zunshine, *Why We Read Fiction: Theory of Mind and the Novel* (Columbus: Ohio State University Press, 2006); and Blakey Vermeule, *Why Do We Care about Literary Characters* (Baltimore: Johns Hopkins University Press, 2009).

23. Joseph Carroll, "An Evolutionary Paradigm for Literary Study," *Style* 42, nos. 2–3 (2008): 103–37; quotation is from p. 105. This double issue of *Style* constitutes a comprehensive statement of the state and ambitions of Darwinian literary study circa 2008. Carroll's essay serves as the occasion and target for no fewer than thirty-five respondents, to whom Carroll responds in a monumental, 104-page "Rejoinder to Critics" (308–411). Online at http://www.umsl.edu/~carrolljc/Documents%20linked%20to%20indiex/Target%20Pieces/1_Target_article.htm (accessed April 24, 2010). Carroll is also a coeditor of *The Evolutionary Review*, a new journal promoting, among other things, Darwinian literary criticism.

24. Steven Pinker, *How the Mind Works* (New York: W. W. Norton & Co., 1997), 525. See chap. 20, "The Arts," 400–20 passim.

25. Joseph Carroll, "Steven Pinker's Cheesecake for the Mind," *Philosophy and Literature* 22, no. 2 (1998): 478–85; quotation is from p. 478.

26. E. O. Wilson, *Consilience: The Unity of Knowledge* (New York: Knopf, 1998), 224–25.

27. See Joseph Carroll, "An Evolutionary Paradigm for Literary Study," *Style* 42, no. 4 (Winter 2008): 103–35; quotation is from p. 122. Pinker is impressed by the energy of Darwinian literary criticism and delighted at the prospect of a consilient theory of literature, which might, he thinks, save literary studies from its current "critical condition—politicized, sclerotic, and lacking a progressive agenda"—despite being dominated by superstars and "having had several centuries to get

it right." But he is unimpressed by the scientific competence of the literary Darwinians, believing that by insisting on the adaptive function of literature, they are responding to what they perceive as a slight rather than addressing a real issue. See Steven Pinker, "Toward a Consilient Study of Literature," *Philosophy and Literature* 31, no. 1 (April 2007): 161–77; quotation is from p. 163.

28. Denis Dutton, *The Art Instinct: Beauty, Pleasure, and Human Evolution* (New York: Bloomsbury Press, 2009).

CHAPTER 5

1. In "The Decline of the English Department," William M. Chace, former president of Wesleyan and Emory universities, notes (with consternation) that over the period from 1970 to 2004, English, Foreign Language, and History have all lost nearly 50% of their undergraduate majors by percentage, while Business has grown by over one-third, to 21.9%. *The American Scholar* (Autumn 2009); online at http://www.theamericanscholar.org/the-decline-of-the-english-department/ (accessed April 24, 2010). The statistics may give a misleading impression with regard to the humanities, which had a spike in enrollments around 1970, and have remained fairly steady over the past generation. Still, the trend toward Business is unmistakable.

2. John Locke, *Some Thoughts concerning Education*, ed. John W. Yolton and Jean S. Yolton (New York: Oxford University Press, 1989), 157, 230, 217.

3. John Henry Newman, *The Idea of the University*, ed. Frank M. Turner (New Haven, CT: Yale University Press, 1996); citations are to this edition and given in the text. For a recent approach to the perennial question of utility, see Michael Bérubé, "The Utility of the Arts and Humanities," in *Rhetorical Occasions* (Chapel Hill, NC: University of North Carolina Press, 2006), 71–90.

4. Bruce Kuklick, *The Rise of American Philosophy: Cambridge, Massachusetts, 1860–1930* (New Haven, CT: Yale University Press, 1977), 453.

5. Laurence Veysey, "The Plural Organized World of the Humanities," in *The Organization of Knowledge in Modern America, 1860–1920*, ed. Alexandra Oleson and John Voss (Baltimore: Johns Hopkins University Press, 1979), 51–106; quotation is from p. 53.

6. An entry, no longer available, on a now-defunct version of the Movers and Shakespeares Web site (accessed September 1, 2009).

7. Ibid.

8. Online at http://www.vanityfair.com/politics/features/2007/01/neocons200701 (accessed April 24, 2010).

9. Jesper Eckhardt Larsen, "The Role of the Humanities in the Bologna Idea of the University: Learning from the American Model?" *Revisita Española de Educación Comparada* 12 (2006): 309–27; quotations are from p. 320; online at http://www.sc.ehu.es/sfwseec/reec/reec12/reec1211.pdf (accessed April 24, 2010).

CHAPTER 6

1. Indeed, the nation that Adams and others built after the success of the Revolution was consciously constructed, as Eric Slauter has argued, "as a work of art." *The State as a Work of Art: The Cultural Origins of the Constitution* (Chicago: University of Chicago Press, 2009).

2. Richard Rorty, "Wissen Deutsche Politiker, wozu Universität da sind?" *Frankfurter Allgemeine Zeitung*, August 31, 2004.

3. M. Hesseldahl et al., *Humanistiske kandidater og arbejdsmarkedet* (Copenhagen: Ministeriet for videnskab, teknologi og innovation, 2005); cited in Jesper Eckhardt Larsen, "The Role of the Humanities in the Bologna Idea of the University: Learning from the American Model?" *Revisita Española de Educación Comparada* 12 (2006): 309–27: quotations are from p. 321; online at http://www.sc.ehu.es/sfwseec/reec/reec12/reec1211.pdf (accessed April 24, 2010).

4. Eleonora Belfiore, "Beyond Utility and the Markets: Articulating the Role of the Humanities in the 21st Century," manuscript.

5. "The Arts and Humanities Research Council's (AHRC) Knowledge Transfer (KT) Strategy 2008–2011": http://www.ahrc.ac.uk/About/Policy/Documents/KT%20Strategy.pdf (accessed April 24, 2010).

6. Higher Education Funding Council for England, cited in Stefan Collini, "Impact on Humanities," *Times Literary Supplement* 5563 (November 13 2009): 18–19.

7. Collini, "Impact on Humanities."

8. See Charles Vest, keynote Address to the National Humanities Alliance, March 3, 2008; online at http://www.nhalliance.org/bm~doc/charlesvest_2008.pdf (accessed April 25, 2010).

9. See Mara Hvistendahl, "Less Politics, More Poetry: China's Colleges Eye the Liberal Arts," *Chronicle of Higher Education*, January 3, 2010;

online at http://chronicle.com/article/Less-Politics-More-Poetry-/
63356/ (accessed April 25, 2010).

10. See Richard Brodhead, "The U. S. Edge in Education," *Washington Post*, September 4, 2006; online at http://www.washingtonpost
.com/wp-dyn/content/article/2006/09/03/AR2006090300742.html (accessed April 25, 2010).

11. Criticizing programs of "education for profit" or "education for economic growth," Martha C. Nussbaum points out that "political liberty, health, and education are all poorly correlated with growth," but insists that growth should not be the only measure. "One sign of what that [growth] model leaves out is the fact that South Africa under apartheid used to shoot to the top of development indexes." "The Liberal Arts Are Not Elitist," *Chronicle of Higher Education*, March 5, 2010, A88.

12. *General Education in a Free Society: Report of the Harvard Committee*, with an introduction by James Bryant Conant (Cambridge, MA: Harvard University Press, 1945). Citations hereafter Redbook and given in text.

13. Ernest L. Boyer, *College: The Undergraduate Experience in America* (New York: Harper & Row, 1987), p. 65.

14. Daniel Bell, *The Reforming of General Education: The Columbia College Experience in Its National Setting* (New York: Columbia University Press, 1966), 39.

15. The commitment of the Redbook to these two principles produces at times a nearly comical style of hesitation and qualification. "However," one characteristically equivocal passage begins, "the emotions and the will cannot be trained by theoretical instruction alone. . . . Yet values cannot be learned solely from books. . . . To be sure, thinking is stimulated by discussion with other people, but in the last resort one has to make up one's mind by oneself. Yet living is a cooperative process. . . . But the task of learning to get along with people is infinitely more difficult" (170).

16. Richards's biographer, at least, is convinced that Richards is essentially the sole author of the portions of the Redbook that deal with literature, and the dominant voice in all the sections on the humanities. See John Paul Russo, *I. A. Richards: His Life and Work* (Baltimore: Johns Hopkins University Press, 1989), 486–88.

17. For Richards's impact on the "Cambridge School" of literary

study, see Stefan Collini, "The Study of English," in *Cambridge Contributions*, ed. Sarah J. Ormrod (Cambridge: Cambridge University Press, 1988), 42–64.

18. John Forrester, "The Idea of a Moral Science, State Funding and Teutonophobia: The Creation of the Humanities in Early Twentieth Century Cambridge," manuscript.

19. Ralph Waldo Emerson, entry for April 20, 1834; in Joel Porte, ed., *The Journals and Miscellaneous Notebooks of Ralph Waldo Emerson* (Cambridge, MA: Harvard University Press, 1982), 123.

20. *Establishing the Goals*, vol. 1 of *Higher Education for Democracy: A Report of the President's Commission on Higher Education* (New York: Harper & Brothers, 1947), 49. The section containing all passages quoted here is excerpted in Wilson Smith and Thomas Bender, eds., *American Higher Education Transformed, 1940–2005: Documenting the National Discourse* (Baltimore: Johns Hopkins University Press, 2008), 83–89.

21. Ibid., 7.

22. J. H. Plumb, ed., *Crisis in the Humanities* (Baltimore: Penguin Books, 1964).

23. *Report of the Commission on the Humanities* (New York: ACLS, 1964), 4 (citations hereafter *Report* and given in text); online at https:// www.acls.org/uploadedFiles/Publications/NEH/1964_Commission_ on_the_Humanities.pdf (accessed April 25, 2010).

24. Vannevar Bush, *Science—The Endless Frontier. A Report to the President by Vannevar Bush, Director of the Office of Scientific Research and Development, July 1945*; online at http://www.nsf.gov/about/history/ vbush1945.htm (accessed April 25, 2010).

25. For example, this passage from the act that created the endowment: "Democracy demands wisdom and vision in its citizens. It must therefore foster and support a form of education, and access to the arts and the humanities, designed to make people of all backgrounds and wherever located masters of their technology and not its unthinking servants. . . . The arts and the humanities reflect the high place accorded by the American people to the nation's rich cultural heritage. . . . The world leadership which has come to the United States cannot rest solely upon superior power, wealth, and technology, but must be solidly founded upon worldwide respect and admiration for the Nation's high qualities as a leader in the realm of ideas and of the spirit." National Foundation on the Arts and Humanities Act of 1965, Public Law 89–209; online

at http://www.neh.gov/whoweare/legislation.html (accessed April 25, 2010).

26. For examples of such discourse from the culture wars of the 1990s, see Dinesh D'Souza, *Illiberal Education: The Politics of Race and Sex on Campus* (New York: Free Press, 1991); and Roger Kimball, *Tenured Radicals: How Politics Has Corrupted Our Higher Education*, 3rd ed. (Chicago: Ivan R. Dee, 2008).

27. See "What We Do" on the NEH's Web site: http://www.neh.gov/whoweare/overview.html (accessed April 25, 2010).

28. Todd Gitlin, *The Sixties: Years of Hope, Days of Rage* (New York: Bantam, 1978), 178.

29. See Jimmy Carter, "Crisis of Confidence," online at http://www.pbs.org/wgbh/amex/carter/filmmore/ps_crisis.html (accessed April 25, 2010).

30. *The Humanities in American Life, Report of the Commission on the Humanities* (Berkeley and Los Angeles: University of California Press, 1980); citations hereafter *Humanities* and given in text.

31. Henk Wesseling, "The Idea of an Institute for Advanced Study: Reflections on Science, Art, and Education," Uhlenbeck Lecture 20, given June 14, 2002 (Wassenaar: Netherlands Institute for Advanced Study in the Humanities and Social Sciences, 2002), 15.

32. Mel A. Topf, "Smooth Things: The Rockefeller Commission's Report on the Humanities," *College English* 43, no. 5 (1981): 463–70; quotation is from p. 468.

33. Helen Vendler, *Invisible Listeners: Lyric Intimacy in Herbert, Whitman, and Ashbery* (Princeton, NJ: Princeton University Press, 2005). One striking difference between the ACLS and the Rockefeller Commissions is that the earlier panel had just one woman out of twenty members, while the later one had five powerful women, including, in addition to Vendler, Jill Ker Conway, president of Smith College; Nannerl Keohane, then an associate professor at Stanford but soon to be president of Wellesley and then of Duke; and Aida Barrera, president of Southwest Center for Educational Television.

34. The 2004 report from the AAU, *Reinvigorating the Humanities*, was produced by a very distinguished group of people chaired by John Casteen, president of the University of Virginia; but the report itself is conceptually thin, and focuses on statistics, instances of "best practices," and specific recommendations. Online at http://www.aau.edu/policy/article.aspx?id=7182 (accessed April 25, 2010).

35. Irving Babbitt cites the Late Latin writer Aulus Gellius's complaint that *humanitas* had come to mean "promiscuous benevolence, what the Greeks call philanthropy," whereas the true meaning was "doctrine" or "discipline." See Irving Babbitt, *Literature and the American College: Essays in Defense of the Humanities* (Boston: Houghton Mifflin, 1908), 6. By the fifteenth century, when the word *humanity* appeared in the English language, this secondary or tertiary meaning connecting the term with philanthropy had disappeared altogether.

36. Richard J. Franke, "The Power of the Humanities and a Challenge to Humanists," *Daedalus* (Winter 2009): 13–23; subsequent citations are given in the text.

37. He refers, specifically, to *Report of the Task Force on General Education* produced by the Task Force on General Education (Cambridge, MA: President and Fellows of Harvard College, 2007), v; online at http://www.fas.harvard.edu/~secfas/General_Education_Final_Report .pdf (accessed April 25, 2010).

38. Michael Wood, "A World without Literature?" *Daedalus* (Winter 2009): 58–67.

39. J. M. Coetzee, "Zbigniew Herbert and the Figure of the Censor," in *Giving Offence: Essays on Censorship* (Chicago: University of Chicago Press, 1996), 151; quoted in ibid., 62.

40. A fellow traveler in this regard is Toril Moi, who has recently given an appreciative reading of Simone de Beauvoir's understanding of the importance of identification. "For reading to 'take,'" Beauvoir says, "I have to identify with someone: with the author; I have to enter into his world, and his world must become mine." Simone de Beauvoir, Contribution to *Que peut le literature?* ed. Yves Buin (Paris: 10/18-Union Générale d'Editions, 1965), 82; quoted in Toril Moi, "What Can Literature Do? Simone de Beauvoir as a Literary Theorist," *PMLA* 124, no. 1 (January 2009): 189–2005; quotation is from p. 193.

41. Ralph Waldo Emerson, "Circles," in *The Essays of Ralph Waldo Emerson* (Cambridge, MA: Harvard University Press, 1987), 177–90; quotation is from p. 185.

42. This was the title of a memo written by Abraham Flexner in 1921. It was published in *Harper's Magazine* in October 1939 (544–52), and is available online at http://www.ias.edu/hs/da/UsefulnessOfUseless Knowledge.pdf (accessed April 25, 2010). It was taken as the founding document of the Institute for Advanced Study, which Flexner helped to found in 1930.

43. Andrew Delbanco, *The Real American Dream: A Meditation on Hope* (Cambridge, MA: Harvard University Press, 1999). Citations are given in text.

44. Delbanco quotes Clifford Geertz's evocation of the gnawing sense that life is purposeless, pointless, directionless, and futile, "a formless monster with neither sense of direction nor power of self-control, a chaos of spasmodic impulses and vague emotions." Clifford Geertz, "Religion as a Cultural System," in *The Interpretation of Cultures* (New York: Basic Books, 1973), 99; quoted in ibid., 1.

45. Compare Iris Murdoch's representation of the image of the psyche offered us by "modern psychology": "The psyche is a historically determined individual relentlessly looking after itself. . . . One of its main pastimes is daydreaming. It is reluctant to face unpleasant realities. Its consciousness is not normally a transparent glass through which it views the world, but a cloud of more or less fantastic reverie designed to protect the psyche from pain." *The Sovereignty of Good* (London: Routledge & Kegan Paul, 1970), 78–79.

46. Alexis de Tocqueville, *Democracy in America*, trans. Phillips Bradley (New York: Vintage, 1990), 2:139; quoted in Delbanco, *The Real American Dream*, 2.

47. Delbanco dilates appreciatively on the kind of American citizen Jefferson envisioned, a man at once intensely practical but also educated in music, mathematics, and nature; in firm possession of a moral framework; self-possessed, self-controlled, and self-realized; and committed to the common good. For an account of Jefferson's vision of the citizens for the new Republic, see James Gilreath, ed., *Thomas Jefferson and the Education of a Citizen* (Washington, DC: Library of Congress, 1999).

48. William James, *The Varieties of Religious Experience* (1903), in *William James: Writings, 1902–1910*, ed. Bruce Kucklick (New York: Library of America, 1987), 250; quoted in Delbanco, *The Real American Dream*, 6.

49. Herman Melville, *White-Jacket; or, The World in a Man-of-War* (1850), chap. 36; quoted in Delbanco, *The Real American Dream*, 57–58.

50. Max Weber, *The Protestant Ethic and the Spirit of Capitalism*, trans. Talcott Parsons (New York: Charles Scribner's Sons, 1976).

CHAPTER 7

1. King Leopold II, "The Sacred Mission of Civilization," in Joseph Conrad, *Heart of Darkness*, ed. Paul B. Armstrong, Norton Critical Edi-

tions (New York: W. W. Norton & Company, 2006), 25. All subsequent citations are to this edition.

2. George W. Bush, presidential message, online at www.cnn.com/ 2003/ALLPOLITICS/12/25/eleco4.prez.bush.letter.index.html (accessed April 29, 2010).

3. Edward W. Said, "Two Visions in *Heart of Darkness*," in Conrad, *Heart of Darkness*, 422–29; quotation is from p. 428.

4. George W. Bush, presidential message December 24, 2003; online at http://www.whitehouse.gov/news/releases/2003/12/20031225.html (accessed June 25, 2008).

5. Chinua Achebe, "An Image of Africa: Racism in Conrad's *Heart of Darkness*," in Conrad, *Heart of Darkness*, 226–49.

6. Conrad, *Heart of Darkness*, 19–20.

7. *Department of English and Fine Arts*. United States Air Force Academy; online at http://www.usafa.edu/df/dfeng/?catname=dfeng (accessed April 29, 2010).

8. *War, Literature, and the Arts* 20, nos. 1–2 (2008): 24–29. Citations are given in the text.

Index

Heritage Foundation, 82
"Heroes of History" (National Endowment for the Humanities), 91
Herzog (Saul Bellow), 177
Hesse, Carla, 27–28
Hesseldahl, M., 228n3
Higher Education for American Democracy (Truman Report), 161–64; and crisis, 163–64; rejection of racial or religious quotas in, 162
Higher Education Funding Council (UK), 149
Hoevelar, J. David, 206n15
Hollinger, David A., 14
Holquist, Michael, 75, 219n73
Homer, 10, 33, 49, 54, 76, 155, 161
Houseman, John, 132
Hudson Institute, 141
humanities, the, 1–42; and American dream, 182–88; assumption of depth in, 31–33; compared with study of law, 29; connection to the state of, 189; contrasted to science, 101; contrasted to social science, 87–88; contribution of philanthropy to, 173–78, 182; as core of liberal arts, 144; and crisis, 15–16, 18, 21–42, 82–83, 88, 163–64, 172; cultural specificity of, 7–9; and cultural studies, 106; and development of character, 14, 150, 155; effect of "impact agenda" on in Great Britain, 149–51; emergence in American context of, 6–9, 14–15, 17–18, 145–47; as expression of American national character, 17, 81, 89–91, 145–47, 156–57, 167–68, 185–90; fields comprising, 14, 207n6; focus on text of, 6–7, 24–29; as a form of philanthropy, 186–87; golden age of, 15; historical orientation of, 24;

humanity as subject of, 6–8, 19, 28–32, 81, 91, 94–95, 97–98, 163; and human self-understanding, 6, 19, 23, 35–37, 39; importance of tradition in, 90–91; and individual self-realization, 167; and the inner life, 172; and liberal education, 150; and melancholy, 184, 186–87; as mingling of liberal-free and *artes liberales* traditions, 17; and modernity, 14, 98, 161; origin in philology of, 3–4, 188; and religion, 98; and transformation, 17, 181; and wisdom, 3, 165, 185
Humanities in American Life, The (Rockefeller Commission Report), 24, 28, 168–73; in context of American "malaise," 169, 172; criticism of, 171; need for funding asserted in, 172–73; and private sensibility, 172
Humboldt, Wilhelm von, 65, 69–70, 88, 221n8; on education and the state, 85; on language as key to national characteristics, 50, 63; on superiority of Sanscritic languages, 55–56
Hutchins, Robert Maynard, 206n12
Hutton, Christopher M., 69, 216n57
Hvistendahl, Mara, 228–29n9

Indo-European language, 54, 61–63, 69
Indo-European race, 61–63. *See also* Aryan race
Indo-Germanic language. *See* Indo-European language
Inherit the Wind, 138
Institute for Advanced Study, 232n42
Iraq, 199; invasion of, 141
Isocrates, 10. See also *artes liberales*
Istanbul, 1–4; and the humanities, 3, 11. *See also* Constantinople

National Humanities Center, 8, 28
National Institutes of Health, 94, 170
National Science Foundation, 91, 170
Nelson, Cary, 224n10
New Criticism, 103–4, 158, 176
New Humanism, 14
Newman, John Henry, 17, 87, 126–28,
    135, 144; opposition to research, 13;
    and tradition of humane letters, 12
New Medievalism, 218n66
New Philology, 46–47, 74–75, 78,
    218n66
Nichols, Stephen G., 74, 218n66
Nietzsche, Friedrich, 43, 47–48, 51, 69,
    77; *Daybreak*, 47–48; "We Philolo-
    gists," 43, 47, 209n8
Northrop Grumman, 139
Nott, Josiah Clark, 213n38
Nussbaum, Martha C., 229n11

Oakley, Francis C., 10, 12
Obama, Barack, 141
Ogden, C. K., 157
Old Testament, 33, 161
Olender, Maurice, 214n40, 215n48
Ondaatje, Michael, 29
Operation Iraqi Freedom, 201
Oxford English Dictionary, 9
Oxford University, 125–26, 135

Pamuk, Orhan, 4–5
Paper Chase, The, 132, 137
Patterson, Lee, 74
Pericles, 155
Petrarch, 83, 95
Phi Beta Kappa, 163
philanthropy, 134, 181–82, 189–90;
    as American phenomenon, 187;
    support for humanities by, 173–74,
    178, 186–87. *See also* Franke,
    Richard J.
philhellenism, 48–49, 68

philology, 3–4, 43–79, 85; and Ameri-
    can pedagogy, 47; as antecedent of
    modern humanities, 19, 188; and
    anti-Semitism, 3–4, 55, 71, 78; and
    Aryan race, 61–69, 76; classifica-
    tion of languages into families,
    46–47, 55, 58–59, 62–63; compared
    to geology, 53; as empirical science,
    45–47; and evolution, 56–61; and
    feminism, 75; focus on Greek lan-
    guage and culture of, 48–50; and
    human nature, 50, 73; inability to
    establish itself as an academic dis-
    cipline, 71; influence of Darwinian
    thought on, 56–60; and linguistics,
    71–73; and literary study, 71, 73–74,
    76; as master discipline, 50–51; and
    medieval studies, 74–75; and mod-
    ern scholarship, 76–77; and
    "the modern spirit," 51–52; and
    "mother-tongue fascism," 69–70;
    and national characteristics, 50;
    and power, 52, 75; and quest for
    origins, 50–51, 188; and race, 3–4,
    54–71, 213n38; reasons for return
    to, 43–45; role of speculation in,
    47–51; and Romanticism, 70; and
    Sanskrit, 55, 61; as a science, 53,
    60–61, 64, 70–72; search for origi-
    nal human language of, 61; and
    Semitic languages, 54–55; as solu-
    tion to problems of scholarship,
    76; supported by Prussian state,
    49; use of tree diagrams in, 58–59,
    71. *See also* de Man, Paul; Müller,
    Max; New Philology; Nietzsche,
    Friedrich; radical philology;
    Renan, Ernest; Said, Edward
Pico della Mirandola, 83
Pilgrim's Progress (John Bunyan), 192
Pinker, Steven, 118–21; on Darwinian
    literary criticism, 226–27n27